Collaborative Learning
in a Global World

A Volume in:
Literacy, Language and Learning

Series Editors

Claudia Finkbeiner
Wen Ma
Peter B. Mosenthal
Patricia Ruggiano Schmidt

Literacy, Language and Learning

Series Editors

Claudia Finkbeiner
Universitaet Kassel

Wen Ma
Le Moyne College

Peter B. Mosenthal
Syracuse University

Patricia Ruggiano Schmidt
Le Moyne College

Collaborative Learning in a Global World

Edited by

Miri Shonfeld
David Gibson

INFORMATION AGE PUBLISHING, INC.
Charlotte, NC • www.infoagepub.com

Library of Congress Cataloging-in-Publication Data

The CIP data for this book can be found on the Library of Congress website (loc.gov).

Paperback: 978-1-64113-465-1
Hardcover: 978-1-64113-466-8
eBook: 978-1-64113-467-5

CONTENTS

ACKNOWLEDGEMENTS

The editors and authoring leads, Miri Shonfeld and David Gibson, would like to acknowledge the support of the Kibbutzim College of Education, Technology and the Arts in Tel Aviv for initiating the communities of writing and for their financial support. We would also like to acknowledge Curtin University in Perth, as well, for their support of the time, people and resources needed for this book. In addition, resources and time of the UNESCO Chair of Data Science in Higher Education Learning and Teaching and TEC, MOFET, assisted the editors in tele-communications, meetings and travel, without which the book could not have been completed. We also would like to acknowledge the guidance, patience and wonderful care of the series editor Prof. Claudia Finkbeiner and her colleague Prof. Wen Ma. Finally, we'd like to acknowledge the wonderfully gifted prac-titioners and research authors and their colleagues for joining us in the journey from ideas to completed statements of their practices, ways of thinking and their sources of inspiration. We share with them a belief that collaborative learning in a global world is more than a teaching method; it is a way of respecting, honoring and including others in the work of knowledge-building.

FOREWORD

Since the mid-1960s, when we started training teachers in how to implement co-operative learning (Johnson, 1989), cooperative learning has progressed from an almost unknown, virtually unused instructional procedure to a pervasive teaching method known by almost every educator throughout the world. In the 1970s, Sir James Britton (1990) and others in England developed collaborative learning aimed at being "natural," that is, student-directed with almost no guidance or instructions from the teacher. Britton viewed the more structured cooperative learning as being "manipulative," controlling, and interfering with students' learning. Over the decades, however, the terms "cooperative learning" and "collaborative learning" have become interchangeable, with the differences between them becoming unclear. This book represents the advances that have occurred in cooperative/collaborative learning over the past 45 years or so.

There are four major reasons why cooperative/collaborative learning will remain a prominent instructional method for the foreseeable future. The first is the quality of theory underlying it. While there are many theories about cooperation, social interdependence theory has provided the most clarity and generated the most research (Deutsch, 1949; Johnson & Johnson, 2005).

The second reason that cooperative/collaborative learning will stay prominent is the amount of research conducted to document its effectiveness and validate social interdependence theory (Johnson & Johnson, 1989, 2005). Whenever the

Collaborative Online Learning in a Global World, pages ix–ix.
Copyright © 2019 by Information Age Publishing

question, "What works?" is asked, an answer has to be cooperative/collaborative learning due to the quantity and quality of the existing research. As the research grows ever stronger, the use of cooperative/collaborative learning becomes more and more inevitable and foundational. The multitude of resulting outcomes not only includes higher achievement and productivity, but also more positive relationships among collaborators and greater psychological health in collaborators.

Third, cooperative/collaborative learning has been implemented in a variety of classrooms in different countries and diverse cultures. The many cooperative learning procedures being used by teachers, all of which seem to work, provide support for the theories and the power of the underlying dynamics.

Finally, cooperative/collaborative learning continues to evolve and change along with society, students, teachers, and instructional technology. Cooperative/collaborative learning procedures and methods are different today compared with the cooperative learning procedures of the 1970s (such as Teams-Games-Tournaments and STAD). As technology, student diversity, and the broadening of education's purposes and goals in the 21st century have changed, so have cooperative/collaborative learning procedures and methods (Johnson & Johnson, 2010).

Miri Shonfeld and David Gibson have brought together chapters focusing on the future of cooperative learning. This is a forward-looking book that not only presents the variety of ways in which cooperative/collaborative learning is being used in contemporary schools but it also reflects the trends leading to the future use of cooperative/collaborative learning as it evolves and changes. This book aptly presents the ways in which cooperative/collaborative learning is evolving to adapt to the new technologies and programs that are becoming available. It not only presents models for using cooperative/collaborative learning online but also offers examples of how cooperative/collaborative learning promote cross-cultural understanding, more positive relationships with individuals with handicapping conditions, more positive relationships among traditional enemies, cross-cultural contact with others with whom one would never interact on the local level, the use of cooperative/collaborative learning in a wide variety of subject areas, and the impact of cooperative/collaborative learning on outcomes beyond achievement. These chapters illustrate the use of cooperative/collaborative learning in response to global interdependence, the diversity and pluralism of students and cultures reflected in schools, the need for 21st-century skills, and the expansion of democracies. This book is a must-read for all those who are interested in or are currently using cooperative/collaborative learning.

David W. Johnson
Roger T. Johnson
University of Minnesota

REFERENCES

Britton, J. (1990). Research currents: Second thoughts on learning. In M. Brubacher, R. Payne, & K. Richett (Eds.), *Perspectives on small group learning: Theory and practice* (pp. 3–11). Oakville, Ontario: Rubicon.

Deutsch, M. (1949). A theory of cooperation and competition. *Human Relations, 2,* 129–152.

Johnson, D. W., & Johnson, R. T. (1989). *Cooperation and competition: Theory and research.* Edina, MN: Interaction Book Company.

Johnson, D. W., & Johnson, R. T. (2005). New developments in social interdependence theory. *Genetic, Social, and General Psychology Monographs, 131*(4), 285–358.

Johnson, D. W., & Johnson, R. T. (2010). Cooperative learning and conflict resolution in the 21st century. In J. Bellanca & R. Brandt (Eds.), *Bridges to 21st century skills: A collection* (pp. 201–220). New York, NY: Solution Tree Press.

Johnson, D. W., & Johnson, R. T. (2014). Cooperation in the 21st century. In J. M. Serrano & R. M. Pons (Eds.), *Anales de Psicologia* [*Annals of Psychology*] (Special Issue on Cooperative Learning), *30*(3, October), 841–851.

INTRODUCTION TO COLLABORATIVE LEARNING IN A GLOBAL WORLD

Miri Shonfeld and David Gibson

The 21st century has brought about changes in every aspect of life through ubiquitous technology and Internet-based social media. The distances between cultures and continents have narrowed, the world has become flatter, and multicultural, international work-teams have become a daily reality in global businesses. For example, Israeli media specialists, U.S. marketing professionals, and Chinese chip makers might work as a team, using information and communication technologies and group processes that require online collaboration skills. Importantly, these global changes in work practices have only begun to have an impact on education. In spite of the power of Web 2.0 platforms to help people create and share information online, the impact of online collaboration tools and practices is not yet widespread in education.

To better prepare students for the information age, researchers and policy makers are beginning to reach agreement about the skills needed for shared knowledge construction that is ubiquitous in online collaborative learning. Indeed, the education systems in several different countries have begun to integrate these skills into teaching and learning and are beginning to place emphasis on their

Collaborative Online Learning in a Global World, pages xiii–xvi.

implementation (Melamed et al., 2010; Resta et al., 2011). For example, in 2015 the OECD PISA exam included assessment of collaborative problem-solving in its country-by-country comparisons for the first time. Collaborative teaching and learning approaches are thus gaining in popularity, and an "Online Collaborative Learning" (OCL) theory has recently been developed to better reflect the skills required in the information age (Harasim, 2012).

Since the 1980s, individual practitioners have made attempts to implement collaborative online learning, and a growing number of researchers since that time have analyzed relevant theories, practices, and challenges (e.g. Sharan & Sharan, 1992). Today, collaborative learning involves interaction between learners through both social and professional communications, which are enabled by the accessibility and affordances offered by online networks. Online learning communities are increasingly part of school experiences. Nowadays, any student can be a part of an international online discussion group where they can collaboratively create, process, and produce knowledge. Multicultural study-groups from different countries can collaboratively explore, develop, and discover cultures they would not otherwise encounter in traditional study practices (Shonfeld, Hoter, & Ganayem, 2013). Such learning practices better prepare students for the 21st-century's realities.

However, online collaborative learning is not a trivial challenge, nor is it intuitive for all teachers and learners. New tools and practices become available at a rate that outpaces the abilities of many higher-education institutions to adopt and implement, so practices in teacher education lag behind industry in using global communications technologies. However, teachers must acquire and practice essential skills in both collaboration and communication technologies in order to successfully teach students how to work in global teams. Consequently, it is essential to train teachers so they can then serve as role models for students.

This book surveys the current state of online collaborative learning and provides theoretical guidance and practical examples to help meet the gaps in research, development, and practice. It is hoped that the book can serve as a compendium of ideas for research faculties of education, classroom instructors, and practitioners to find rationales, ideas, and teaching approaches that support collaborative learning in a global context.

COLLABORATION—THEORY, ATTITUDES, AND IMPLEMENTATION

In the first chapter, "My Personal and Professional Involvement with Cooperative Learning," pioneering practitioner Yael Sharan responds to questions framed by Zippora Zelkovitch, a veteran teacher educator. The questions include what is cooperative learning (CL)?; What causes teachers to object to CL?; and What is the role of CL in today's education?

Elaine Hoter, one of the early promoters of collaborative learning in Israel, shares her personal journey in Chapter 2, "Developing a Model for Online Collaborative Learning." The journey includes the central role of writing and reflection, setting up roles within a collaborative environment, and a discussion of the interactions among the roles.

In Chapter 3, "Technology-Enabled, Challenge-Based Learning in a Global Context," David Gibson, Leah Irving, and Katy Scott describe how a new scalable educational technology helps digital learning experiences to reach a global audience. The design principles of challenge-based learning in a global context come from an extension of problem-based, project-based, and contextual teaching and learning. Case examples are provided from Curtin University's *Challenge* platform, which enables and supports scalability, self-organizing and self-directing teams, automated assessment methods, and the support of creative transmedia narratives.

COLLABORATIVE LEARNING CONNECTING CULTURES

Rivi Carmel, in Chapter 4, "Learning About the 'Other': Encounters between Arab and Jewish Students in Israel," describes a study of a one-year "shared citizenship" collaborative intervention program offered during the 2013–2014 academic year between the English teaching departments in two colleges in Israel. The program aimed to provide future English teachers with the opportunity to promote openness and understanding towards the "other": Arab towards Jews and Jews towards Arabs, while using English as the mutual language of communication.

The use of blended contact between schools to promote community cohesion on both sides of the border in Ireland has been a feature of education policy and practice for over 30 years and is discussed by Roger Austin in Chapter 5, "Blended Contact for Community Cohesion in Northern Ireland and the Republic of Ireland." This chapter analyzes the thinking underpinning the work and summarizes the research evidence of its impact.

In Chapter 6, "Online collaboration between Israeli and Slovak students," Tsafi Timor presents findings of a study of a collaboration that introduced the teacher-education students to collaborative global learning and global educational understanding, allowing them to develop critical thinking with regard to their local practices.

Miri Shonfeld and Paul Resta discuss "Competitive Game Effect on Collaborative Learning in a Virtual World" in Chapter 7. They examine the learning theory, the design and execution of a competition in a collaborative project, and student reactions to the experience. The chapter evaluates the project's successes and the problems encountered. It suggests ways to enhance this binational and multicultural educational approach.

COLLABORATION IN THE K12 CLASSROOM

In Chapter 8, "TEC4SCHOOLS TEC: An Online Collaborative Learning Model in a Multicultural Environment," Miki Kritz and Efrat Bachar discuss the TEC model (Technology, Education, and Cultural Diversity). The model is based on the gradual increase in exposure and approaches to communication among participants. They describe elementary school students who undertook collaborative tasks over the Internet and examine the impacts on the participating teachers and students in the following areas: multi-cultural outlook, pedagogical contribution, and technological and social aspects. Their research shows a significant impact on the students, teachers, and community.

Betty Shrieber and Rachel Peled describe cooperative learning among young adult pupils (ages 19–21) with Cerebral Palsy (CP) in Chapter 9, "Cooperative Online Research Meetings of Cerebral Palsy and Graduate Students to Promote Web Accessibility." Questionnaires completed by the postgraduates working with these students revealed that they developed an increased awareness of the special needs of pupils with disabilities. For the CP students, this opportunity to participate in cooperative learning gave them a place to present themselves, demonstrate the technological needs important to them, and indicate that they deserve equal rights.

Dalit Levi shares results from observations of classroom dialogs among peers and offers a model for documenting conceptual change in Chapter 10, "Collaborative Conceptual Change in the Computer-Science Classroom." She found that the model for organizing preconceptions and change over time illustrates the ways in which students relate to the interdisciplinary concept of recursion, the particular learners' language concerning recursive phenomena, and the nature of the conceptual change that might take place in the course of the collaborative learning activity.

COLLABORATION IN TEACHER-EDUCATION PROGRAMS

In Chapter 11, Miri Shonfeld and Yehudith Weinberger discuss the question "What Influences Teacher Educators' Use of Collaborative Learning?" These researchers found that since the most influential factor on lecturers' use of CL is their willingness to incorporate it in their classes, which is based on their competency and readiness, it is crucially important to raise their consciousness of CL.

In Chapter 12, "Online Collaborative Learning: Connecting University Students from Israel and Germany," Claudia Finkbeiner, Miriam Muchow, Einat Rozner, and Miri Shonfeld analyze the quality and frequency of communication as well as the results of tasks produced by two systematically selected groups during a one-semester online course involving a collaboration between graduate students from Israel and Germany. The chapter focuses on both pedagogy and the technology. The basic principle of the class was learning by doing, as exemplified in the Learner-Moderator-Researcher plus (LMR Plus) Model, rather than just reading or listening. The interaction was based on the Technology, Education, and Cultural diversity (TEC) Model in which collaboration and communication take place. This experience suggests that synchronous meetings in online courses should be implemented more often and more systematically.

Tina Waldman and Efrat Harel, in Chapter 13, "Promoting Online Collaboration Competence among Pre-service Teachers of English as a Foreign Language," present an online collaborative project between pre-service teachers of English as a foreign language (EFL) studying at a teacher-training college in Israel and a university in Germany. The chapter reports on research carried out on the 33 Israeli students based in part on quantitative data collected in a survey distributed both pre- and post-collaboration, as well as on qualitative data collected via personal interviews conducted with the students following the collaboration. The findings show that online collaboration integrated into teacher training contributes to teacher development.

In Chapter 14, "The Forum of Excellent Students: A Model for Cooperative Learning in a Multicultural Environment," Liat Eyal, Rama Klavir, and Naomi Magid describe the implementation of cooperative learning in a multicultural student forum, where pre-service teachers participated as part of their training-in-excellence program. The mixed-methods study, which was based on questionnaire responses from 110 graduates of the forum, examines the contribution of the cooperative-learning environment to their learning experience and the forum's influence on their perceptions as future teachers. The results indicate that the students experienced empowering and enjoyable dialogical learning which affected their perceptions of multiculturalism as a valuable resource, removing barriers and prejudices and enriching the learning.

ASSESSMENT AND EVALUATION

Chapter 15, "Assessing Personal Learning in Online, Collaborative Problem-Solving," outlines a domain model for planning the assessment of individual contributions to an online, collaborative problem-solving effort. Because of the complex social context of the task, the observations of learning in online, collaborative problem solving can provide evidence of higher-order creative, critical thinking, and communication skills. The model brings together definitions of personalized learning, collaboration, and problem solving and provides a framework for a chain of reasoning based on a network of claims about what learners know and can do. Authors David Gibson, Leah Irving, and Tami Seifert discuss how assessing personal learning in online, collaborative problem solving entails observing the actions, communications, and products created by group members in a designed task space as they engage in coordinated activity to construct and maintain a shared conception of an open-ended problem and achieve a goal related to the problem.

The research in Chapter 16, "The Impact of an Online, Collaborative Learning Program on Attitudes toward Technology in Two Education Colleges'

M.Ed. Programs," by Noga Magen-Nagar compared collaborative learning in a traditional online course with a designed intervention online course, examining for impacts on attitudes towards technology including technological anxiety, self-confidence, and technology orientation among M.Ed. students. The results indicated significant differences between the intervention group and the control group. Collaboration in the intervention group had a more meaningful indirect effect on predicting attitudes towards technologies compared to the control group.

REFERENCES

Harasim, L. (2012). *Learning theory and online technology: How new technologies are transforming learning opportunities.* New York, NY: Routledge Press.

Melamed, U., Peled, R., Mor, N., Shonfeld, M., Harel, S., & Ben Shimon, I. (2010). *A program for adjusting teacher education colleges to the 21st century.* Ministry of Education, Israel.

Resta, P., Searson, M., Patru, M., Knezek, G., & Voogt, J. (2011). *Building a global community of policy-makers, researchers and teachers to move education systems into the digital age.* Edusummit Report, International summit on Education, Unesco, Paris.

Sharan, Y., & Sharan, S. (1992). *Expanding cooperative learning through group investigation.* New York, NY: Teachers College Press.

Shonfeld, M., Hoter, E., & Ganayem, A. (2013). Improving collaborative online learning using the TEC model. In R. McBride & M. Searson (Eds.), *Proceedings of Society for Information Technology & Teacher Education International Conference 2013* (pp. 1028–1033). Chesapeake, VA: AACE.

CHAPTER 1

MY PERSONAL AND PROFESSIONAL INVOLVEMENT WITH COOPERATIVE LEARNING

Yael Sharan

WHAT IS COOPERATIVE LEARNING?

In the 1960s, several educational researchers and psychologists sought ways to actively engage students of all ages in learning by what became known as cooperative learning (CL). Since then, this approach has grown to be an umbrella pedagogy that covers a diversified body of methods, models, and instructional procedures with increasingly diverse applications. The many ways of organizing a CL classroom raise the question of what they have in common. Brody and Davidson (1998) offer a succinct and helpful definition:

> CL methods, models and instructional procedures organize students to: work in groups toward a common cooperative learning goal or outcome, or share a common problem or task, in such a way that they can only succeed in completing the work through [behavior] that demonstrates interdependence, while holding individual contributions and efforts accountable. (p. 8)

Collaborative Online Learning in a Global World, pages 1–8.
Copyright © 2019 by Information Age Publishing

DOES THIS DEFINITION FIT ANY PARTICULAR THEORY OF CL?

This definition integrates the central elements of the main theories that contribute to making CL what it is today. CL was never a uniform, homogenous approach to teaching and learning; it was born of several "parents" who nurtured it with complementary educational, psychological, sociological, and motivational theories. Together, these theories provide a powerful rationale as to why CL successfully promotes academic and social skills and contributes to meaningful learning. Prominent pioneers of the theories and practice are John Dewey, Morton Deutsch, David Johnson and Roger Johnson, Shlomo Sharan, Robert Slavin, Elizabeth Cohen, and Spencer Kagan (Sharan, 2015). Researchers continue to enrich our understanding of how the various theoretical and practical elements contribute to the mosaic that is the CL pedagogy of today. Researchers and practitioners also continue to contribute to the design and development of classroom and school action plans that include the seminal elements of CL in all subjects and at all levels.

Researchers have also turned their attention to teacher education for CL (see, for example, Cohen, Brody, & Sapon-Shavon, 2004). While there is no single way to teach teachers how to implement CL, there is consensus that experiential learning is an essential feature of any teacher-education program for CL (Sharan, 2002). Teacher education for CL seeks to help teachers move from the traditional transmission model that calls for imparting prescribed facts and ideas, to the transaction model that invites students to actively participate in the learning process, and, beyond, to the transformation model that invites learners to contribute to the formation of knowledge (Brody, 1998; Sharan, 2010b). Experiential workshops avoid merely "learning about" CL, which by itself cannot bring about the necessary change in teachers' perception of their role in cooperative learning. Experiential workshops enable teachers to encounter the many personal and professional implications of cooperative learning; they afford teachers many opportunities to experience learning together as partners or in small groups for various purposes and periods of time (Damini, 2014; Koutselini, 2008; Pescarmona, 2014; Sharan, 2002, 2004).

WHY DO YOU THINK CL HAS
SPREAD THROUGHOUT THE WORLD?

From the second half of the 20th century onward, CL has caught the attention of educators, universities, and governments in many countries and today is implemented and researched all over the world. Several reasons for this come to mind. For one, cooperative learning procedures combine and promote academic as well as social skills—two universal educational goals. Secondly, the increasing diversity in classrooms everywhere propels teachers to turn to the large body of CL methods and procedures as being among the most flexible modes of instruction for the intercultural classroom. There are multiple programs for educational interventions that strive to turn classrooms into intercultural learning communities, where teachers weave learners' differences and similarities into the curriculum and create opportunities for meaningful contact and interaction among students of diverse backgrounds (Portera, 2008). Moreover, CL practice is consistently supported by research that leads to continuous examination of its effectiveness along with constant refinement of theory and cooperative procedures. CL researchers and practitioners also offer a wealth of books, guidebooks, and teacher-training programs. Teachers draw on the power of CL when they seek ways to enhance all students' involvement in their learning and endeavor to refine their ability to create an interactive and nurturing learning environment (Sharan, 2010a).

HOW DID YOU DISCOVER THE NEED FOR INTERACTIVE LEARNING?

My own journey began in 1954 when I took my first teaching job in a public school in a farming village near the southern border of Israel, where new immigrants from Iran lived. They hardly knew the Hebrew language and weren't used to modern, informal relationships between teachers and students. My fellow teachers and I were novice teachers, fresh out of a teachers' college, where we learned to teach by the time-honored transmission approach. We had never learned that teaching and learning depended on the connection between learners and the curriculum.

It quickly became obvious that my third-grade students were not interested or involved in what we were teaching. A vivid turning point in my teaching took place in a lesson about the sun. After my saying that as far as they may think the sun is from earth, it's even farther, one girl said, "You mean it's as far as Iran is from Israel?" I immediately realized that *what* I was teaching and the *way* I was teaching had nothing to do with her world. This short incident propelled me to seek a different approach to teaching, one that included encouraging the children to ask more questions about what they were learning, to express orally and in writing their understandings of what they were learning, and to work in pairs so they could share their learning with one another.

At the time, I knew nothing about cooperative learning or individualized learning (both had yet to be popularized), yet gradually the need for a whole new approach to teaching became clear to me: the need to make learning meaningful by tailoring learning materials and teaching methods to learners' needs and interests (Sharan, 2015).

HOW DID THIS LEAD TO COOPERATIVE LEARNING?

After teaching for two years, I went on to study education at the university, where I came across a book, sadly no longer in print, that greatly influenced me: Miel's (1952) thorough study of cooperative planning in 57 schools throughout the U.S. The study covers every aspect of CL, explains in great detail the challenges involved in carrying it out and the solutions offered by teachers and students alike, and is surprisingly relevant to this day. In addition, a two-year stay in California in the early 1970s was an opportunity to learn about a great deal of educational experimentation in various forms of group work. As a result, Shlomo Sharan and I wrote a book, in Hebrew, called *Small Group Teaching*, based on the various interactive teaching methods we had witnessed in several schools in California and on the literature available at the time. In Israel, Shlomo Sharan researched one particular CL model, group investigation (GI), whose many components, together and separately, have become an integral part of educational practice, especially in the higher grades (Sharan & Sharan, 1992; Sharan, Sharan, & Tan, 2013). A unique feature of Shlomo's research projects was that all teachers in a school participated in all the training workshops, regardless of whether they took part in the study or not. I was part of the team of teacher trainers in these projects and have remained a teacher-educator for group investigation and cooperative learning.

"Small group teaching" became known as cooperative learning, and the number of researchers and practitioners grew. In 1979, Shlomo Sharan convened the first international conference, in Israel, that brought together many of these researchers and practitioners for the first time. People came from Australia, England, America, and the Philippines, and many Israeli teachers of English also attended. (In most countries, the teachers of a foreign or a second language are the first to adopt cooperative learning to facilitate learners' communication skills). At the end of the conference, delegates decided to form an association, and the International Association for the Study of Cooperation in Education (IASCE) was born and to date has convened 15 international conferences in all parts of the world.

HOW DID YOU COMBINE GROUP INVESTIGATION AND COOPERATIVE LEARNING IN YOUR TEACHER TRAINING?

For several years, I facilitated workshops that focused on GI. Sometimes a workshop would last two or three consecutive days, which allowed participants to investigate this model step by step. They experienced GI as they learned about it and reflected on the various facets of carrying it out. I adapted this experiential way of learning about GI to one-day workshops and even to three-hour workshops.

One of the unique features of this type of workshop is that participants are given a general topic to investigate, divide the investigation among group members, and, finally, share their findings with teammates and with the whole class. Both the knowledge gained from the investigation process and participants' personal and professional reflections about their experience contribute to learning about GI and about CL. As Thelen (1981) wrote, the content that groups create must be made public, shared with the whole class; the groups' combined knowledge becomes the class's capital. The dividends are the knowledge everyone gains from individual and group contributions. The experience is quite exciting and very new for most teachers, especially for those who are used to the traditional transmission approach to teaching.

DO TEACHERS FIND IT DIFFICULT TO ACCEPT GROUP INVESTIGATION IN PARTICULAR AND COOPERATIVE LEARNING IN GENERAL?

Learning GI and other CL methods and models by actually carrying them out is an eye-opening experience for teachers. In addition to introductory workshops, teachers new to CL generally benefit from a great deal of practice that is monitored by teachers who have more experience using CL. They also benefit from observing one another and from exchanging their experiences and ideas with one another (Brody, Damini, & Pescarmona, 2016).

In recent decades, CL has spread to educational settings in Asian countries, where traditionally the teacher is a supreme authority. Students are not used to asking questions and are not viewed as potential sources of knowledge. In Hong Kong, Singapore, and parts of India, for example, my workshops were based on short-term activities that allowed for the incremental experience of and reflection on CL components and principles. Little by little, activity after activity, participants understood how positive interdependence and individual accountability contribute to the completion of a group task and to learning. And, of course, we discuss the teacher's role, which I model throughout the workshop.

WHAT IS IT THAT CAUSES TEACHERS TO OBJECT TO COOPERATIVE LEARNING?

In many countries, CL is often introduced by supervisors, or by university education departments, or by outside experts who are invited to change the way teachers teach. Rarely is the change initiated by the teachers or schools themselves and their own assessment of their needs. One result is that often teachers believe that by being told to implement CL they are being asked to give up all the other ways of teaching that they know. Though no one explicitly tells them this, it remains a pervasive attitude and one that requires time and experience to overcome. What they come to accept is that once they have understood CL they have the autonomy and responsibility to judge when it is appropriate to apply and at what pace to apply it to their specific curricula and classrooms. Basically, they go through a change process, and, as in any area, change is a slow process.

HAVE YOU FOUND SIMILAR QUESTIONS WHEREVER YOU'VE WORKED WITH TEACHERS?

It's been my good fortune to conduct cooperative learning workshops in Italy, Thailand, Finland, Greece, Israel, Canada, India, Singapore, Lithuania, and the U.S., among other places. It's a striking phenomenon that in all these countries teachers raise the same questions about CL in general and about GI in particular.

Some of the ubiquitous questions are: "How much decision making should we leave to students? How can we prepare students for group discussion? How can individual work be assessed?" Obviously, countries differ in language, in teaching traditions, and in culture. It seems that as people, teachers in different countries present a wide variety of backgrounds and interests that contribute to the energy and creativity in the workshop. In contrast, as teachers, they present a more homogeneous front, with similar professional concerns and hesitations about CL (Sharan, 2001).

HOW DO YOU SEE COOPERATIVE LEARNING'S ROLE IN EDUCATION TODAY?

CL elements continually surface in different interactive and inquiry-based learning models designed by practitioners and researchers. I think that today CL is a firmly established part of teachers' toolbox, even if they aren't aware of the origin of a particular CL procedure. We've come a long way from the days when a teacher would learn only one method, like Jigsaw (Aronson, Blaney, Stephan, Sikes, & Snapp, 1978) or a few structures. Today, there is a broader understanding of the CL approach and its applications and of the benefits of including full methods and models or their components in a vast variety of settings, including post-secondary, vocational, and university ones (Baloche, 2011; Sharan, 2012). Elements of CL are also found in various forms and levels of digital and online, collaborative learning environments (De Wever, Schellens, Valcke, & Van Keer, 2006; Jacobs & Seouw 2015; Nam 2016; Shonfeld & Ronen, 2008).

CL practice continues to be supported by research that examines its effectiveness under different conditions and subject matter and constantly refines cooperative learning theory and practice (Johnson & Johnson, 2009; Slavin, 2010). Researchers too numerous to mention here continue to examine the effects of the specific methods and models and of CL in general on achievement, social interaction, cognitive processes, motivation, school organization, and, more recently and urgently, on the cultural diversity of today's classrooms (Sharan, 2010b). Also studied are the similarities and differences between methods; students' and teachers' perceptions of CL; the connections between CL procedures and methods and inclusion, group composition, size, discussion, task structure, helping behaviors, and teacher education for CL (Sharan, 2012).

It is my firm belief that when implemented responsibly, cooperative learning affords learners and teachers the experience of learning in an environment where knowledge is not a stilted, externally prescribed and measured product, but a dynamic, creative process that grows out of the interaction between students, however diverse their backgrounds, interests, experiences, and ideas. Teaching becomes a vibrant and enriching experience and often results in unexpected discoveries and insights for the teachers as well as for students.

(Zippora Zelkovitch interviewed Yael Sharan to form the basis for this article.)

REFERENCES

Aronson, E., Blaney, N., Stephan, C., Sikes, J., & Snapp, M. (1978). *The jigsaw classroom.* Beverly Hills, CA: Sage.

Baloche, L. (2011). A brief view of cooperative learning from across the pond, around the world, and over time. *Journal of Co-operative Studies, 44*(3), 25–30.

Brody, C. (1998). The significance of teacher beliefs for professional development and cooperative learning. In C. M. Brody & N. Davidson (Eds.), *Professional development for cooperative learning: issues and approaches* (pp, 25–48). Albany, NY: SUNY.

Brody, C., Damini, M., & Pescarmona., I. (2016). Teacher education for CL. *IASCE Newsletter, 34*(2), 4–5.

Brody, C., & Davidson, N. (1998). Introduction: professional development and cooperative learning. In C. M. Brody, & N. Davidson (Eds.), *Professional Development for Cooperative Learning: Issues and Approaches*, (pp. 3–24). Albany, NY: SUNY.

Cohen, E., Brody, C., & Sapon-Shavon, M. (Eds). (2004). *Teaching cooperative learning: The challenge for teacher education.* Albany, NY: SUNY.

Damini, M. (2014). How the Group Investigation model and the Six-Mirrors model changed teachers' roles and teachers' and students' attitudes towards diversity. *Intercultural Education. 25*(3), 197–205.

De Wever, B., Schellens, T., Valcke, M., & Van Keer, H. (2006). Content analysis schemes to analyze transcripts of online asynchronous discussion groups: A review. *Computers & Education, 46*(1), 6–28.

Jacobs, G., & Seouw, P. (2015). Cooperative learning principles enhance online interaction. *Journal of International and Comparative Education, 4*(1), 28–38.

Johnson, D. W., & Johnson, R. T. (2009). An educational psychology success story: Social interdependence theory and cooperative learning. *Educational Researcher, 38*(5), 365–379.

Koutselini, M. (2008). Teacher misconceptions and understanding of cooperative learning: An intervention study. *Journal of Classroom Interaction, 43*(2), 34–44.

Miel, A. (1952). *Cooperative procedures in learning.* New York, NY: Teachers College Press.

Nam, C. W. (2016). The effects of digital storytelling on student achievement, social presence, and attitude in online collaborative learning environments. *Interactive Learning Environments, 24*(1), 1–16.

Pescarmona, I. (2014). Learning to participate through Complex Instruction. *Intercultural Education, 25*(3), 187–196. doi:10.1080/14675986.2014.905360

Portera, A. (2008). Intercultural education in Europe: Epistemological and semantic aspects. *Intercultural Education, 19*(6), 481–492.

Sharan, S., Sharan, Y., & Tan, I. (2013). The Group Investigation approach to cooperative learning. In C. Hmelo-Silver, C. Chinn, C. A. O'Donnell, & C. Chan (Eds.), *International handbook of collaborative learning* (pp. 351–369). New York, NY: Routledge.

Sharan, Y. (2001). Have cooperative learning, will travel. *IASCE Newsletter, 20*(2), 5–6.

Sharan, Y. (2002). Essential features of a teacher education programme for cooperative learning. *Asia Pacific Journal of Education, 22*(1), 68–74.

Sharan, Y. (2004). Forward: A teacher educator's perspective. In E. G. Cohen, C. Brody, & M. Sapon-Shavon, (Eds.), *Teaching cooperative learning: The challenge for teacher education* (pp. ix–xii). Albany, NY: SUNY.

Sharan, Y. (2010a). Cooperative learning for academic and social gains: Valued pedagogy, problematic practice. *European Journal of Education, 45*(2), 300–310.

Sharan, Y. (2010b). Cooperative learning: A diversified pedagogy for the diverse classroom. *Intercultural Education, 21*(3), 195–203.

Sharan, Y. (2012). From the journals, to the field and back. *IASCE Newsletter, 31*(1), 15–16.

Sharan, Y. (2015). Meaningful learning in the co-operative classroom. Education 3–13. *International Journal of Primary. Elementary and Early Years Education, 43*(1), 83–94.

Sharan, Y., & Sharan, S. (1992). *Expanding cooperative learning through group investigation.* New York, NY: Teachers College Press.

Shonfeld, M., & Ronen, I. (2008). Online learning adaptable for students with diverse skills. *Proceedings of IUT.* Glasgow, Scotland.

Slavin, R. E. (2010). Instruction based on cooperative learning. In R. Mayer (Ed.), *Handbook of Research on Learning and Instruction* (pp. 344–360). London: Taylor and Francis.

Thelen, H. (1981). *The classroom society.* London: Croom Helm.

CHAPTER 2

DEVELOPING A MODEL FOR ONLINE COLLABORATIVE LEARNING

Elaine Hoter

By the early 1980s, "cooperative learning" methods were emerging as an accepted and effective way of teaching. Cooperative methods such as Jigsaw (Aronson, Blaney, Stephan, Sikes, & Snapp, 1978) and STAD (Slavin, 1995) were gradually being introduced into the classroom. However, most classrooms were not set up to be conducive to the logistics of cooperative learning (CL) which, among other procedures, requires working in groups and changing group composition, a marked change in the roles of teachers and students.

I found these procedures useful while teaching EFL reading-comprehension courses at the university level. They engaged the learner and allowed the students to interact with each other and with the text on a deeper level. The students built up their collaboration skills through various activities, and the classroom became a very active place for learning. Students sat in small groups and had assignments to carry out together. An example is Jigsaw activities, in which each member becomes an expert in a different part of the text and explains his or her understanding to others. However, at that time university studies were either formal large lectures or smaller seminars led by the lecturer. On one occasion at

Collaborative Online Learning in a Global World, pages 9–24.
Copyright © 2019 by Information Age Publishing
All rights of reproduction in any form reserved.

the beginning of my teaching at the Hebrew University, the students were working in jigsaw groups and having intense discussions on the material. A well-known professor was teaching in the room next door. He stormed into the room and shouted, "What is all this noise about? This is supposed to be a university. Can't you wait quietly until the lecturer comes?" One of the students was brave enough to say, "But the lecturer is in the class." The professor turned to me and yelled, "This is what you call learning?" Needless to say, I didn't try to tell him that the noise was productive and this was collaborative learning.

When I served as joint coordinator of spoken-English programs at the Open University, we instructors were able to experiment and base our teaching on co-operative/ collaborative learning techniques (Bejerano, 1987). At this time, the two terms were used interchangeably. However, the favored terminology today is collaborative learning (CL). Students worked in groups of four seated around small tables. As the Johnsons explain, "[CL] is not simply a matter of putting students into groups to learn, but involves positive interdependence, face-to-face interaction, individual accountability, and appropriate use of interpersonal and small group skills" (Johnson, 1984). The learning was not individualistic or competitive; the students needed to communicate and work together in order to accomplish shared goals. So much more communication goes on in this type of class, and improvement in the students' speaking ability—particularly in fluency—quickly became apparent.

Another consideration in a language classroom is the content of the lessons. Should the content be organized around reading comprehension topics, for example, grammar and text structure, or around themes? In content-based instruction (CBL), language is used as a means for teaching a subject or content area. The common ground for all CBL models is the use of meaningful content as a vehicle for language teaching and as a catalyst for language practice (Brinton, Snow, & Wesche, 1989, 1997; Mohan, 1986; Snow & Brinton). Kasper (1998) explains that in a content-based ESL course, students use the English language to acquire content knowledge through a variety of academically based tasks. He explains that these tasks are designed to teach students discipline-based content, while at the same time help develop proficiency in basic language skills (Kasper, 1998).

The advantages of using content-based units are many: they use authentic materials, allow for the integration of appropriate skill instruction, and serve as a unifying thread that spans multiple genres and skill areas (Brinton, 2000).

IMPORTANCE OF WRITING

In the early days of the Internet, writing was the main form of communication. CMC at its best encourages participants to become involved in authentic projects and write for a real audience: communicating with real people throughout the world, instead of writing assignments for the teacher. There are a number of advantages to the writing mode. Obviously, when learning a language, this is an ideal opportunity to use the language in a meaningful way. Writing has another advantage, and that is that it diminishes external differences of race, color, age, or physical challenge. All participants are equal. However, social cues, and cultural differences become problematic when people are not in a face-to-face (F2F) situation. Many misunderstandings can occur due to lack of information in the writing mode, such as whether a person is joking or being cynical, for example.

Writing has long been seen as an interactive process between the writer and herself/himself. The teacher's role is to supply feedback. Feedback, according to Zamel (1985), has two components, assessment and correction. An interesting case study in using e-mail to improve writing in German (St. John & Cash, 1995) shows how modelling the correct language on the part of the teacher and unobtrusive correction can considerably improve the grammar structure and vocabulary use of the student writer.

Research in written discourse shows that the computer writing environment has a number of advantages over the F2F environment (Chun, 1994; Kelm, 1992; Kern, 1995; Warshauer, 1996). The written discussions produced longer turns, more complex language, slightly greater equality of participation, more content focus, greater proportion of social talk, and more directness, whereas the F2F discussions produced more language, a greater proportion of meaning-negotiating functions, and more efforts at active group-building. In another online collaborative learning course carried out over an 11-year period between hearing and deaf students from Israel and Gallaudet University in the USA, the online writing component equalized the populations and reduced communication limitations for the deaf students (Hoter, 2006).

TERMINOLOGY

It seems appropriate here to understand the terminology used and the progression of the use of the Internet for collaborative learning. In the 1990s, there were two trends that have since diverged, the first in distance learning and the second in computers in education. Initially, distance learning referred primarily to the delivery of programs to remote students who never met each other or the lecturer. The first online courses followed this format, but they have since developed to allow for more interaction among the participants. The second trend was computer-assisted instruction (CAI), in which computers were being used in the classrooms as an addition to textbook course material. Traditionally, the use of CAI was associated with self-contained programs such as tutorials, drills, simulations, instructional games, tests, etc. With the additional technologies supplied through the introduction of the Internet in education, the scope of the role of computers in the classroom has widened considerably, going beyond simple CAI.

The customary approach in most on-campus courses at universities and teaching colleges involves a lecture/tutorial format in which material is delivered as lectures and discussed in tutorials. This is called the transmission approach, and the assumption is that the delivery of the "lecture" results in the learning of the material (Brody, 1998). For external students, beginning in the 1990s, materials delivered through the web allowed access to easily updated textual materials, some limited interactivity with programs on the Internet, and access to audio and video that could be streamed in real time. This made it technically possible for external students to watch a lecture in real time without being physically present at the university. This is also a transmission mode of teaching.

According to a report by the Office of Technology Assessment (1995) to the U.S. Congress, most technology instruction in colleges of education involved teaching about technology as a separate subject, so that the technology was not being integrated into other coursework. This assessment was applicable to teachers' colleges throughout the world. This was a far cry from the vision of Dede (1999) and other pioneers advocating integrating the Internet into education, who suggested that alternative pedagogical models should include guided inquiry learning with active construction of knowledge, collaborative learning, social exploration of multiple perspectives, and apprenticeship mentoring relationships.

Alternative approaches that encompass collaboration and build a sense of community by the use of the Internet became an important focus of research (Dillenbourg & Schneider, 1995; McMahon, 1997). Goldsworthy (1999–2000) claimed that four components are required to ensure real collaboration within a project: positive independence, individual accountability, group processing, and social skills.

Computer-mediated communication (CMC) is divided into two communicative modes: asynchronous and synchronous. Asynchronous communication does not take place in real time. This enables the participants to take time to read and respond to the messages. For language students, this has considerable advantages as they are not under pressure to write and read quickly and have a chance to monitor and edit their or other participants' text-based dialogue structures. Lee (1999) explains that the asynchronous mode has been widely used in the domain of collaborative writing, brainstorming, and fostering critical thinking. He says that the main disadvantage is that students cannot expect immediate feedback from the other participants and that this delayed response can cause frustration and affect the spontaneity of the communication.

Synchronous communication is a real-time mode, allowing two or more people to participate in simultaneous communication. The options available at the end of the 1990s were textual: IRC (Internet Relay Chat) and Multiple User Dungeons (MUDs). The advantages are that communication is taking place in real time and students can get used to a speech-like linguistic strategy (Ko, 1996). This type of communication is similar to real speech patterns with partial sentences and inter-ruptions. However, the disadvantages for the foreign-language learner are that they not only have to think in the target language but also, due to the time con-straints, have to type quickly, often at the expense of the standard of the written text. In these synchronous situations, students tend to provide simplified linguistic or syntactically broken inputs (Ko, 1996).

Electronic communities share some elements of traditional communities, including social interaction based upon geographical proximity, shared consciousness, and common goals. Rheingold (1993) defines electronic communities as "[s]ocial aggregations that emerge ... when enough people carry on those public discussions long enough with sufficient human feeling, to form webs of personal relationships in cyberspace" (p. 5). In the educational sense, an electronically networked community is one bound by common use or purpose rather than by physical location, technological orientation, institutional affiliation, grade level, or subject area (Kurshan, Harrington, & Milbury, 1994).

Distributed learning is a combination of face-to-face (F2F) instruction and learning in the classroom with an Internet component. The Internet component can be an on-line project with another school or on-line learning for part of the course. Students may only attend the F2F lessons and fulfill the other course requirements on-line. This type of learning is also referred to as the hybrid or blended model. E-learning is the generic term for learning using the Internet and it incorporates on-line learning, distributed learning, CMC, and learning using the tools of the Internet. Mason (1998) talks about the "integrated model," which consists of collaborative activities, learning resources, and joint assignments. In this model, the distinction between content and support dissolves, and a learning community is created. This is what Alexander (1999) refers to as the collaborative model.

However, in 1995 we were working in a vacuum. The Internet only became public in 1993, and online collaborative learning hadn't been tried out except as an extension of pen-pal projects, although some those pioneers envisioned the impact CMC would have on learning and teaching. One of these pioneers was Hiltz, who already saw in 1990 that computer-mediated communication was "particularly suited to the implementation of collaborative learning strategies or approaches." She foresaw it as a collaborative learning experience in which the teachers and students are both active in the building of knowledge, not delivered learning as in the transmission model but something that "emerges from active dialogue" (p. 135).

CMC was viewed as having the potential to facilitate communication and information-sharing among scholars, experts, parents, and students; help teachers implement new teaching techniques and improve student learning; expand the walls of the classroom by exposing students to a wide range of experts and resources; promote collaborative and active learning; enable student-directed investigation; encourage group development and electronic distribution of curriculum materials; and assist with teachers' professional development (Kurshan et al., 1994; Office of Technology Assessment, 1995). For this to occur, the use of technology must be coupled with a change in the beliefs of the teachers themselves, and only then can CMC encourage collaboration. Proponents of CMC promote the constructivist approach, using cooperative learning and collaborative problem solving and project-based learning (PBL). The philosophy is based on three basic characteristics stemming from constructivist Vygotskyan theories (Vygotsky, 1978):

1. Knowledge is not a product to be accumulated but an active process in which the learner attempts to make sense of the world.
2. People acquire knowledge in forms that enable them to use the knowledge later.
3. The construction of knowledge is based on the collaboration and social negotiation of meaning. Common understandings and shared meanings are developed through interaction among peers and teachers (Alexander, 1999).

THE ONLINE COLLABORATIVE-LEARNING MODEL

The typical online course given at the start of the use of the Internet in teaching in the mid-1990s, when the Internet became public, was a reproduction of the teacher-based or textbook-based learning used in class or at various open universities: the transmission mode. The students had some of the material online and submitted their assignments electronically. The learners in many cases had large forums and discussions among themselves and channels to communicate with the instructors. This model did not suit the teaching styles of collaborative teachers. In order to use the Internet to connect between students (in this specific course between student teachers in the teaching college and pupils in the classroom), a new model was needed.

The online collaborative learning model (OCL) presented here developed as a blended course in which the student teachers met with the instructor every week in the computer room. The OCL model has three overriding elements: the buddy/mentor system; collaborative, content-based pedagogy; and ongoing and holistic assessment (Figure 2.1). Class time was allocated to learn the technology, and the students immediately practiced what they had learnt through working together and teaching real pupils in the school through the Internet. The role of the instructor was incorporated into four areas: pedagogical, social, managerial, and technical (Collins & Berge, 1996).

The subject matter in the course was learning about advanced literacy skills and also teaching these skills. Learning about reading and writing skills does not mean that the student teacher can necessarily apply this knowledge in a teaching situation. The practicum with the online EFL pupil was therefore a necessary component of the model.

The year-long course included 20 student teachers studying to be English teachers and 35 junior-high-school pupils. The course was optional at the junior-high school, which was one of the first schools in Israel to be connected to the Internet. Many more students wanted to take the course than there were places, and pupils were selected from those who needed to improve their English, not simply the top pupils.

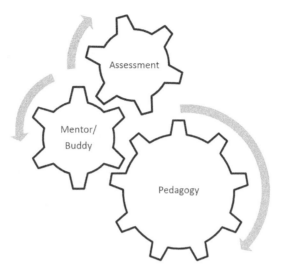

FIGURE 2.1.   Elements of the OCL Model

Technophobia

The first major barrier that needed to be combated was the fear and lack of confidence of the student teachers in using the technology. This might be hard to understand today, when few young people have technophobia, but at the start of the Internet, it was new to everyone. The course model tried to combat these barriers by giving the student teachers time to learn and use the technology and plan their teaching using technology. In addition, the course model attempted to give the participants a sense of achievement to raise their level of confidence by providing a supportive environment. It was decided that the course would involve distributed learning, with the student teachers meeting face to face in the classroom for four hours weekly in one block to enable them to use the Internet for communication and teaching their online pupils. The Internet was very slow, and more time had to be allocated to complete assignments.

Teacher Collaboration

The success of this type of course begins with the teaching-partner collaboration. The qualities required are dedication and willingness to learn on the job. This is how the system worked. The instructor (the teacher in the teaching college) worked with the student teachers in the classroom, who in turn taught a class of junior-high-school pupils, who also met in a classroom with their teacher. This junior-high-school teacher was the instructor's teaching partner.

Buddy-Mentor Approach

The basic premise of the COL model was the "buddy-mentor" approach. (Hoter, 2000; Oliver et al., 2001) This is very similar to the "Havruta" learning method in Jewish yeshiva education in Talmud, in which two pupils learn and discuss the material. In this model, the student teacher works as an online partner with an EFL pupil to complete joint assignments and also acts as a mentor. As a mentor, the student teacher gives feedback and helps the pupil with reading and writing in English, as well as providing additional tasks for the language learner. The idea of veteran teachers mentoring new teachers has become popular in the field of education through the Internet as well as F2F (Altany, 2001), but here it is the student teacher who is the mentor. The student teacher is at the same level as the pupil on issues of technology, where most of the tools of the Internet are new to both groups, but in the field of English, the student teacher has more knowledge than the EFL pupil.

The buddy part of the relationship between the pupil and the student teacher is similar to an email or key-pal exchange. This is when the student teacher communicates online with a student in much the same way that pen pals have communicated in the past. The difference is that there are more opportunities for interactive communication than with key pals because the letters are transmitted more quickly and there are more options for collaboration.

There were many reasons for choosing the buddy-mentor system as the basis for the model. First, learning and teaching is a communicative process which requires and prescribes partners (Rafaeli, 2001). Second, the student teachers had real pupils to work with and teach. By initially understanding one student's learning style and problems with learning English, the student teachers were able to concentrate on the individual and not deal with an entire class of learners. In addition, working with one pupil allowed the student teachers to build a personal relationship with the pupils. They were able to be part of the pupils' lives for the duration of the course and were able to empathize with the pupils and provide both academic and personal support. Having real pupils to work with also gave the student teachers a feeling of responsibility to their online partners to write back promptly and make sure that they had letters, tasks, and joint activities waiting in the pupils' e-mail boxes for the next lesson (very few students and pupils had Internet access out of class time).

A number of problems were associated with the buddy-mentor model. The major problem was administrative. Sometimes, student teachers or pupils were absent, and then the partners found themselves unable to continue working alone. On some occasions, one group was on vacation and joint collaboration had to wait. Another problem was that one of the partners just didn't do the task or did not do it properly and was not willing to put the effort into the learning process of writing. This greatly affected the work of the partner in quality, quantity, and motivation. Other problems arising in the one-on-one relationship involved e-mails not arriving, mainly due to misspelled addresses. Personality conflicts, however, were minimal. Some partners developed close relationships, which carried on after the course, whereas others never got off the ground. A contingency plan had to be made to overcome any technical problems, and all the instructors and student teachers learned the value and importance of flexibility. In later courses, the student teachers committed themselves to working on writing assignments with the pupils every week, come what may.

PEDAGOGY

To move from collaborative classroom learning to online collaborative learning, it is necessary to consider the principles of good practice and adapt them to the new learning environment. These principles are student-centered, experiential, holistic, authentic, expressive, reflective, social, collaborative, democratic, cognitive, developmental, constructivist, and challenging, (Zemelman, Daniels, & Hyde, 1998). All these elements can be found within the framework of the new model.

The tasks designed for the course were varied and required different cognitive competencies from listing, ordering, sorting, classifying, comparing, and matching to problem solving, sharing personal experiences, anecdote telling, and creative project work. The majority of tasks in the course were collaborative. Carrying out the collaborative tasks required time from the student teachers and pupils. Without sufficient time for planning, the work lacked accuracy, fluency, and complexity (Skehan, 2000). The logistics for planning how long to allow for each task were deliberated on as the course was being written and were open to negotiation during the course.

As the purpose of the course was also to familiarize the student teachers with the tools of the Internet and integrate them into the classroom, a number of these tools were introduced, and each was connected to a different module of the course content. The matching was cumulative: once a tool was introduced, it could be applied later in other areas of content. Online discussions were an important component for the student teachers, to enable them to participate (and, in the case of one group, another student teacher in Italy). It soon became apparent that online discussions needed moderating to be effective and to allow multiple participation (Collins & Berge, 1996; Hoter & Vermel, 1999). Student teachers took turns moderating the discussions and learning its intricacies through practice.

From the beginning of the course, motivation to learn about the Internet was high, with the student teachers realizing that it was important for their careers. Initially, learning about the technology became the main component of the course, overriding all the content-area aims. The need to know the technology and the frustration which abounded produced a barrier for many student teachers. Some of the frustration was caused by technological problems—for example, a slow server or the Internet connection falling—but most of the frustration in the early stages was from not feeling confident about using the tools of the Internet. Once the student teachers gained confidence from completing tasks successfully and mastered the basic functions of the email program, they were able to concentrate on the subject matter. They had to overcome the initial stages in the adoption of technology to see how the integration of the Internet could be beneficial for them as teachers-to-be.

For a number of student teachers, there was a critical incident in the process that served as a breakthrough. One of them wrote:

> I never thought I would be able to teach Yair over the Internet. I had a great deal of doubts about the program. How could you possibly teach a pupil that you had never met or even seen? How would the student feel comfortable with me… and what would be his motivation for learning? My doubts were all in vain. Yair was initially motivated by the sheer fact that he was using the computer and the Internet. I don't believe it mattered to him, or that he even noticed that he was actually learning. I must admit that I really didn't feel like I was teaching. It feels like I have a pen pal... The poem exercise was the most fun out of all. Once again I was afraid that it would be too difficult a task for Yair. The process of asking questions, and getting to know one another was fun. Yair composed a poem before I got a chance to compose mine. The poem was brilliant….[O]nce again I have underestimated his abilities. I learnt not to be afraid of challenging my student… worst case scenario he would ask for assistance. Yair's poem was brilliant, so brilliant in fact that I was afraid that my poem would not be good enough...So I rewrote it.

The high-school pupil working with Loise expressed this communication and collaboration among people through the Internet in his poem about her:

> Loise likes sport and I like sport too.
> Loise lives in the city and I do too.
> We are both human beings and we are learning English
> And at the same time we are learning about each other.
> Loise is a teacher and I am a pupil.
> But in this course we can be friends.
> You see, we are very similar people
> So it's good you are my unseen teacher.

"Unseen" is a pun made by the pupil. "Unseen" is the term used for texts read in the English classroom as well as the literary meaning of being a teacher the pupil does not see.

In short, the course required the student teachers to learn about the tools of the Internet and apply their knowledge in joint assignments with pupils through the Internet. The student teachers were required to micro-teach using the tools of the Internet and then, after reflection with peers, teach their pupil-partner through the Internet. The students were free to choose the content which would most motivate their online pupils. The student teachers learned about teaching the subject matter and using reflection to analyze the learning experience.

Deliberations on Assessment and Evaluation

At the time the OCL model was formulated, traditional summative evaluation was the norm in teaching colleges. The student took an exam at the end of the course and/or handed in a paper, and this constituted the grade he/she received. However, in order to assess the ongoing progress of the student teacher, as well as what the student has learned from the experience of learning and teaching online, formative, ongoing assessment is needed. If assessment can be seen as a movie, then a test is a freeze frame: it gives a picture of the learner's language at a particular point in time (MacGregor, 2000). In our case, we wish to see the whole movie.

For this alternative model, a multitude of elements needed to be assessed. They are listed in Table 2.1. In the first column, the area to be assessed is stated, and the second column indicates what needs to be assessed in that area.

The issue became more complex when some teachers had extremely good working relationships with their pupils and really managed to help them improve their literacy skills in English, but, on the other hand, they did not complete the technology requirements of the course and did not integrate the technology into their online teaching. Other student teachers did excellent work on the technology side but got no reaction or at most a few words from their junior-high-school partners. They were not able to give feedback and work as a team with their online partners. Should they be penalized for this?

Portfolio, or in our case Webfolio, assessment was used for the pupil and student teacher pairs. Portfolio assessment is the systematic collection of student work measured against predetermined scoring criteria, which often takes the form of scoring guides, rubrics, check lists, or rating scales (O'Malley & Pierce, 1996).

TABLE 2.1   Assessment Needs.

The Content Matter	Has the student teacher learned the content area of reading and writing skills and strategies?
Teaching the Content Area	Is the student teacher able to apply his/her knowledge about reading and writing skills in a teaching situation?
The Use of Technology	Does the student teacher feel competent in using the tools of the Internet?
Using Technology to Teach	To what extent does the student teacher feel confident using the tools of the Internet to teach?
Pair Work	How well did the student teacher collaborate with the pupil partner to produce the joint assignment?
Mentoring	How well did the student teacher mentor the EFL pupil?
Reflection	To what extent was the teacher able to reflect on the process he/she was going through? How were these reflections implemented in the online teaching?

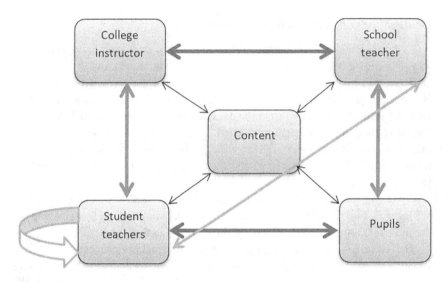

FIGURE 2.2. The Online Collaborative Learning Model interactions

Each Webfolio contained compulsory and optional elements including the pictures and introductions of both participants, the bio-poems written about each other, the separate and joint mini-projects, select email exchanges, the articles they had summarized, the address of the personalized newspaper and exercises to go with it, and extracts from the real-time meetings between the pairs. The pairs presented the portfolio to their own classes and reflected on the process they had gone through. The Webfolios were then posted on the Internet. In short, the area of assessment within the model is central and ongoing. The assessment is part of the learning cycle and needs to be reconsidered each time the model is used.

INTERACTIONS IN THE OCL MODEL

The OCL model involves interactions between the participants to themselves and between participants and the content. Each interaction is expanded on below:

College Instructor and Course Content

The instructor decided on the content and technologies needed for the course and wrote the course rationale and syllabus, taking into account the pedagogical, social, managerial, and technical areas.

Junior-High-School Class Teacher and Instructor

The correspondence between the teachers began from the moment a suitable classroom teacher was found. In this case, suitable meant with regard to the teachers' backgrounds (they had to have a high level of CMC literacy), the English level of the pupils, the teachers' timetable (they had to meet their pupils on a weekly basis F2F and have a similar semester as far as dates are concerned). The next stage was for the classroom teachers to become familiar with the course content and negotiate any aspects they wished with the instructor. A joint time schedule was set up. During the course, correspondence with the instructor took place on an almost daily basis. This correspondence included updates on lessons, technical problems, and administrative issues as well as personal correspondence.

Instructor and the Student Teachers

The instructor met the student teachers on a weekly basis in the classroom. However, a large proportion of the lessons included explanations and demonstrations of how to use and adapt the technology for the online pupils they were teaching. All the work in the content area was carried out via online class discussions, as were the interactions among the student teachers. The student teacher used the course site as a resource for all the material in the content area and were required to write a weekly reflective dialogue journal.

Pupils and the Classroom Teacher

The junior-high-school teacher met the pupils once a week for three to four hours. This lengthy time was found to be necessary due to technical problems and waiting for connections through the Internet. At that time, many thought the "www" stood for the World Wide Wait! In the sessions, the teacher gave technical instruction and help to the pupils and ultimately graded the student together with the online student teacher. Although the EFL teacher gave hints and advice, the school pupils knew that their teacher was their online student teacher who sent them individualized assignments to do alone or as a partner with the online teacher on a weekly basis.

Student Teacher and Junior-High Pupil

Each student teacher worked on a one-to-one basis with one or two junior-high-school pupils. The main interaction in the course was between the pupils and the student teacher. The student teacher mentored the pupil and gave assignments and feedback to improve the reading and writing skills of his or her partner. The pairs carried out joint collaborative tasks which required them to use the Internet.

Classroom Teacher and Student Teacher

The classroom teacher and student teacher interacted throughout the year, sharing information about the pupil's progress through email. The classroom teacher reported on any issues during the class time, and the student teacher enlisted the help of the teacher when needed.

CONCLUSIONS

Research studies have shown that using CMC in different subjects has resulted in increased motivation in one or more aspects; for example, either in terms of increased commitment to the learning task, enhanced enjoyment and interest, an enhanced sense of achievement, achievement of specific goals, or an increased sense of self-worth and a determination to achieve long-term goals (Cox, 1997).

In addition, Dede sees learner motivation increasing when guided inquiry, project-based collaboration, and mentoring relationships are introduced into the curriculum. This is manifested by better attendance, higher concentration, and greater time on task (Dede, 1999).

In the course described, motivation was very high. Pupils refused to take a break and continued the assignments whenever they could find a computer connected to the Internet. This was "infectious," and the student teachers also felt they had to outdo themselves to develop even more interesting tasks and assignments to work together and get to know their pupil partners. The feedback also attested to the high level of enjoyment this course generated and the extent to which the participants felt that they had improved their English. It was an experience the participants remembered as one of the most challenging and enjoyable in their learning experience.

Since this first course in 1996, numerous collaborative online courses have been taught using the basic model described in this chapter to connect different populations who would not normally have the opportunity to work together: hearing and deaf, children in Israel and overseas, students in Israel and abroad, and Arabs and Jews. These courses are much harder to teach and are far more demanding on the teachers, but the learning experience and the reward for those who participate far outweigh the disadvantages.

REFERENCES

Alexander, J. O. (1999). Collaborative design, constructivist learning, information technology immersion, & electronic communities: A case study. *Interpersonal Computing and Technology*, *7*, 1–28.

Altany, A. (2001). *The poetics of mentoring: Teachers teaching teachers.* Paper presented at "Opening Gates in Teacher Education" online conference, Mofet Institute, Israel. Retrieved from http://vcisrael.macam.ac.il/site/eng/files/E4A019_paper.htm

Aronson, E., Blaney, N., Stephan, C., Sikes, J., & Snapp, M. (1978). *The jigsaw classroom.* Beverly Hills, CA: Sage.

Bejarano, Y. (1987). A cooperative small-group methodology in the language classroom. *Tesol Quarterly*, *21*(3), 483–504.

Brinton, D. (2000). Out of the mouths of babes: Novice teacher insights into contentbased instruction. In L. Kasper, M. Babbitt, & R. Mlynarczyk (Eds.), *Content-based college ESL instruction* (pp. 48–70). Mahwah, NJ: Erlbaum.

Brinton, D. M., Snow, M. A., & Wesche, M. B. (1989). *Content-based second language instruction.* Boston: Heinle & Heinle.

Brody, C. (1998). The significance of teacher beliefs for professional development and cooperative learning. *Professional development for cooperative learning: Issues and approaches*, 25–48.

Chun, D. (1994). Using computer networking to facilitate the acquisition of interactive competence, *System*, *22*(1), 17–31.

Collins, M. P., & Berge, Z. L. (1996). *Facilitating interaction in computer mediated online courses.* Proceedings of the FSU/AECT Conference on Distance Learning. June 20–23, Tallahassee, FL.

Cox, M. (1997). *The effects of information technology on student motivation: Final report.* London, UK: King's College.

Dede, C. (1999). *Emerging learning technologies in higher education: Implementation strategies for practitioners.* Paper presented at the Conference on Learning Technologies @ the Service of Higher Education in Israel. Van- Leer Institute, Jerusalem.

Dillenbourg, P., & Schneider, D. (1995). *Collaborative learning and the Internet ICCAI.* Retrieved from http://tecfa.uniitge.ch/tecfa/research/CMC/colla/iccai95_1.html

Goldsworthy, R. (1999–2000). Collaborative classrooms, *Learning and Leading with Technology*, *27*(4), 6–9.

Hiltz, R. S. (1990). Evaluating the virtual classroom. In L. Harasim (Ed.), *Online education: Perspectives on a new environment* (pp. 133–183). New York, NY: Praeger.

Hoter, E. (2000). The effectiveness of student teacher training through the internet. In D.A. Willis, J. Price, & J. Willis (Eds.), *Technology and teacher education annual* (pp. 2250–2260). Charlottesville, VA: Association for the Advancement of Computing in Education.

Hoter, E. (2001). *A model for learning how to teach advanced literacy skills via computer mediated communication* (Doctoral dissertation). The Hebrew University, Jerusalem, Israel.

Hoter, E. (2006). Building community or a collaborative project? Connecting the Hearing and non-hearing communities. *Information Technology, Education and Society, 7*(1), 45–58.

Hoter, E., & Vermel, J. (1999). *An academic listserv: Useful or a waste of time?* Presentation at Mofet international conference for teacher educators, Bet Berl College, Israel.

Johnson, D. W. (1984). *Circles of learning. Cooperation in the classroom.* Alexandria, VA: Association for Supervision and Curriculum Development.

Kasper, L. (1998). *ESL and the internet: Content, rhetoric, and research.* Paper presented at Rhetoric and technology in the next millennium: An asynchronous online conference. Retrieved from https://sites.google.com/a/rsu71.org/the-global-classroom-linking-the-world-one-classroom-at-a-time/esl-and-the-internet

Kelm, O.R. (1992). The use of synchronous computer networks in second language instruction: A preliminary report. *Foreign Language Annals*, *25*(5), 441–454.

Kern, R. G. (1995). Reconstructing classroom interaction with networked computers: Effects on quantity and characteristics of language production. *Modern Language Journal*, *79*(4), 457–476.

Ko, K. K. (1996). Structural characteristics of computer-mediated language: A comparative analysis of interchange discourse. *Electronic Journal of Communication/La Revue Electronique de Communication, 6*(3). Retrieved October 5, 2018 from https://www.learntechlib.org/p/83178/

Kurshan, B., Harrington, M.A., & Milbury, P. (1994). *An educator's guide to electronic networking: Creating virtual communities.* Clearinghouse on Information and Technology, Syracuse University (ERIC Document Reproduction Service No. ED 372 772).

Lee, C. (1999). An exploration of pedagogical implications of using networked-based computer mediated communication in the communicative language classroom. *Interpersonal Computing and Technology: An Electronic Journal for the 21st Century, 7*(1), 1–16.

MacGregor, D. (2000). *Second language proficiency assessment.* ERIC/CLL Resource Guides. Online Center for Applied Linguistics. Retrieved from

Mason, R. (1998). Models of online courses. *ALN Magazine, 2*(2), 1–10.

McMahon, M. (1997, December). *Social constructivism and the World Wide Web-A paradigm for learning.* In ASCILITE conference. Perth, Australia (Vol. 327).

Mohan, B. A. (1986). *Language and content.* Reading, MA: Addison-Wesley.

Office of Technology Assessment. (1995). *Teachers and technology: Making the connection.* United States Government Printing Office, (Report No: 052-003-01409-2. Retrieved from http://www.ota.gov:80/T128

Oliver, D., Davis, R., Hoter, E., Kelly, C., Sperling, D., & Vilmi, R. (2001). Six Internet pioneers teach English to the world. *ESL Magazine, 4*(1), 10–14.

O'Malley, J. M., & Pierce, L. V. (1996). *Authentic assessment for English language learners: Practical approaches for teachers.* Boston, MA: Addison-Wesley Publishing Company.

Rafaeli, S. (2001). Are teachers superfluous? Keynote presentation. *Opening gates in teacher education online conference for teacher educators.* Retrieved from http://vcisrael.macam.ac.il/site/eng/show_file.asp?propid=7&subject=ks&page=people

Rheingold, H. (1993). *The virtual community: Homesteading on the electronic frontier.* New York, NY: HarperCollins.

Skehan, P. (2000). *Influences on task performance: The impact of different task conditions.* Paper presented at Trabajo presentado en American Association for Applied Linguistics Annual Conference, Vancouver, Canada.

Slavin, R. E. (1995) *Cooperative learning: Theory, research and practice* (2nd ed.) Boston, MA: Allyn and Bacon.

Snow, M. A., & Brinton, D. M. (1997). *The content-based classroom: Perspectives on integrating language and content.* New York, NY: Longman.

St. John, E., & Cash, D. (1995). German language learning via e-mail: A case study. *ReCALL, 7*(2), 47–51.

Vygotsky, L. S. (1978). *Mind in society.* Cambridge, MA: Harvard University Press.

Warschauer, M. (1996). Motivational aspects of using computers for writing and communication. In M. Warschauer. (Ed.), *Telecollaboration in foreign language learning* (pp. 29–46). Honolulu, HI: University of Hawai'i Second Language Teaching and Curriculum Center.

Zamel, V. (1985). Responding to student writing. *TESOL Quarterly, 19*(1) 79–101.

Zemelman, S., Daniels, H., & Hyde, A. (1998). *Best practice: New standards for teaching and learning in America's schools.* Portsmouth, NH: Heinemann.

CHAPTER 3

TECHNOLOGY-ENABLED, CHALLENGE-BASED LEARNING IN A GLOBAL CONTEXT

David Gibson, Leah Irving, and Katy Scott

WHAT IS COLLABORATIVE, CHALLENGE-BASED LEARNING?

Challenge-based learning is a new teaching model that incorporates aspects of collaborative problem-based learning, project-based learning, and contextual teaching and learning while focusing on current real-world problems (Johnson, Smith, Smythe, & Varon, 2009). Online, global learning challenges engage students' curiosity and desire to learn by making central the solving of open-ended problems as a member of a self-organizing and self-directing international team (Harris & Nolte, 2007). In particular, when delivered as a mobile learning experience using an application platform developed at Curtin University in Western Australia, such challenges can integrate 21st century tools, require collaboration, and assist students in managing their time and work schedules, while effectively scaling to large numbers of students. Set in the environment of a friendly competition where people experience game-like attributes such as automated feedback, points, leader boards, badges, and leveling up for rewards, challenge-based learning increases motivation to achieve high performance (Gibson & Grasso,

Collaborative Online Learning in a Global World, pages 25–39.
Copyright © 2019 by Information Age Publishing

25

2007). Research on challenge-based learning is beginning to show impacts such as increased engagement, increased time working on tasks, creative application of technology, and increased satisfaction with learning (Johnson & Adams, 2010; Roselli & Brophy, 2006).

Similar to problem-based and project-based learning, and borrowing liberally from those well-established approaches (see Gibson et al., 2011, and the Buck Institute for Education (www.bie.org)), the additional structure of global relevance, international collaboration, and team-based competition leads to a unique objective, expressed well in a recent report by the New Media Consortium (Johnson et al., 2009).

At the center of challenge-based learning is a call to action that inherently requires students to make something happen. They are compelled to research their topic, brainstorm strategies and solutions that are both credible and realistic in light of time and resources, and then develop and execute one of those solutions that addresses the challenge in ways both they themselves and others can see and measure.

The term "challenge-based learning" arose in the U.S. with the support of innovative technology groups such as Apple Education, the New Media Consortium, The Society for Information Technology and Teacher Education, and the U.S. Department of Education Office of Educational Technology. Here, we describe for the first time a unique application of challenge-based learning in higher education, supported by a new cloud-based mobile technology platform that can be used for bridging informal to formal learning, recruiting students into university, reaching larger numbers of people with game-based approaches, envisioning student engagement in work-integrated learning; and assisting students to acquire evidence of attainment of graduate capabilities such as leadership, critical thinking, creativity, communication skills, and experience in international team collaboration.

To explain how collaborative, challenge-based learning can work in higher education, we will first present an organizational overview of how our implementation addresses a wide range of structures, human resources, and symbolic, semantic and policy issues and embodies the philosophy of our technical framework. These four perspectives will be familiar to students of organizational behavior (Bolman & Deal, 1991) and are useful as a frame of reference for understanding challenge-based learning as a transformative organizational innovation in higher education. In each of the perspectives, we will explain how the collaborative, challenge-based approach relates to a range of teaching and learning methods; we then comment on what learners experience, what new roles are implied for instructors, and how the institution of higher education is changing to meet the new global imperatives of teaching and learning in the light of each perspective. We conclude the article by sharing a set of tenets for the design of collaborative challenges and introducing some details of a challenge-based learning-technology platform.

Structural: Well-Defined vs. Open-Ended Challenges

The structural perspective refers to the *architecture* and *mechanisms* of the roles and responsibilities in learning. For well-defined problems, the traditional role of the learner is a novice who is listening, watching, and learning from an expert. The expert knows the answer and can check the veracity of the novice's solution. In contrast, with open-ended or ill-structured problems, any participant on the problem-solving team is as likely as any other to have something to add to and help create the solution (Jonassen, 1997). Experts don't have all the answers, even if they do have more wisdom about how to construct meaningful and relevant solutions. Feedback on well-defined problems is thus often relatively easy to automate, since there are usually finite right and wrong answers in a limited range of expressions. But in open-ended challenges, feedback on detailed criteria is needed, which requires new methods of expression of the learner's understanding, such as visualizations and causal maps (Eseryel, Ifenthaler, & Ge, 2013). As in performance assessment, a scoring matrix aids in the evaluation of open-ended solutions when used by the learner, peers, and experts (Kelsey, 2001).

Learners undertaking a collaborative challenge might experience either end of the spectrum from well-defined to ill-structured problems or a cycling between those ends, depending on how much scaffolding of process and content as well as timing of support is desired to help learners create, communicate, think critically, and collaborate. For example, in the *Curtin Leadership Challenge*, a self-guided, challenge-based, digital learning experience, individuals first learn in a structured way about their own values and preferences and compare their thoughts with what the literature says about socially responsible leadership and then are introduced to more open-ended decisions about leadership.

In the *Balance of the Planet* sustainable-development challenge, the process of building a team is scaffolded, but the choice of which global problem to solve is left to the team to decide, and product rubrics with criteria for solution elements guide the team's decisions. For example, the team knows that it has to produce a seven-minute video as one of its products, and the video must convince the audience of the value of the team's solution, but no other help or advice is given, and the team must figure out not only what to represent but how to go about creating a video to meet those criteria.

Instructors in the world of collaborative, challenge-based teaching and learning have a special role in constructing a problem space with key ideas, essential questions, resources, and evaluation criteria. Subject matter experts (SMEs) in a discipline work with a digital-media team and game-creation team to engineer the learning experience. For *Balance of the Planet,* for example, the UNESCO Bangkok office, Curtin University's Sustainability Policy Institute, and the Australian Sustainable Development Institute, with the support of the Deputy Vice Chancellor Academic, engaged in the design thinking process that led to the challenge. In the next section, we explain the human-resource journey of SMEs in leadership into the new world of challenge-based learning. The point we are making here is that a new structure of teaching, created via collaborations among SMEs working with learning-experience designers and technical teams, is arising as an innovation to create new structures of teaching and learning in response to the myriad changes taking place in higher education today (Grummon, 2010). Challenge-based learning is seen in this context as one of Curtin University's innovative responses.

Human Resources: Individuals and Groups

The human-resource perspective refers to the people in the system: learners who form collaborative international teams, mentors who give advice to the teams, challenge authors who create and continuously adapt the digital learning experience, the platform creators and administrators, and the senior executives and external partners who support the challenge. This is the new face of instructional design teams in higher-education, challenge-based learning.

Learners experience a challenge as individuals but are also involved in the social processes of their group. Team members in the *Balance of the Planet,* for example, must agree on a team name and a key problem they wish to solve. They must choose an approach and point of view toward their solution or proposal and collaborate to create key artefacts that are submitted for feedback and judging. The team can reach out to any expert in the world to help them with their solution. The challenge has numerous activities and scaffolds at the team's disposal to help with group development and team learning processes, based in five disciplines of organizational learning (Senge et al., 1994) as well as with individual exploration and personal growth in a community of practice (Lave & Wenger, 1991; Li et al., 2009).

Individual and group experiences are integrated over time as team members undertake activities of their own choosing within the five disciplines of personal mastery, shared vision, mental models, team learning, and systems thinking (Senge, 1990). Students anonymously score each other's submissions and artefacts and gain extra points by offering elaborative comments that are accepted and used by others. Students on winning teams are invited to become mentors to future teams, are guided in their role, and are rewarded for their work. As mentors, they are observers on several teams and can share ideas, offer assistance, and promote exchanges of ideas among teams.

Instructors in the challenge-based learning framework are designers of the digital learning experience who put in most of their time in up front and then take a back seat during the implementation while individuals and teams are learning, working, communicating, creating, and submitting artefacts. Most of the input from subject-matter-expert authors is gathered during the design phase and is embedded into the digital experience through the public scoring rubrics, artefact descriptions for final submission, and scaffolding activities, which the team members can choose to experience or ignore. Some research indicates that students undertake more than is expected because the quest for points and attaining the winning condition are strong attractors for performance (Haskell, 2013). Instructors do not intervene during implementation, which allows the individual and team to self-teach; SMEs on the design team return to active duty at the end of the challenge when they form into panels to judge final submissions. This dramatic shift of focus goes beyond the "sage on the stage" as well as the "guide on the side" (Wiggins, 1989) to a stance where students learn by grappling with a problem or challenge using designed resources and experiences. Other subject experts in the world at large are human resources who serve at the pleasure of the team (Carroll, 2000).

A great variety of human resources can be found in higher education, and they span a wide range, from subject experts with deep knowledge of research and discipline content but little knowledge of learning theory and teaching, to teaching experts who combine subject knowledge, to learning scientists, digital media and instructional designers, tutors, student-life counselors, scholarship and admissions staff, administrators, career counselors, and many more. In a challenge-based, higher-education system where there is a shared vision and aspiration for producing global impacts, nearly all of these human resources can play helpful, targeted roles before, during, and after each phase of design, implementation, and evaluation. Subject specialists can respond with advice when a team asks. Teaching-focused experts can co-design the challenge-based digital experiences with media and instructional designers. Counselors and leadership experts can help train and support the mentors. Learning scientists can assist in researching the cognitive and non-cognitive effects and analyzing the data collected automatically by the technology. Scholarship leaders can be part of the reward structure; and so on. There is room for everyone to gather around the metaphorical circle of the issues at the center of technology-enabled, challenge-based learning in a global context.

Symbolic: Dramatic Aspirations

The symbolic perspective refers to the soul of the program, its aspirational vision and the stage it sets for creativity, meaning, and the importance of the effort (Bolman & Deal, 1995). The symbolic dimensions of challenge-based learning in a global context include addressing complex societal, economic, and environmental problems and fragmentation (Conklin, 2001); saving the world from destruction; and raising the hopes, learning capacities, and economies of all people. These are a set of aspirational objectives that might at first seem impossible to reach, but note: the game-like nature of a challenge creates a new virtual space for thinking and action where any kind of inquiry and expression is possible, similar to the virtual illusion of a fine art form (Langer, 1954). A global challenge is a call to dream, create, and be entrepreneurial in spirit for the good of others, which draws upon and requires one to integrate competence, autonomy, and relatedness (Ryan & Deci, 2000).

Learners who have participated in global, challenge-based learning programs relate that they were attracted by the idea of making new global friends, creating a new idea or solution that could change the world, and by the hopes of being recognized and rewarded for being the best in the world in the competition (Gibson & Grasso, 2007). These symbolic hopes for increased intercultural understanding, improved skills and powers of influence, and enhanced self-efficacy and confidence are real, measurable impacts that follow from the playful learning and effort in challenge-based learning (Harris & Nolte, 2007).

Instructors in fields such as theatre, music, film, digital media, creative writing, and performance art are experienced in the integration of genres common to many creative processes. Especially useful in innovation and entrepreneurial thinking are the skills of improvisation, brainstorming, and trusting one's instincts that are so central to the construction of expression and evaluation in the arts (Amabile, 1996). These interdisciplinary, team-based creation processes are critical paths for the symbolization of any inquiry and expression and now need to be codified into a new method of curriculum design for challenge-based learning. The design method for the future of digital learning experiences is a team-based effort of people knowledgeable in subject matter, dramatic narrative, mechanics of game-like interactions and rewards, digital-media artists and communicators, and computational science tools for algorithms and visualizations (Gibson, Aldrich, & Prensky, 2007). The mission of such interdisciplinary teams when creating challenge-based learning experiences is to create a symbolic space for transmedia narrative (Passalacqua & Pianzola, 2011) to be introduced as well as to evolve through the participatory culture (Jenkins et al., 2006) shared by those who take up the challenge.

Challenge-based learning is an approach to teaching that is well suited to the aspirational aims of higher education, and when focused on a global context, it is particularly fit to support its global mission. Supporting the structural and human resources and symbolic perspectives is the technological know-how to reach and engage people at scale around the world.

Technical: High Tech—High Touch

Technology enables collaborative, challenge-based learning in a global context to be authentic and fully empowered for creating, testing, and sharing ideas on a scale and speed of impact that was unimaginable a few years ago. However, this is not an argument from the standpoint of intoxication with technology (Naisbitt, Naisbitt, & Philips, 1999) with its attendant desire to find a quick fix, or as part of professing a love of gadgets, or the desire for a magical, automated solution. Instead, there are three pragmatic rationales for thoughtfully and carefully integrating technology into challenge-based learning in a global context.

First, computational tools and methods have transformed the landscape of science and our understanding of complex phenomena, leading to the observation that social and psychological research, including the learning sciences, have a new game-changing foundation (Gibson, 2012) that will advance as interdisciplinary teams construct challenges for learners. Second, social network tools such as Facebook and Twitter, as was evident in the Arab Spring (Lotan et al., 2011), illustrate the self-organizing power of some technology enablers, which has the potential to be harnessed for deliberative democracy and social-change leadership (Boeder, 2005; Habermas, 1990; Neilsen, 1990) to make the world a better place. Higher education has an ethical imperative to provide students with opportunities, guidance, and rewards for using technology for these ends. Third, powerful computational tools and global social networks are evidence of how computers change the way we think (Turkle, 2004). In *Balance of the Planet,* for example, by the use of technology to form and manage a work team, reach an international scientist for comment, find a solution and adapt it, and create complex communications and artefacts for others to judge, technology is a lens to see the world in new ways as well as a tool to envision, create, and take action for social, environmental, and economic justice, the triple bottom line of sustainable development (Sachs, 2012).

Second, learners on a globally distributed team are remote from each other in time and space, so technology is critical to the team's success. Learners in *Balance of the Planet* must use a wide variety of technologies for communication, creating documents and media, sending files, and keeping track of progress in order to submit a final product such as a video and a substantial, well-referenced, co-authored paper. The challenge-based learning philosophy of enabling technologies is to use them to introduce options but not to confine learners to any particular method, tool, or process. The sole driver of production is a highly detailed description of final submissions with publicly available scoring guides for both the video and extended report. This stance gives the learner and team maximum flexibility to find and creatively use technologies to meet their own aims. The digital-learning-experience design embeds a core set of technology requirements but leaves open how high tech and high touch the team envisions its solution.

Third, not only can instructors determine the expectations and resource constraints and set the digital stage for performance by working with a multidisciplinary design team, but so can the students. This kind of intensive, team-based design makes economic and pedagogic sense because one goal of *technology-enabled,* collaborative, challenge-based learning is to reach massive, open, online scale with a new kind of blended learning. Instead of blending face-to-face with online learning, the new blend is 1) well-structured and ill-structured problems, 2) individual and team learning, 3) dramatic transmedia narrative experience (Passalacqua & Pianzola, 2011) and practice-based acquisition, and 4) high tech and high touch. The economics of creating such a stage for challenge-based learning make sense in the long run because of scale, repeatability, and taking advantage of socially and algorithmically driven automation during the implementation phase. Pedagogically, a challenge is an invitation to perform to criteria, similar to a performance assessment or capstone project, and is therefore intended neither to be all things to all people nor to deliver all of education for all purposes.

DESIGN PRINCIPLES

In this section, key design principles for challenge-based learning are presented before a brief discussion of Curtin's Challenge platform. The principles are grouped into *ubiquitous and transformative technology* and *game-inspired teaching and learning* and build on the four perspectives outlined above. The tenets have emerged based on observations of innovative technologies being applied to the design problem of building a supportive technology infrastructure for challenge-based learning at Curtin University.

Ubiquitous and Transformative Technology

The first group of tenets concerns the embedded, anytime, anywhere nature of technology and information combined with the radical impacts this access and structure have had on the way we think about work, creativity, and the nature of thought itself. For example, embedded computers (Wolf, 2001) in the kitchen might mean that the refrigerator knows when milk and eggs are needed, can place and pay for the order at the store, and will notify the owner to pick them up on the way home from work. Access to information at any time has changed entertainment; for example, people can now "binge watch" (Jenner, 2014) an entire season of a show in one sitting, which was impossible a few years ago. Access to information on the go, anywhere has led to telecommuting (Ye, 2012) as well as to "Internet addiction" (Yellowlees & Marks, 2007). These kinds of cultural and psychological changes reflect a growing reliance on a new form of technology-enabled knowledge and thought which is mobile, distributed across one's social connections, media, and devices (Pea, 1993) and which requires as well as develops transmedia narrative expression and navigation skills, among other new media skills (Jenkins et al., 2006).

These two ideas–ubiquitous mobile computing and the transformation of work, creativity and thinking–suggest a need to rethink the digital environment for teaching and learning to be fit for purpose in this new landscape. In challenge-based learning by global teams, we have found four specific ways to reshape digital learning experiences.

Computational Thinking, Tools, and Toys

This approach assumes that people will learn better in a technology environment if given interactive, highly visual, and playful ways of engaging with and exploring ideas. The foundations of the idea have roots in the algorithmic and data revolution in science (Stanton, 2012) as well as in philosophy through computational epistemology (Thagard, 2002). As a design principle, words are minimized, and doing something with one's hands and mind is maximized. Directions about how to do something are kept to a minimum. Interactions are made as obvious as possible or easily discoverable, and the goal is to get the person to move things around, try things out, and to create his or her own words and concepts while displaying a real-time view of the data of interest.

Groups Self-Organizing Around Shared Goals

This approach acknowledges the social adhesion of knowledge production and creative problem solving when there is a shared vision (Senge et al., 1994). Instruction about and presentation of knowledge is kept to a minimum. Groups are allowed to form, adjust membership, and disband at will. Groups decide upon and develop their own specific focus (e.g., influencing the future of transportation) within a larger challenge concept (e.g., saving the world from various impacts of global warming). Unification of the group's production efforts is facilitated by having a concrete submission format for a final product that has been formed to provide evidence of highly detailed criteria with enough structure to ensure a fair comparison across groups. For example, a challenge might be to produce a seven-minute video explaining how the group's concept will save the world, which must show the concept in action, explain how it works, and convince the audience to join in, help, or try the solution. The video will be scored using a 10-point rubric with highly specific elements that help guide the group's decision-making about the video.

Find and Use Any Knowledge, Person, or Thing at Any Time

This principle acknowledges the ubiquitous, distributed nature of knowledge (Wenger, McDermott, & Snyder, 2002) and allows the group to reach out across the globe as well as through space and time to find any idea from any time or to engage with any mind or resource they can find. Points are subtracted for not acknowledging sources of reference, while significant extra points are given for utilizing and elaborating on the ideas, works, and words of others. Supports are given concerning how to acknowledge others. Encouraging this outreach, uptake, synthesis, and inclusion into the group's work is seen as key to collaboration and is a training ground for assembling ideas, scholarly thought, agents, and allies into one's creative, team-based problem solving and products.

Social, Epistemic, and Bayesian Networks as the New Teacher's Aide

This principle acknowledges a common feature of social network communities and in fact all kinds of networks. Thumbs up on Facebook, five-star ratings on Netflix, and publicly displayed trust measures on eBay are examples from industry and telecommunications of a kind of social currency that can be part of a digital learning-experience design. Coursera, a massive open online course

(MOOC) company, for example, utilizes social voting to help scale its assessments (Pappano, 2012). As people engage with a particular digital learning experience, the data network of which resource nodes they used and how they used them begins to form a basis for analysis. The general form of the data, when properly collected and stored, is called a Bayesian network (Mislevy, Steinberg, & Almond, 2003) from the practice of changing the weights associated with each node during the training of the data network (Baker, Chung, & Delacruz, 2008); and when the digital learning experience has been designed to replicate an authentic professional frame of thinking and action, then the analysis of the network can be considered an "epistemic network analysis" (Shaffer et al., 2009). Since the network can be used to make predictions, guide people to new resources, and make assessment judgments, we can think of this design element as supporting a new digital teacher's aide.

Game-Inspired Teaching and Learning

The student experience in challenge-based learning is inspired by elements of game-based learning. The following principles underscore how the context of a game with worthwhile rewards motivates people to undertake a challenge.

You Are The Hero of Your Own Story

This tenet addresses relevance and heroic action as the core of motivation to undertake a challenge. It also ties to personalization, while at the same time giving over to the person the authority to create the path he or she chooses to follow (in contrast to personalizing by selecting the next item for the person based on what has recently been accomplished). What games do well is give the feeling of heroic action quite often (e.g. once every few seconds or minutes) rather than only at the time of choosing to enroll in the experience (Prensky, 2001).

Work on Your Own Time, on Your Own Path

This element addresses freedom, creativity, and choice. Since the person can leave at any time, and might come back for only short stays, the learning design has to be thoughtfully constructed to allow short bursts of activity as well as meaningful sequences that unfold during concentrated periods of time. The heart of a game is having interesting decisions to make and complex consequences for one's actions (Aldrich, 2005). Digital learning design thus needs many decision points and many alternative ways to re-experience a setting, problem, or task.

Failure is Expected and Welcomed

This principle captures the idea that through dedicated practice, people gain skill and can become experts. In games, the player is given ample resources, which, while limited, are not so precious as to stifle risk. By sacrificing or losing from time to time, one learns how to win big at a later time. This is learning by trial and error, in which the cycle of learning is quick and the endorphin rush of winning small keeps people engaged (Howard-Jones et al., 2011).

Feedback, Points, Leader Boards, and Winning

These elements rest upon transparency of goals, access to data about progress, and comparison data that contextualizes to others and to accumulated gains. These principles have historically been explored as part of assessment theory (Black & Wiliam, 1998; Wiggins, 1989) and recently have been re-configured within the computational environment of digital learning environments (Baker et al., 2008; Gibson & Clarke-Midura, 2013).

Next, we briefly outline a case of combining the learning theories and design principles just outlined into a new online e-learning platform developed to support challenge-based learning at Curtin University in Perth, Western Australia.

BRIEF EXAMPLE: CURTIN CHALLENGE PLATFORM

Challenge is a web-based, mobile-ready application platform for active digital learning experiences and event-level data collection (Gibson & Jakl, 2013). Digital learning experiences launched on the platform present content in short, interactive tasks and track a learner's behaviors, products, and decisions at the event level in high resolution (many frames per second) allowing near real-time as well as post-hoc analysis of cognitive and behavioral change over time.

The teaching and learning approach of the platform uses *challenge-based learning* (Johnson & Adams, 2010) to shape the learning process and *evidence-centered design* (Mislevy, 2011) to inform the assessment process. Students largely teach themselves through self-organized activity, open-ended inquiry during exploratory learning, and creative self-determined expression within the bounds of required products that will be judged by peers, the world at large, and experts. The Curtin teaching and learning platform supports any number of people from thousands to tens or hundreds of thousands via technology-enhanced, digital learning experiences.

Challenge is designed to support self-directed learning, self-organizing international teams, open-ended problem solving, automated documentation and assessment of learning, social network validation processes, expert judging, and a variety of levels of recognition and awards. *Challenge* enables individuals to build up a private, safe, and trusted longitudinal record of digital engagement and to make progress at the individual level while working alone or with others. Individuals can participate numerous times in several different challenges and can gain a collection of micro-credentials that stand as evidence of meeting university-level progress and achievement.

SUMMARY

A new blend of e-learning approaches known as challenge-based learning supports the development of capabilities for global leadership, entrepreneurship, and ethical decision-making. Students in challenge-based learning experience a mixture of 1) well-structured and ill-structured problems, 2) individual and team learning, 3) dramatic transmedia narrative experience and practice-based acquisition, and 4) high tech and high touch technology approaches. Higher education has the requisite organizational resources–the structures, human resources, ethical aspirations and technical know-how–to create and support scalable, self-organizing learning communities and semi-automated processes for content creation and assessment feedback to bring these experiences and their content experts to the world. Design principles from ubiquitous computing, transformational uses of technology, and game-inspired engagement elements form a new basis for teaching and learning.

REFERENCES

Aldrich, C. (2005). *Learning by doing: The essential guide to simulations, computer games, and pedagogy in e-learning and other educational experiences.* San Francisco, CA: Jossey-Bass.

Amabile, T. M. (1996). *Creativity in context: Update to the social psychology of creativity.* Boulder, CO: Westview Press.

Baker, E. L., Chung, G. K., & Delacruz, G. C. (2008). Design and validation of technology-based performance assessments. In J. Michael Spector, M. David Merrill, Jeroen van Merriënboer, & Marcy P. Driscoll (Eds). *Handbook of research on educational communications and technology* (pp. 595–604). London, UK: Routledge.

Black, P., & Wiliam, D. (1998). *Inside the black box: Raising standards through classroom assessment.* London, UK: King's College.

Boeder, P. (2005). Habermas' heritage: The future of the public sphere in the network society. *First Monday, 10,* 1–15. doi:10.5210/fm.v10i9.1280

Bolman, D., & Deal, T. (1991). *Reframing organizations.* San Francisco, CA: Jossey-Bass.

Bolman, D., & Deal, T. (1995). *Leading with soul: An uncommon journey of spirit.* San Francisco, CA: Jossey-Bass.

Carroll, T. (2000). If we didn't have the schools we have today, would we create the schools we have today? Paper presented at *AACE/SITE conference.* San Diego, CA.

Conklin, J. (2001). *Wicked problems and fragmentation.* Retrieved from http://cognexus. org/wpf/wickedproblems.pdf

Eseryel, D., Ifenthaler, D., & Ge, X. (2013). Validation study of a method for assessing complex ill-structured problem solving by using causal representations. *Educational Technology Research and Development, 61,* 443–463.

Gibson, D. (2012). Game changers for transforming learning environments. In F. Miller (Ed.), *Transforming learning environments: Strategies to shape the next generation*

(Advances in Educational Administration, Volume 16, pp. 215–235). Bingley, UK: Emerald Group Publishing Ltd. doi:10.1108/S1479-3660(2012)0000016014

Gibson, D., Aldrich, C., & Prensky, M. (Eds.) (2007). *Games and simulations in online learning: Research and development frameworks.* Hershey, PA: Information Science Publishing.

Gibson, D., & Clarke-Midura, J. (2013). Some psychometric and design implications of game-based learning analytics. In D. Ifenthaler, J. Spector, P. Isaias, & D. Sampson (Eds.), *E-learning systems, environments and approaches: Theory and implementation* (pp. 201–208). London, UK: Springer.

Gibson, D., & Grasso, S. (2007). The global challenge: Save the world on your way to college. *Learning & Leading with Technology, 5191*(November), 12–16.

Gibson, D., & Jakl, P. (2013). *Data challenges of leveraging a simulation to assess learning.* West Lake Village, CA: Pragmatic Solutions. Retrieved from http://www.curveshift.com/images/Gibson_Jakl_data_challenges.pdf

Gibson, D., Knezek, G., Mergendoller, J., Garcia, P., Redmond, P., Spector, J. M., & Tillman, D. (2011). Performance assessment of 21st century teaching and learning: Insights into the future. In M. Koehler & P. Mishra (Eds.), *Proceedings of Society for Information Technology & Teacher Education International Conference 2011* (pp. 1839–1843). Chesapeake, VA: AACE.

Gibson, D. C., Ostashewski, N., Flintoff, K., Grant, S., & Knight, E. (2013). Digital badges in education. *Education and Information Technologies*, (November), 1–8. doi.org/10.1007/s10639-013-9291-7

Grummon, P. (2010). Trends in higher education. *Planning for Higher Education., 6,* 51–61. doi:10.2307/1974977

Harris, D., & Nolte, P. (2007). *Global Challenge Award: External evaluation year 1 2006–2007.* Montpelier, VT: Vermont Institutes Evaluation Center.

Haskell, C. (2013). 3D GameLab. In *Cases on Digital Game-Based Learning* (pp. 302–340). IGI Global. http://doi.org/10.4018/978-1-4666-2848-9.ch016

Howard-Jones, P., Demetriou, S., Bogacz, R., Yoo, J. H., & Leonards, U. (2011). Toward a science of learning games. *Mind, Brain, and Education, 5*, 33–41.

Jenkins, H., Purushotma, R., Clinton, K., Weigel, M., & Robison, A. (2006). *Confronting the challenges of participatory culture: Media education for the 21st Century.* Cambridge, MA: MIT New Media Literacies Project. Retrieved from http://mitpress.mit.edu/sites/default/files/titles/free_download/9780262513623_Confronting_the_Challenges.pdf

Jenner, M. (2014). Is this TVIV? On Netflix, TVIII and binge-watching. *New Media & Society, 18*(2), 257–273. doi.org/10.1177/1461444814541523 doi:10.1177/1461444814541523

Johnson, L., & Adams, S. (2010). *Challenge based learning: The report from the Implementation Project* (pp. 1–40). Austin, TX: New Media Consortium.

Johnson, L., Smith, R., Smythe, J., & Varon, R. (2009). *Challenge-based learning: An approach for our time.* Austin, TX: The New Media Consortium.

Jonassen, D. H. (1997). Instructional design models for well-structured and ill-structured problem-solving learning outcomes. *Educational Technology Research and Development, 45*, 65–90.

Kelsey, K. D. (2001). Overcoming standardized testing with authentic assessment strategies in the classroom. *The Agricultural Education Magazine, 73*(5), 4.

Langer, S. (1954). *Philosophy in a new key: A study in the symbolism of reason, rite and art.* Cambridge, MA: Harvard University Press.

Lave, J., & Wenger, E. (1991). Situated learning: Legitimate peripheral participation. In J. S. Brown, (Ed.), *Learning in doing: Social, cognitive and computational perspectives* (p. 138). Cambridge: Cambridge University Press.

Li, L. C., Grimshaw, J. M., Nielsen, C., Judd, M., Coyte, P. C., & Graham, I. D. (2009). Evolution of Wenger's concept of community of practice. *Implementation Science IS, 4*(1), 11.

Lotan, G., Graeff, E., Ananny, M., Gaffney, D., Pearce, I., & Boyd, D. (2011). The Arab Spring| the revolutions were tweeted: Information flows during the 2011 Tunisian and Egyptian revolutions. *International Journal of Communication, 5,* 31. Retrieved from http://ijoc.org/index.php/ijoc/article/view/1246

Mislevy, R. (2011). *Evidence-centered design for simulation-based assessment.* Los Angeles, CA: The National Center for Research on Evaluation, Standards, and Student Testing.

Mislevy, R., Steinberg, L., & Almond, R. (2003). On the structure of educational assessments. *Russell: The Journal of the Bertrand Russell Archives, 1*(1), 3–62.

Naisbitt, J., Naisbitt, N., & Philips, D. (1999). *High tech, high touch: Technology and our search for meaning.* New York, NY: Broadway Books.

Nielsen, T. (1990). Jurgen Habermas: Morality, society and ethics: An interview with Torben Hviid Nielsen. *Acta Sociologica, 33,* 93–114. doi:10.1177/000169939003300201

Pappano, L. (2012). The year of the MOOC. *New York Times.* Retrieved from http://www.nytimes.com/2012/11/04/education/edlife/massive-open-online-courses-are-multiplying-at-a-rapid-pace.html?pagewanted=all&_r=0

Passalacqua, F., & Pianzola, F. (2011). Defining transmedia narrative: problems and questions. Dialogue with Mary-Laure Ryan. *ENTHYMEMA,* 65–71. doi:10.13130/2037-2426/1188

Pea, R. D. (1993). Practices of distributed intelligence and designs for education. In G. Solomon (Ed.), *Distributed cognitions: Psychological and educational considerations* (pp. 47–87). Cambridge, UK: Cambridge University Press.

Prensky, M. (2001). *Digital game-based learning.* New York, NY: McGraw-Hill.

Roselli, R., & Brophy, S. (2006). Effectiveness of challenge-based instruction in biomechanics. *Journal of Engineering Education, 95*(4), 311–324.

Ryan, R., & Deci, E. (2000). Self-determination theory and the facilitation of intrinsic motivation, social development, and well-being. *Contemporary Educational Psychology, 25,* 54–67.

Sachs, J. (2012). From millennium development goals to sustainable development goals. *Lancet, 379*(9832), 2206–11. doi:10.1016/S0140-6736(12)60685-0

Senge, P. (1990). *The fifth discipline: The art and practice of the learning organization.* New York, NY: Doubleday.

Senge, P., Kleiner, A., Roberts, C., Ross, R., & Smith, B. (1994). *The fifth discipline fieldbook: Strategies and tools for building a learning organization.* New York, NY: Currency Doubleday.

Shaffer, D., Hatfield, D., Svarovsky, G., Nash, P., Nulty, A., Bagley, E., & Mislevy, R. (2009). Epistemic network analysis: A prototype for 21st-century assessment of learning. *International Journal of Learning and Media, 1*(2), 33–53.

Stanton, J. (2012). *An Introduction to data science.* Syracuse, NY: Syracuse University Press.

Thagard, P. (2002). *Coherence in thought and action.* Boston, MA: MIT Press.

Turkle, S. (2004, January 30). How computers change the way we think. *Chronicle of Higher Education, 51*, B26–28.

Wenger, E., McDermott, R., & Snyder, W. M. (2002). *Cultivating communities of practice.* Cambridge, MA: Harvard Business Press.

Wiggins, G. (1989). Teaching to the (authentic) test. *Educational Leadership, 46*, 41–46.

Wolf, W. H. (2001). *Computers as components: Principles of embedded computing system design.* San Francisco, CA: Morgan Kaufmann Publishers.

Ye, L. Richard. (2012) Telecommuting: Implementation for success. *International Journal of Business and Social Science, 3*, 20–30.

Yellowlees, P. M., & Marks, S. (2007). Problematic Internet use or Internet addiction? *Computers in Human Behavior, 23*, 1447–1453.

CHAPTER 4

LEARNING ABOUT THE "OTHER"

Encounters Between Arab and Jewish Students in Israel

Rivi Carmel

Israel is a country where Jews and Arabs live together as citizens but in fact are two different ethnic groups. The Israeli-Jewish population constitutes the "majority," while the Israeli-Arabs constitute the "minority." The two groups hold different cultural, social, and national identities, thus forming two different, often opposing societies living together within one state. The relationship between Israeli Jews and Israeli Arabs has long been tense and conflict-ridden, laden with negative emotions and mistrust towards each other (Oren & Bar-Tal, 2007). Social scientists, educators, and practitioners on both sides of the Arab-Jewish conflict have been engaged in educational efforts aiming to improve relations between Israeli Jews and Israeli Arabs, intending to lessen the hostility between these two groups. Many governmental and non-governmental organizations have initiated and developed a variety of coexistence interventions, face to face (F2F), online intergroup encounters, and educational training programs (Maoz, 2004; Sagy, 2002, 2006; Walther, Hoter, Ganayim, & Shonfeld (2015). Designing such interventions

Collaborative Online Learning in a Global World, pages 41–58.
Copyright © 2019 by Information Age Publishing
All rights of reproduction in any form reserved.

between Arabs and Jews is particularly difficult as the tension between the groups is high and trust is low (Ross, 2000).

Based on the belief that education is an important key for any changes in a society, intergroup encounters between Jewish and Arab preservice teachers, who come from culturally diverse backgrounds, are therefore particularly significant. Educational processes in such encounters aim to create positive experiences designed to bring about change in participants' attitudes and stereotypical perceptions towards each other (Shonfeld, Hoter, & Ganayem, 2013). The encounters provide opportunities for collaboration, enabling groups to learn about the "other" and discuss and explore interpersonal feelings and national, social, cultural, and ethnic identity, with the aim of achieving a deeper understanding and better cooperation (Maoz, 2004, 2011).

This chapter describes a study of a one-year "shared citizenship" collaborative intervention program which occurred during the 2013–14 academic year between the English-teaching departments in two colleges in Israel: Al Qasemi Academy College of Education located in Baqa El-Gharbiyye and Kibbutzim College of Education located in Tel Aviv. The overall aim of the program was to improve the relationship between Jewish and Arab students living in Israel, seeking to provide future English teachers with the opportunity to promote openness and understanding towards the "other"–Arabs towards Jews and Jews towards Arabs– while using English as the mutual language of communication between them.

CONTEXT OF THE STUDY

The English departments in Al Qasemi Academy College of Education and Kibbutzim College of Education recognized a need and developed the collaborative "Shared Citizenship" program. The program included 12 Arab and 12 Jewish college students. Students in the program met in a series of separate and joint encounters and collaborated with each other via an online platform. They engaged in planning English lessons, which they taught in schools of the other community. One day a week for five consecutive weeks, Arab students taught adolescents in "The Ginmazia," a Jewish junior high school in Tel Aviv, and Jewish students taught adolescents in "Al Qasemi," an Arab high school in Baqa al-Gharbiyye.

The combination of three dimensions of the program–F2F encounters, online collaboration and the practical component of teaching pupils in schools–enabled close contact over a period of nine months. Participants learned about each other and exchanged ideas for teaching English while integrating ideas of multiple identities, democratic citizenship, respect, and tolerance in the classroom.

The collaborative-learning program began with a lecture followed by workshops given to all students in each of the two English departments on the topic of "Shared Citizenship." The lectures and workshops highlighted the issues of civic responsibility, accepting the "other," coexistence and multiculturalism, and tolerance and understanding. Following this introduction, an invitation was sent to all students studying in the English departments of the two colleges.

Twelve students in each college chose to participate. Academic credit was offered to participants. Two pedagogical instructors (Arab and Jewish) and two facilitators (Arab and Jewish) led the face-to-face encounters. Four separate single-group encounters and four intergroup encounters were held at the two colleges. In addition, the program included a joint tour of the bilingual school "Bridge Over the Valley" in Kfar Kara in the northern part of Israel, which included social gatherings held in a public park and at the pedagogical advisor's private home.

An online Moodle site was set up for participants, facilitators, and the pedagogical instructors. The site was a common space for sharing and discussing lesson plans, collaborative work, reflections, and online forum discussions. English was the language of communication between all parties involved: students, facilitators, and pedagogical advisors. Topics discussed in group encounters and taught in the classrooms included multiple and conflicting identities, multiculturalism, customs, similarities and differences, stereotypical views and prejudice, and understanding the "other."

Jews and Arabs in Israel

The complex and long-standing Arab-Israeli conflict goes back to the turn of the 19th century, years before the establishment of the State of Israel, and continues today, 68 years after its establishment. At the heart of the conflict are disputes over land and landmarks, which hold cultural, historical, and religious significance for Jews, Muslims, and Christians. Over the last decade, there have been periods when hope for peace appeared more realistic and other times when the conflict peaked and no prospects for peace were seen on the horizon. Nowadays, Israel is experiencing a re-escalation of the conflict leading towards intractable situations that result in deep mistrust between the two groups living in the country. Since its establishment in 1948, the State of Israel has been steadily developing and growing in economics, industry, high tech, and more. Yet, due to the changing political environment and political tension, relations between Israeli Jews and Arabs remain intensely conflicted, with serious gaps in understanding each other (Hasson, 2012).

Following Israel's independence, Arab citizens of the new state transformed from being a majority (in pre-1948 Palestine) to a minority of no more than a fifth of the total population of the new state (Spolsky & Shohamy, 1999). Today, the population in Israel is 8.522 million, of which 74.8% (6.377 million) are Jews, 20.8% (1.771 million) are Arabs or Druze, and 4.4% are Christians (Central Bureau of Statistics, 2016). Over the years, the Arab citizens integrated slowly and unevenly into Israeli society, and today, the two sectors live in separate, different societies. They live in different cities, attend different schools, follow different cultural codes and customs, speak different languages, and espouse different political ideals. Schools in Israel are thus separated by both religion and race. Jewish pupils attend Jewish schools (secular, religious, or ultra-religious) where the language of instruction is Hebrew, while Arab pupils attend separate

Muslim, Christian, or Druze schools where the language is Arabic. Hebrew (the language of the majority) is taught as a second language, and English is taught as a third language in Arab schools.

Life in separate cities and the split education system where pupils are taught in their own language and according to their own cultural norms, coupled with additional economic and socio-political factors, have intensified the division and tension between Israeli Jews and Arabs. Tension between the two groups is based on extreme viewpoints coming from a particular perspective, containing certain inherent assumptions that build up into negative stereotypes and prejudice towards one another. This is a worrying situation that calls for intense, active involvement in peace-education programs with the aim to promote communication and dialogue between Jews and Arabs. The main objective behind such active initiatives is to develop awareness and tolerance and improve attitudes towards each other. Over the years, many governmental and non-governmental organizations have been working steadily to promote "shared citizenship" and a "shared society" in different areas of everyday life: economic development, the labor market, and particularly education (Maoz, 2011).

The Contact Hypothesis: Reducing Stereotypes

Research on connecting people from different or conflicting cultures is based on the contact hypothesis, first presented by Allport (1954). The contact hypothesis provides the background, rationale, and conditions for bringing together people across different geographic, religious, and cultural boundaries in the interest of reducing prejudice. According to this hypothesis, the best and perhaps only way for people to break down their stereotypes and preconceived ideas about others is by actually meeting them and getting to know them. According to Allport (1954), under the right conditions, contact among people holding different identities characterized by conflict, hatred, or violence can reduce bias between them.

The hypothesis claims that the gradual development of contact between individuals, understanding life on the other side of the border, helps in reducing stereotypical views held by groups, particularly groups in conflict. In these intergroup interactions, participants increase their knowledge of the other group and at the same time reduce their intergroup anxiety. This, in turn, broadens participants' awareness and perceptual field to allow impressions of the other group to become more accurate and positive, thus reducing previously held stereotypes (Stephan & Stephan, 1984, 2001). The rationale behind this idea is that under particular conditions, when members of two conflicting groups meet and the experience is a positive one, both groups' members will undergo an attitude change on two different levels. On the personal level, the negative stereotypical views held by the individual will be replaced by a more positive perception towards the other. On a more general level, the positive associations with the other which the individual experiences will have an additional positive effect on other group members, thus reducing the negative stereotypical views held by the entire group. In other words, the positive experience is magnified. Additionally, these constructive encounters, held under particular conditions, will help reduce interpersonal threats and social distance that group members may feel towards each other.

Allport (1954) outlined four fundamental conditions necessary for ideal, successful collaborative meetings. These are (1) equal-group status within the situation, (2) common goals, (3) intergroup cooperation, and (4) institutional support. In traditional face-to-face settings, these requirements are difficult to put into practice. Some of the challenges are logistical or financial and are related to the practicality of organizing and executing F2F meetings. Other barriers can be emotional or psychological and related to possible anxiety and apprehension people may have during F2F intergroup encounters. Recently, the contact hypothesis has been revisited and adapted in a large body of research that focuses on new, modern, and cheaper ways of collaboration between people using the Internet and up-to-date information technologies (Amichai-Hamburger & Mckenna, 2006; Austin, 2006; Austin & Anderson, 2008; Hoter, Shonfeld, & Ganayim, 2009). Indeed, the Internet has created a suitable and fitting environment for people from different parts of the world to communicate with each other, becoming a significant facilitator for collaborative projects between diverse people and cultures around the world. The Internet can be used to meet the challenges posed by traditional F2F encounters, and in many cases, it improves the contact when specific online tools for specific situational needs are used (Amichai-Hamburger & Mckenna, 2006).

It is important to note that much of the research on such updated, online, web-based interactions indicates that it can only work effectively when meaningful pedagogical models are implemented (Austin & Anderson, 2008; Ligorio & Veermans, 2005). In Israel, similar research efforts are carried out between Jews and Arabs using online communication projects (Hoter, Shonfeld, & Ganayim, 2009; Walther et al., 2015). Hoter et al. (2009) developed the *Online Inter-Group Contact Hypothesis (OICH)* model, which became the *TEC* model (Shonfeld et al., 2013), based on the extension of the contact hypothesis, aiming to use the model effectively for on-line communication between groups in conflict. The TEC model has been in use since 2005 and offers Israelis from diverse religions and cultures opportunities to collaborate, interact, and learn about each other, aiming to reduce stereotypical views and enhance mutual understanding (Shonfeld et al., 2013). The "Shared Citizenship" intervention program, for example, contained an online component that served as a useful and important platform where meaningful communication and interaction took place. This comprehensive design was necessary to meet the necessary conditions for meaningful collaboration.

Collaborative Learning

Collaborative learning is a widely established pedagogical approach and is associated with "high impact" learning practices (Kuh, 2008). It is based on the premise that dialogue and personal responsibility drive learning. The rationale behind this approach is that students work with each other towards the same goal, mutually constructing knowledge while sharing their understanding through the process of collaborating with each other. Collaborative learning capitalizes on the value of peer interaction and is based on modern cognitive theory: learners must be "actively engaged" in the learning process (Barkley, Cross, & Major, 2005). Collaborative-learning practices provide effective environments for learning and are designed to enhance interaction between peers engaged in a common task. Kuh (2008) identifies two key goals of collaborative learning: "learning to work and solve problems in the company of others, and sharpening one's own understanding by listening seriously to the insights of others, especially those with different backgrounds and life experiences" (p. 10). In our increasingly diverse society, it is of vital importance that teacher-educators prepare future teachers to listen carefully, think critically, collaborate productively to solve conflicts or problems, and be constructive participants in the society they are part of. Designing collaborative projects between diverse populations is therefore a notable goal.

Reaching a high level of engagement between students with different backgrounds is indeed one of the challenges for educational researchers and practitioners in teacher education. Guenther and Miller (2011) cite five broad strategies that promote student engagement: (1) promoting diversity experiences, (2) creating shared-learning opportunities, (3) maximizing student-faculty interaction, (4) involving students in active learning, and (5) setting high expectations. Students in teacher-education programs are potentially major agents of social change in society because they will be teaching the next generation. This highlights the significance and value of programs that involve learning about diversity via open discussions and collaborative interaction.

Shonfeld et al. (2013) report on numerous educational initiatives that bring together diverse groups in Israeli society involving both online and face-to face meetings based on the Contact Hypothesis (Allport, 1954; Pettigrew & Tropp, 2006). They further elaborate on collaborative projects that integrate information and communication technologies (ICT), highlighting the advantages of online meetings between cultures in conflict such as Arabs and Jews. Shonfeld et al. (2013) argue, "[S]ince 2007, Internet-based workshops have gained momentum in Israel and the Middle East since the Internet is both attractive to young people and is regarded as neutral ground for meeting" (p. 60). Educational projects between Jews and Arabs such as Yad2Yad, interactive computer games such as "Peacemaker," the "Yahla" youth movement which uses social networks to bring together Arab and Jewish youth from ages 15 to 30, and on-line academic courses taught in various teaching colleges are some examples of collaborative frameworks that promote open dialogue towards understanding the "other," as mentioned by Shonfeld et al. (2013). Many of these projects are followed by research, and initial findings are encouraging (Shonfeld et al., 2013; Walther et al., 2015).

The Contact Hypothesis (Allport, 1954), which posits that intergroup contact tends to contribute to the reduction of prejudice given certain conditions, in combination with the principles of collaborative learning as aforementioned, form the theoretical framework of the "Shared Citizenship" program.

Goals and Research Questions

The motivation behind this program was to help participants understand the attitudes, perceptions, and beliefs they held towards each other and have them gain a deeper understanding of their own ethnic identity as Israeli Jews and Arabs. The goal of the study was to check whether participating in such a program resulted in changes in participants' stereotypical views, interpersonal feelings, and attitudes. This chapter will focus on two research questions:

- What were participants' perceptions and attitudes towards the "other": Jews towards Arabs and Arabs towards Jews?
- What changes occurred in participants' perceptions and attitudes as a result of the program?

RESEARCH METHODS AND DATA COLLECTION

Both quantitative and qualitative approaches were important in this study in order to gather varied and rich data. Consequently, a mixed-method approach was used for data collection. The quantitative data, in the form of a pre-post questionnaire on attitudes and stereotypical perceptions, were important to collect totally objective data using controlled variables. The qualitative data were important for a few reasons. First, the number of participants was small (n=24), and therefore any generalization made from the controlled variables in the pre-post questionnaire would be limited. Second, the aim of this program was not only to compare and quantify changes in participants' attitudes but also, and of no less importance, to obtain a deeper and wider picture of the experience participants underwent. Furthermore, the nature of the program, with its varied components, focused on process and collaboration, and thus the study lent itself to the collection of data such as reflective journals, online communication, and observations. The aforementioned goals of the project were presented to the participants and clarified for them.

Quantitative Data

The questionnaire administered in this study was based on a tool used by Bar-Tal and Teichman (2005) to study attitudes and stereotypes, Arabs towards Jews and Jews towards Arabs, in a variety of contexts. The questionnaire used in this present study included four closed questions, which were presented on a Likert scale. Question one related specifically to the topic of attitudes: Arabs towards Jews and Jews towards Arabs. This question included 11 sub-question items relating to cultural, social, and personal attitudes ranging on a scale from 1 (agree completely) to 5 (totally disagree). For example: "I feel sympathy towards Arabs/Jews"; "I feel animosity towards Arabs/Jews." Question two related to the topic of social distance. This presented six situations relating to the extent one is ready to be with Arabs/Jews, on a scale from 1 (ready/positive) to 7 (not ready at all/negative). For example: "to live in an Arab/Jewish neighborhood"; "to work with Arabs/Jews"; "to marry an Arab/Jew." Question three related to the topic of interpersonal threat and included 11 descriptors of feelings one may have when encountering Arabs/Jews, on a semantic differential scale from 1 (positive) to 9 (negative), for example, feeling anxious (1) versus relaxed (9), estranged (1) versus friendly (9). Question four related to the topic of stereotypes. This question included a list of 14 stereotypical characteristics such as "smart," "clean," and "intelligent," using a scale from 1 (completely agree) to 5 (totally disagree), to evaluate the extent to which they agreed or disagreed with such characteristics of the "other." It will be noted that negatively worded question items were converted and underwent statistical decoding, so the higher the number on the scale the more positive the attitudes.

Qualitative Data

The qualitative data aimed to capture a thick description of the program–what took place during encounters, what was the nature of the collaboration on the online site, what occurred in schools–seeking to understand the content that emerged from all components of the program. The qualitative data were collected and assembled on a continuous basis throughout the duration of the project (November to June). The data comprised (a) notes from six observations from both single-group and mixed-group encounters and two informal meetings, (b) 24 personal reflective essays, (c) notes from eight classroom observations in both Arab and Jewish schools, and (d) a variety of data generated on the Moodle site. Examples of the topics discussed on the Moodle site are: "What are your expectations from the programs?"; "In what way were your expectations met or not met?; "Describe what you felt during and following the encounters."; "What are you taking away from this experience?"; "What did you learn about yourself?"; "What would you do differently if you had the opportunity to participate in a similar project?" In addition, ideas for lesson plans and a variety of activities relating to Arab and Jewish cultures were regularly posted on the site, thus focusing on both pedagogical and content issues. These data shed light on their collaborative work in preparation for the student-teachers' practice experience.

DATA ANALYSIS

Descriptive statistics and t-tests were conducted on the data collected from the pre-post questionnaire. The four parameters and sub-items were analyzed separately for statistical significance. Analysis included a comparison between Jewish and

Arab students at the outset and at the end of the program. Given the small number of participants (n=24), the analysis focused on descriptive statistics in order to exemplify participants' attitudes or any changes that may have occurred as a result of the program.

The analysis of the qualitative data was an on-going process (Holliday, 2010). Using an inductive approach, data were coded according to key words and phrases that were repeatedly used by the participants, orally and in writing. Participants' personal reflective essays and their communication generated on the Moodle site were coded and analyzed thematically. The codes that appeared with significant frequency were grouped into themes. Observation notes from single and intergroup encounters were analyzed in a similar manner. This was done while going back and forth with the data, formulating arguments that were supported by the data. Some examples of the commonly used words and phrases were: "Basically we are the same"; "I gained their trust"; "we" versus "them"; "us"; "conflict"; "better world"; "similar and different"; "mutual respect"; "enjoy our differences"; "common problems"; "stereotypes"; "anxiety"; "fears and worries"; "offensive attitude"; "prejudice"; "acceptance and rejections"; "judging people/ judgmental"; "first impression"; "multiple perspectives."

FINDINGS

The findings will be presented following the research questions while relating them to both the quantitative and qualitative data.

Quantitative Data

The two research questions were: (1) "What are participants' perceptions and attitudes towards the 'Other': Jews towards Arabs and Arabs towards Jews?" and (2) "What changes occurred in participants' attitudes and perceptions as a result of the program?"

Findings from the questionnaire analysis reveal that at the outset of the program both the Arab and the Jewish students held similar perceptions about the "other" with regard to the four parameters: Attitudes, Social Distance, Interpersonal Threat, and Stereotypes. In other words, at the starting point, the participants began the program with very similar perceptions of the "other." At the end of the program, the Jewish students generally saw the Arabs in a more positive light in all four parameters. In other words, overall, the program affected the Jews in a positive way more than it affected the Arabs. More specifically, the findings indicate no considerable change in participants' attitudes and perceptions from the beginning of the program (pre-test) when compared to their perceptions at end of the program (post-test) with regard to three of the four parameters: Attitudes, Social Distance, and Interpersonal Threat. Significant change was found amongst the Jewish students in one parameter, namely Stereotypes ($t=2.03$, $p<0.05$). Figures 4.1 through 4.4 below present the findings on each parameter.

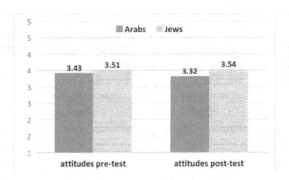

FIGURE 4.1.   Attitudes Pre & Post Tests

Figure 4.1 presents the findings on the first parameter, namely, Attitudes, which relates to what participants think and feel about the other in terms of people their language and culture (respect, hostility, superiority, etc.). It can be noted that at the outset of the program, participants' attitudes about each other were not particularly positive and that both Arabs and Jews seemed to lean towards the "safe" middle. At the outset of the program (pre-test) Jewish students' attitudes towards the Arabs were slightly more positive, but not significantly so (M=3.43 amongst the Arabs and M=3.51 amongst the Jews).

Figure 4.2 below presents the findings of the second parameter, namely Social Distance. This issue relates specifically to the extent to which Arabs or Jews were ready to be with each other. It can be noted that both Jews and Arabs felt some distance towards each other and here, too, the Jewish students' feelings towards the Arabs were slightly more positive (higher), yet not significantly so (M=4.29 amongst the Arabs and M=4.70 amongst the Jews). Findings further reveal that both Arabs and Jews were quite willing to "host a Jew/Arab at home" (M=5.77

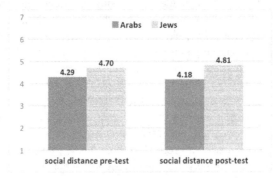

FIGURE 4.2.   Social Distance Pre & Post Tests

amongst Arabs and M=6.10 amongst the Jews in the pre-test) or to "work with Arabs/Jews" (M=5.23 amongst the Arabs and M=5.9 amongst the Jews). However, when it came to more intimate connections such as marriage in the family, their positive views dropped drastically (M=2.75 amongst the Arabs and M=3.9 amongst the Jews). Their views were yet more negative when it came to their feelings about "Marrying a Jew/Arab" (M=1.85 amongst the Arabs and 3.20 amongst the Jews). These sharp differences may be the reason for the mediocre mean result which leans towards the middle (M=4.18 amongst the Arabs and M=4.81 amongst the Jews in the post-test). As can be noted from Figure 4.2, no significant change occurred following participation in the program.

Figure 4.3 below presents the findings of the third parameter, namely Interpersonal Threat, which checked participants' feelings when encountering Arabs/Jews (fear, anxiety, hostility, joy, etc.). It can be noted that at the outset of the program, both Arabs and Jews held similar views and both reported some feeling of discomfort when coming into contact with the other (M=5.34 amongst the Arabs and M=5.25 amongst the Jews on a scale from 1–9, when 1 is negative and 9 is positive). Though there was slight improvement in their feelings towards the other, no significant change occurred following participation in the program. Here too the Jewish students' feelings towards the Arabs were slightly more positive (higher).

Figure 4.4 below presents the findings on the issue of Stereotypes. At the outset, when comparing the Arab and the Jewish students, findings reveal that there was no significant difference in perceptions between the two groups (t=1.63, $p<0.05$). However, significant changes were found at the end of the program amongst the Jewish students (t=2.31. $p<0.05$). The Jewish students' stereotypical perceptions improved following participation in the program. In other words, before participating in the program, both Jews and Arabs held some stereotypical views towards each other (M=3.19 amongst the Arabs and M=3.41 amongst the Jews on a scale from 1–5). At the end of the program, participants' overall stereotypical

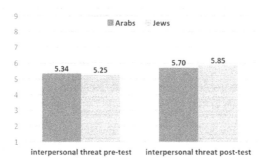

FIGURE 4.3.   Interpersonal Threat Pre & Post Tests

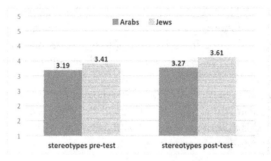

FIGURE 4.4.　Stereotypes Pre & Post Tests

perceptions decreased. Jewish students' views were slightly higher and thus more positive than those of the Arab students.

In conclusion, findings from the questionnaire exemplify participants' tendency to lean towards the "safe middle," which indicates some degree of stereotypical views. The picture emerging from the data is one where, at the outset of the program, both Jews and Arabs held some negative attitudes and some stereotypical views towards each other with regard to all four parameters. Findings indicate no considerable change in participants' attitudes and perceptions from the beginning of the program (pre-test) when compared to their perceptions at end of the program (post-test) in three out of the four parameters. Significant change was found amongst the Jewish students in the parameter dealing with stereotypical perceptions. Overall, there was some (but not significant) general positive change in participants' views and perceptions at the end of the program. The Arab students' perceptions towards the Jews were slightly (but not significantly) less positive.

Data analyzed from the qualitative data such as participants' reflective journals and online discussions revealed rich information about their views, contact, and learning experience. These show expressions of mutual interest, empathy towards the other, desire and hope for the prospect of change. Two main themes emerged: Personal and Educational.

Personal Themes

Reflections in their journals showed a combination of emotions, feelings, beliefs, and reactions; for example:

Learning About Own Identity

Participants reflected on their own private experience and revealed deeper understanding of their personality and feelings: "I have a stronger belief in my society."; "Jews don't have an ideal life, as we were told."; "I thought I was more accepting than I really am."

Overcoming Psychological and Ideological Barriers

Participants described the challenges they had to face and expressed the ways it had affected them: "I feel I am leaving my comfort zone."; "My fear of them did not materialize."; "I opened up to new things."

Building Trust and Bridging Differences

Words and phrases such as "trust," "building trust," and "gaining trust" were frequently used by participants to express the process they felt they were going through: "Little by little I gained their trust."; "I can tell the difference between a friend and an enemy."; "Basically, we are the same."; "The children didn't mind that we were different."

Hope for Change

Participants showed optimism that change between the conflicting Jewish and Arab societies can occur. Although not explicitly stated, their writings exposed a desire for better relations between Arabs and Jews: "It strengthened my hope for a better country."; "You mustn't judge a whole society by one person."; "I want to feel at home."; "It's important to accept people in order to live in a better world."

Educational: Learning and Teaching

Participants reported that they learned new things about each other in terms of customs, rituals and religion and broke some common myths, all of which have had an impact on them as future teachers and educators. Some examples are:

Multiple Identities

The journals revealed their understanding that people hold different identities and therefore they needed to be open to differences. "I can stay neutral and see the bigger picture, be part of something larger."; "I am a person with an open mind and I accept things better than I expected."; "It made me realize a variety of things about life in general, such as the importance of first impression, self-acceptance and accepting the society."

Collaboration/Collaborative Learning

Participants could see the added value of collaborating with a different ethnic group when they have a mutual goal. They understood the meaning of teaching and learning collaboratively and reflected on their own strengths and weaknesses regarding this: "I work well in a group."; "I can work in a group but prefer to work by myself."; "The connection with the different groups was clearer and each one had his own special needs and character in our meetings."; "I will absolutely engage in group work when I teach my class and encourage personal contact with each of my students."

Increased Professional Confidence as Teachers

Both the Jewish and Arab students reported that as a result of participating in the program, their confidence as future teachers had increased significantly and they felt generally more capable to deal with challenges. For example: "It helped me in dealing with the teaching process."; "I now have experience in teaching small groups."; "I have the ability to keep the pupils interested."; "I think that the activities we had with the groups can be used in any lesson."

Conflict Versus Resolution, Reducing Stereotypical Views and Prejudice

In their written reflections, as in the F2F intergroup meetings, participants did not avoid relating specifically to many of the sensitive political issues introduced and discussed in the program, namely the issue of stereotypical views and prejudice between Israeli Arabs and Jews. For example: "What can I do, as an English teacher, to improve the dynamics between Arabs and Jews in Israel?"; "…[I]t is highly important to discuss acceptance and 'other,' which exists everywhere."; "…[T]his process is relevant for everyone with no exceptions, not just Jews-Arabs." Participants additionally mentioned the need for initiating and practicing pro-active dialogue between Arabs and Jews. For example: "We need to do something because the children deserve to live in a world without conflict."

In summary, all 24 participants thought the program was good, effective, and met their expectations. Four Jewish students wrote that it was the best course in their entire teacher-education program. Four Arab students wrote that it exceeded their expectations, two of them saying, "This project gave me more than I gave back."; "I think it was a wonderful experience and I liked it." Many students wrote that they learned to work together and "open up to others." Both Jewish and Arab students said that they were well received by the pupils and teachers in their respective schools. They felt that they were able to appreciate multiple perspectives (of pupils or colleagues) and could develop better skills to address common problems facing a diverse society like the one they live in.

DISCUSSION AND IMPLICATIONS

The "Shared Citizenship" program has significant value for existing research and work done in the field of co-existence between Jews and Arabs for a few reasons. First, all students in the English departments in the two colleges (about 400 students) were exposed to the shared citizenship concept and to the importance of building open and constructive dialogue on democratic citizenship, respect, and tolerance between the two societies. Twenty-four students chose to participate, which displayed their intrinsic motivation and commitment. Additionally, this program had a practical component of teaching in the school of the "other," which is a distinctive element in this program. This gave the participants the unique experiential dimension of interacting with children, teachers, and with other position holders in the schools.

The findings of this study highlight the value of projects that promote collaboration between Jewish and Arab students in teacher-education contexts, in addition to the overall general positive contribution it may have made towards building peace. Educational programs such as this, which include practical involvement in schools and in the community, create the foundation of peace education in preservice teacher education and training. In an article that presents a new model for teacher training whereby teachers become intellectuals involved in the community, Yogev and Michaeli (2011) highlight the importance of initiating programs that enhance political activism and community involvement. They state, "These activities are an integral part of the training process and will alleviate feelings of interpersonal insecurities, aid in shattering stereotypical perceptions, and lay the groundwork for conciliation in Israeli society" (p. 314). These authors further argue that for change to occur in Israel's problematic reality, "teacher training must be directed towards nurturing teachers who are equipped with social and political awareness, possess a sense of self-capability, and are prepared to work in the education system for the advancement of Israeli society" (p. 315).

Creating opportunities for meaningful, positive contact between Arabs and Jews living in Israel is an important pedagogical goal in planning teacher-education programs. According to Stephan and Stephan (1984, 2001), under particular conditions, when members of two conflicting groups meet and the experience is a positive one, members of both groups will undergo an attitude change. In the present study, a significant positive change was observed in participants' stereotypes following participation in the program. The qualitative data reveals that they underwent a positive and meaningful experience. Indeed, it is known that people's attitudes and perceptions are not easily changed and gaining trust between groups in conflict is a long process. Nevertheless, the results of this study indicate that positive attitudes can be strengthened following a positive experience, given particular conditions. While participants didn't change their attitudes dramatically, the contact they made via their ongoing collaboration developed interpersonal closeness both as individuals and as groups. Some of the negative stereotypical views held by the participants were replaced by more positive perceptions towards the "other," as was documented in their reflective journals and in the survey question relating to stereotypes.

In addition, this study has implied a potential significant role of English as a neutral language for intergroup encounters. The contact and ongoing collabora-tion between the Arab and Jewish students brought about an instrumental reason and need to use the English language in speaking, writing, and teaching. English became the language of communication since it was also the language of instruc-tion in the classrooms. This particular setting may have awarded a special status to the English language as a "neutral language" used by both Arabs and Jews. English became the language that brought together and equalized between the language of the majority (Hebrew) and of the minority (Arabic). The significance of the English language becoming a possible bridge in connecting Jewish and Arab students merits additional study.

With regard to the significance and benefits of collaborative learning, the "Shared Citizenship" program is an example of a "high impact" (Kuh, 2008) collaborative project in which all parties worked with each other towards the same goal–promoting openness and understanding towards the "other." The program was designed to provide participants with active engagement and meaningful involvement with each other, thus meeting the four necessary conditions for meaningful contact to take place: equal-group status within the situation, common goals, intergroup cooperation, and institutional support. The program was developed in light of educational and socio-political challenges in Israeli society and can serve as an example for additional practical programs for future teachers or educators in general.

Limitations

The sample was small, consisting of only 24 participants. The program ran for one academic year (nine months) with a practical teaching period of five consecutive weeks. This is a relatively short duration for any significant change to take place or for any clear-cut generalizations. This study should be followed by other, similar continuing studies. Further studies on additional intergroup encounters with a focus on collaborative learning experiences between Arab and Jewish students in Israel are likely to contribute to a deeper understanding of the socio-cultural and socio-political complexities in Israeli society.

REFERENCES

Allport, G.W. (1954). *The nature of prejudice*. Cambridge, MA: Addison-Wesley.
Amichai-Hamburger, Y., & Mckenna K.Y.A. (2006). The Contact Hypothesis reconsidered: Interacting via the Internet. *Journal of Computer-Mediated Communication, 11*, 825–843.
Austin, R. (2006). The role of ITC in bridge building and social inclusion: Theory, policy and practice issues. *European Journal of Teacher Education, 29*(2), 145–161.
Austin, R., & Anderson, J. (2008). Building bridges online: Issues of pedagogy and learning outcomes in intercultural education through citizenship. *International Journal of Information and Communication Technology Education, 4*(1), 86–94.
Bar-Tal, D., & Teichman, Y. (2005). *Stereotypes and prejudice in conflict: Representations of Arabs in Israeli Jewish society*. Cambridge, UK: Cambridge University Press.
Barkley, E. F., Cross. K. P., & Major, C. H. (2005). *Collaborative learning techniques: A handbook for college faculty*. San Francisco, CA: Jossey Bass.
Bogardus, E.S. (1967). *Measuring social distance. A forty-year racial distance study*. Los Angeles, CA: University of Southern California Press.
Central Bureau of Statistics. (2016). *68th Independence Day—8.5 million residents in the State of Israel*. [Media Release]. Retrieved from http://www.cbs.gov.il/www/hodaot2016n/11_16_134e.pdf

Guenther, C. L., & Miller, R. L. (2011). Factors that promote student engagement. In R. L. Miller (Ed.), *Promoting student engagement (1): Programs, techniques, and opportunities* (pp. 10–17). Washington, DC: Society for the Teaching of Psychology.

Hasson. S. (2012). *Relations between Jews and Arabs in Israel, future scenarios.* The Joseph and Alma Gildenhorn Institute for Israel Studies, University of Maryland. Retrieved from http://israelstudies.umd.edu/pdf/hasson-eng.pdf

Holliday, A. (2010). Analyzing qualitative data. In B. Paltridge & A. Phakiti (Eds.), *Continuum companion to research methods in applied linguistics* (pp. 98–110). London, UK and New York, NY: Continuum.

Hoter, E., Shonfeld, M., & Ganayim, A., (2009). Information and communication technology (ICT) in the service of multiculturalism. *IRRODL, 10*(2). Retrieved from http://www.irrodl.org/index.php/irrodl/article/view/601/1207

Kuh, G. D., (2008). *High impact educational practices: What they are, who has access to them, and why they matter.* Washington, DC: AAC&U.

Ligorio, B., & Veermans, M. (2005). Perspectives and patterns in developing and implementing international web-based collaborative learning environments. *Computers and Education, 45*(93), 271–275.

Maoz, I. (2004). Coexistence is in the eye of the beholder: Evaluating intergroup encounter interventions between Jews and Arabs in Israel. *Journal of Social Issues, 60,* 437–452.

Maoz, I., (2011). Does contact work in protracted asymmetrical conflict? Appraising 20 years of reconciliation-aimed encounters between Israeli Jews and Palestinians. *Journal of Peace Research, 48*(1), 115–125.

Oren, N., & Bar-Tal, D. (2007). The detrimental dynamics of de-legitimization in intractable conflicts: The Israeli-Palestinian case. *International Journal of Intercultural Relations, 31,* 111–126.

Pettigrew, T. F., & Tropp, L. R. (2006). A meta-analytic test of intergroup contact theory. *Journal of Personality and Social Psychology, 90*(5), 751–783.

Ross, M. H. (2000). "Good-enough" isn't so bad: Thinking about success and failure in ethnic conflict management. *Peace and Conflict: Journal of Peace Psychology, 6*(1), 27–47.

Sagy, S., (2002). Intergroup encounters between Jewish and Arab students in Israel: Towards an interactionist approach. *Intercultural Education, 13,* 259–274.

Sagy, S. (2006). Hopes in times of threat: The case of Palestinian and Israeli-Jewish youth. In Y. Iram & H. Wohrman, (Eds.), *Educating toward a culture of peace* (pp. 147–160). Charlotte, NC: Information Age Publishing, Inc.

Shonfeld, M., Hoter. E., & Ganayem, A. (2013). Connecting cultures in conflict through ICT in Israel. In R. S. P. Austin & W. J. Hunter (Eds.), *Linking schools: Online learning and community cohesion* (pp. 42–58). New York, NY: Routledge.

Spolsky, B., & Shohamy, E. G. (1999). *The languages of Israel policy, ideology and practice.* Clevedon, UK: Multilingual Matters, Ltd.

Stephan, W. G., & Stephan, C. W. (1984). The role of ignorance in intergroup relations. In N. Miller & M. B. Brewer (Eds.), *Groups in contact: The psychology of desegregation* (pp. 229–255). New York, NY: Academic Press.

Stephan, W. G., & Stephan, C. W. (2001). *Improving intergroup relations.* Newbury, CA: Sage.

Walther, J. B., Hoter, E., Ganayem, A., & Shonfeld, M. (2015). Computer-mediated communication and the reduction of prejudice: A controlled longitudinal field experiment among Jews and Arabs in Israel. *Computers in Human Behavior, 52*, 550–558.

Yogev. E., & Michaeli, N. (2011). Teachers as society-involved "organic intellectuals": Training teachers in a political context. *Journal of Teacher Education, 62*(3), 1–13.

CHAPTER 5

BLENDED CONTACT FOR COMMUNITY COHESION IN NORTHERN IRELAND AND THE REPUBLIC OF IRELAND

Roger Austin

The island of Ireland, with its border separating Northern Ireland and the Republic of Ireland, has probably experienced more ICT-based links between schools than any other comparable part of the world. With a total population of around 4.8 million (3 million in the Republic of Ireland and 1.8 million in Northern Ireland), what is it about Ireland that explains the extensive use of ICT for links between schools? What lessons are emerging from almost 30 years of educational partnerships between schools that have been involved in sustained ICT contact and brief face-to-face encounters?

This chapter examines both a cross-border program, which linked schools between Northern Ireland and the Republic of Ireland between 1999 and 2014, and more recent work within Northern Ireland between schools that were mainly either Protestant or Catholic in ethos. The duration and scale of this work, with foundations laid as early as 1986 and over 140,000 pupils involved, makes this

Collaborative Online Learning in a Global World, pages 59–74.
Copyright © 2019 by Information Age Publishing
59

a unique study for understanding how national education policies have tried to mobilize technology to address longstanding cultural and political differences.

CONTEXT

A previous history of conflict on the island of Ireland and within Northern Ireland provides the backdrop to blended contact work that has been developed in schools to support purposeful curricular contact between young people. In brief, although Ireland and the British Isles are geographically close and share more in common than is often recognized, relationships between the two islands have been marked since the 11th century by intermittent suspicion and at times outright conflict triggered by differences in religion, economic competition, and more recently issues of security. For the purpose of this chapter, the most salient points to understand the present can be seen in the events between 1921 and 1999 (Rees, 1998).

For most of the period from the 11th century to 1921, Britain effectively controlled Ireland and, through the settlement of Scottish and English newcomers in the 17th century Plantation of Ulster, created both new towns and, significantly, a population that espoused the Protestant faith, which was markedly different from the traditional Catholic beliefs of the majority Irish population (Stewart 1997). While the Scottish and English settlers showed continued loyalty to the British crown, Irish nationalists became increasingly vociferous in their demands for some form of autonomy and from 1916 for complete independence. The result, after prolonged fighting, was the partition of the island in 1921 into a mainly Protestant Northern Ireland, which remained part of the United Kingdom, and a mainly Catholic, independent Republic of Ireland (Rees, 1998).

Within Northern Ireland, the discrimination experienced by Catholics in terms of housing and jobs created resentment, which exploded in 1969 with a violent campaign to force a reunification of the whole island, led by guerrilla forces called the Irish Republican Army (IRA). In support of its aims, the IRA drew on the Irish constitution, which at that time laid claim to the whole of the island of Ireland as its sovereign territory (Bew & Gillespie, 1999).

Between 1969 and 1999, the period known as "The Troubles," Protestant loyalist paramilitaries, the local Northern Irish police, and the British Army confronted the IRA. Loss of life, destruction of property, protection rackets, and allegations of torture on both sides created a bitter legacy. Before a peace deal was finally signed in 1999, there were attempts to enable children in school to learn to respect difference, notably through the European Studies (ES) project, which was set up in 1986 and ran until 2014 (Austin & Hunter, 2013).

The ES project was based on the notion that technology could be used to link schools not just on the island of Ireland but between Ireland and Great Britain in the wider context of Europe. Young people were linked together in England, Northern Ireland, and the Republic of Ireland with schools on the European mainland and given opportunities to see that, in addition to their national identity, they all shared a common European identity. The focus for the project was pupils aged 11–18. It is important to underline that this initiative, which included 330 schools in 2015 in 27 European countries with 6,600 pupils, started well before any peace agreement was signed. In total, over its 25-year history, some 90,000 students aged 11–18 took part in the ES project.

When a peace agreement was reached in 1999, its terms included a referendum and subsequent rewriting of the Irish constitution to the effect that Northern Ireland would retain its current constitutional position within the United Kingdom for as long as a majority in Northern Ireland wished this to remain the case. A locally elected assembly and executive were set up in Northern Ireland within a power-sharing framework, and cross-border bodies were created to seek to normalize relations between the two parts of the island. Part of this north-south dimension led to the setting up of a cross-border educational initiative called the Dissolving Boundaries through Education in Technology project.

DISSOLVING BOUNDARIES, 1999–2014

Extensive research has been undertaken on the Dissolving Boundaries (DB) program, which involved teachers and pupils from special, primary, and secondary schools in Northern Ireland and the Republic of Ireland (Austin 2006, 2011: Austin & Hunter, 2013; Rickard, Grace, Austin, & Smyth, 2014). Some of the most important findings from this work are summarized here.

First, the DB program involved 50,000 pupils in 570 schools supported by 2,600 teachers between 1999 and 2014. Links between schools were formed on the basis of one school in Northern Ireland and one school in the Republic of Ireland. This decision was based on the proposition that younger children, and those in special schools in particular, were more likely to be able to develop effective working relationships if the number of partner children was based on one class linked to another class. In terms of scale, it was one of the largest programs of its kind (Austin & Hunter, 2013). Its broad aims were to provide professional development for teachers in the use of information technology and to extend "north-south" understanding.

The DB program used the theoretical construct of the *contact hypothesis* (Allport, 1954) to shape the work that was carried out. In particular, this meant that contact was group to group between linked schools, long term (an entire academic year), cooperative in that there was a common purpose to the work carried out, and undertaken in schools where institutional support was expected. For example, in the early stages of school recruitment, principals were invited to briefing sessions, and when the project started, they received copies of the learning agreements that partner teachers created at the start of the year. When the project team identified schools as potential partners, they took account of the age and ability of the children to try to ensure that contact was perceived as being between young people who were of equal status.

Second, rather than providing teachers with ready-made curricular materials, the teachers were invited to anchor the project work in topics that were already on their curriculum; this meant that teachers had to use considerable creativity since the curricula in each jurisdiction were markedly different. Teachers were given ownership of the choice of topics that were suitable for their classes. At a planning conference held early in the school year, the partnered teachers were given ICT training together, provided with possible venues for holding a face-to-face meeting for the children, and asked to produce a planning agreement which outlined the intended work for the school year. In addition to copies of the agreement going to school principals, the DB program team used the agreements to monitor the flow of information between linked schools. This was made possible by adopting a Virtual Learning Environment (VLE) Moodle, which was secure from outside hacking but allowed the DB team to provide support to any schools where communication appeared to have faltered. The strategy in effect was to provide a modest grant to schools that created opportunities for teachers to gain confidence in the use of ICT for blended, collaborative learning.

Third, the choice of technologies, essentially Moodle and low-cost video-conferencing, was driven by the view that the DB program should not be appropriated by ICT specialists in school but rather should be pitched at a level that was accessible to any and every teacher. This was felt to be the surest way for it to become sustainable. The technologies also provided asynchronous contact and potential for knowledge construction in a "wiki" as well as real-time contact through video-conferencing. In other words, this particular mix of ICT had a good chance of working in a busy school day and was consistent with the DB program's constructivist position.

During the lifetime of the DB program, different platforms and software were used, but these were always selected in consultation with the main ICT providers for schools, so that, in principle, no school in Northern Ireland or the Republic of Ireland would be denied participation. The principles guiding which schools were invited to take part were that half of the schools should be classified as having economic, social, or educational disadvantages and that in Northern Ireland there should be a roughly even split between Catholic and Protestant schools. However, in order to keep within the annually approved budget, 30 schools on each side of the border were initially invited to take part each year and were given the opportunity to continue in subsequent years with reduced levels of support. By 2005, the DB program was supporting about 100 schools on each side of the border. When schools dropped out, a figure that varied from 5% to 15% each year, new schools took their places. In spite of requests by the DB directors to increase the budget to allow more schools to take part, the Departments of Education in Belfast and Dublin were unable to accede to this.

Fourth, two university schools of education ran the DB program: Ulster University in Northern Ireland and Maynooth University in the Republic of Ireland. This meant that insights were rapidly disseminated to the staff and students taking initial teacher-training courses and there was a natural synergy between the need to evaluate the program and the universities' expectations for research output. One specific outcome of this was that Dissolving Boundaries was chosen by Ulster University as a case study of "impact" for the Research Excellence Framework in 2014. This evaluation of research undertaken in all UK universities every five years involves scrutiny of the quality of published work and, for the first time, evidence of the impact of research. The impact case study of Dissolving Boundaries was rated as one of the best in the entire United Kingdom (Research Excellence Framework, 2014). In the following sections, conclusions are drawn concerning the impact of the DB program and its cost effectiveness.

Impact on Teachers

According to a report from the National Foundation for Educational Research on teaching approaches that help to build resilience to extremism among young people (Bonnell et al., 2011), professional development in the use of ICT on the DB program "helped to develop teachers' skills and confidence in this area" and this, in turn, was regarded as "one of a number of significant motivators for teachers' participation in the project." (pp. 97, 99) This was an important conclusion in the sense that teachers were pivotal to its success. Further, a joint inspection report by officials on both sides of the border in Ireland (Assistant Chief Inspector, 2012) said that the professional development provided by the DB program improved the quality of learning. They noted that key findings, such as the insights into what kinds of practice facilitated collaborative learning using ICT, were disseminated in research reports to all teachers and used as the focus for professional development at annual planning conferences. The report added that the DB program "has contributed to and utilized international research to ensure that it is focused on improving the quality of the learning experiences for the participants" (p. 10).

Impact on Children's Learning

Research reported by Austin and Anderson (2008) based on teacher perceptions of the impact of the DB program on children highlighted improved communication skills, improved self-esteem, and for 75% of the teachers in primary schools, "improved north-south understanding." (p. 99) Data from the NFER report (Bonnell et al., 2011) noted that "pupils reported increased awareness and tolerance of pupils from the other side of the border (p. 12)." Evidence from the NI/ROI Joint Inspection report (Assistant Chief Inspector, 2012), confirmed these findings. It noted that 99% of the schools in Northern Ireland strongly agreed or agreed that DB has led to "a positive change in pupils' values and attitudes, e.g., open-mindedness, acceptance, self-confidence, empathy and curiosity" (pp. 10–12). Research by Rickard et al. (2014) based on pupils' confidential and anonymous replies reported that, even one year after their involvement, students who took part were extremely positive about their experiences and far more likely to want to repeat such links compared to pupils in the same schools who had not taken part. These consistent findings, over a period of nine years, need to be understood in the context of the DB program enabling conditions of careful matching of schools, professional development of teachers, regular monitoring of partnerships, and links based on both long-term use of ICT with limited face-to-face contact.

Impact on Educational Policy, ICT Accreditation, and Assessment

The data generated by research into the DB program also led to changes in policy in terms of the accreditation of ICT in Northern Ireland. Evidence from the Council for the Curriculum, Examinations and Assessment (CCEA) in Northern Ireland (REF Impact Case Studies, 2014) confirmed that, since 2009, the scheme run for all schools in NI was amended to include "exchange" because of the work of Dissolving Boundaries. It stated,

> In 2009, CCEA introduced a revised version of the ICT Accreditation Scheme for pupils at Key Stages 1, 2 and 3 which, for the first time, included the requirement that ICT should be used for "exchange." This new focus was introduced as a result of the growing number of schools that were already using ICT for inter-school links through the Dissolving Boundaries Program. (p. 3)

The ICT accreditation scheme became mandatory for all schools in Northern Ireland in 2016 (CCEA, 2015).

Summary and Cost-Effectiveness

The Centre for Cross-Border Studies based in Armagh in Northern Ireland was commissioned by the Department of Education to review all cross-border educational programs. Having assessed all the evidence available, it commented that DB was "the single most outstanding example of mutually beneficial cross-border cooperation... between schools anywhere in Europe, let alone Ireland" (Pollak, 2011, p. 1). The estimated average cost per pupil per annum, based on the overall budget divided by the number of participating pupils, produced a figure of £76. In the absence of comparable data from other programs, it is difficult to be sure whether this is good value or not. This chapter later discusses a similar program linking schools within Northern Ireland which cost around half this figure, with savings from less-expensive planning conferences, shorter distances for teachers and pupils to travel, and without including costs for the ICT infrastructure since that was already in place.

Reflections

The duration of the DB program, some 15 years, was unusual in that the normal practice for research and development initiatives is funding for three to four years. Best practice was disseminated to all schools in the system and embedded in everyday practice. This was certainly the case when citizenship was introduced into the curriculum in Northern Ireland, and it is now taught in every post-primary school. Taken along with the European Studies Program, which was supported by Dublin and Belfast for an even longer period of time, we might see the lengthy duration of the Dissolving Boundaries program as signaling an ambition to reach every school on the island of Ireland, but when the funding was abruptly stopped in 2014, only around 25% of schools in Northern Ireland and some 15% in the Republic of Ireland had been involved. To date, there has been no official explanation for the cessation of funding.

According to some commentators, the initial enthusiasm for north-south cooperation in the wake of the 1999 Good Friday agreement has slowly dissipated in Dublin, where more pressing economic matters have taken precedence. However, it would appear that there remains a willingness on the part of the administrations in both Dublin and Belfast to maintain some level of educational cooperation, including digital literacy. What is clear is that when funding stopped and the external support was removed, even schools that had been in long-term partnerships found it difficult to continue their links. This might be seen as a failure on the part of the DB program to build enough capacity in schools for teachers to continue without external support. But it can also be seen as a sign that work of this sort, linking schools across jurisdictions, is inherently difficult, particularly when there are aspirations for outcomes to go beyond conventional learning goals to embrace intercultural ones. In the case of Dissolving Boundaries, it is clear that while many schools were committed to the program and provided some of their own resources to support it, there was a clear need for external funding to provide outside support and ongoing professional development. Once this funding, as well as the support of the program team, was removed, schools did not have the resources to continue on their own.

It is possible that part of the legacy of the Dissolving Boundaries program will be found in the work that has started in Northern Ireland, where the administration has turned its attention to the question of how to address the fact that 92% of children attend schools that are separated by religious ethos, some attending Catholic schools from the age of five while others attend state schools that are de facto Protestant.

NORTHERN IRELAND

Around 8% of children attend integrated schools in Northern Ireland, where pupils of all faiths as well as those with no professed faith are educated together. To mitigate the effects of separate schooling for the vast majority of young people, a number of policies have been introduced. In the 1970s there were pioneering projects like the Schools Cultural Studies Project (Robinson, 1983) and attempts to make the teaching of history and religious education less divisive (Austin, 1986; Darby, 1974; Greer, 1972). These valuable but piecemeal approaches were all based on the view that curriculum content changes would improve community relations. The same approach was adopted on a system-wide level in the early 1980s, when all schools were required to include Educational for Mutual Understanding (EMU) and Cultural Heritage (Department of Education, 1982) as cross-curricular themes to address the need for mutual respect. A fairly generous budget was created to enable schools from different traditions to have face-to-face meetings to visit museums, places of interest, or in some cases partner schools. But by 2006, there was growing evidence that these various attempts to bring about reconciliation were only reaching 20% of the pupils in primary schools and a mere 3% in secondary schools (Education and Training Inspectorate report for 2002–2004, Department of Education, Northern Ireland, 2006).

In response, the Department of Education introduced citizenship as a mandatory subject in the curriculum in 2007. While the curriculum gave teachers the chance to address key issues of democracy and social justice, the lessons were of course taught in separate classrooms where nearly all the children had the same cultural/ religious background. There was no provision for schools to interact with each other.

O'Connor, Beattie, and Niens (2008), in a study of the effects of citizenship education in Northern Ireland, found that regardless of the intrinsic merits of the course content, the fact that pupils studied only with peers from the same side of the community as themselves was a limitation in the learning environment. More recently, in a detailed evaluation of the extent to which a shared curriculum could enhance community relations, Niens, Kerr, and Connolly (2013) reported that there were notable differences between the schools which studied the same content but also had contact with one another as compared to schools that simply studied the same curriculum. Niens et al. (2013) concluded that while the curriculum has had the effect of making a difference in pupils' attitudes, there was considerable added value for both the pupils and teachers when contact was part of joint study of the curriculum. They noted that,

…the contact element of the program has, patently, been successful in engaging schools; the lessons which were "shared" were predominantly reported as having gone very well in terms of pupil enjoyment, interaction and participation. Additionally, a majority of Curriculum + Contact teachers felt that the joint sessions were very positive exercises, particularly in terms of learning from the other teachers' experience. (Niens et al., 2013, p. 67)

The studies supporting cross-cultural contact provided part of the context for a shift in government policy towards what is now called "shared education," which began in 2005 with a policy document called "A Shared Future." From 2007, small-scale pilot work started and was extended explicitly in 2012 (Department of Education, 2015); it was based on the assumption that there was no political appetite for pushing separate schools to become integrated, a move that would be fiercely resisted by the main churches. Instead, the policy encouraged schools to share facilities. The government has provided funding and defined the process as "two or more schools from different sectors working in collaboration with the aim of promoting equality of opportunity, good relations, equality of identity, respect for diversity and community cohesion" (Department of Education, Northern Ireland, 2015, p. 5). A 2013 Department of Education survey across all schools in Northern Ireland sought to determine the extent to which the schools had participated in shared education. Seventy-six percent of respondents claimed to have been involved in such work, but only 65% was cross-community (Department of Education, Northern Ireland, 2013). It is also worth noting that a significant percentage of these links was with special schools, international or cross-border, rather than with schools of a different denomination within Northern Ireland.

Hughes (2013) commented that even though shared education may have some positive effect on pupils, it remains problematic that teachers' reasons for participating are more focused on educational outcomes than on reconciliation. Duffy and Gallagher (2014), while noting some achievements of shared education, pointed out that most of the work done to date involved the bussing of pupils from one school to another or to neutral venues. It would appear that little or no use has been made of ICT within Northern Ireland to sustain partnerships between schools.

More recently, using evidence presented on the impact of the Dissolving Boundaries Program, an enquiry by the Education Committee in Northern Ireland's devolved assembly on shared and integrated education (Northern Ireland Assembly, 2015) recommended that shared education should "be defined as curriculum-based interactions that always foreground educational improvement and involve children and young people in sustained whole school/organization activities across all educational phases while making optimal use of existing IT infrastructure" (p. 45). This is an important recognition, for the first time, of the role that ICT can play to link schools in Northern Ireland. This report led to the adoption of shared education as government policy in the Shared Education Act of 2016, laying an obligation on the Department of Education to support shared education across all schools in Northern Ireland.

While the Department of Education is refining its strategy for delivering shared education, some work has already started. The Epartners program, for example, started in 2013 by the University of Ulster, provides some evidence about what is emerging on the role of blended learning in linking schools within Northern Ireland.

EPARTNERS

Using broadly the same approach as the Dissolving Boundaries Program but applied to the need to link schools within Northern Ireland, Ulster University launched the Epartners program in 2013. In two important respects, it differed from previous work, first in that it included university students as mentors in the schools that volunteered to take part. Previous work (Austin & Hunter, 2012) had indicated that although students might be studying together at the University, they remained all too often in their cultural silos, avoiding contact with those perceived to be from "the other side." A project using ICT to link schools within Northern Ireland for joint work in the curriculum might provide a valuable experience of collaborative learning for the University students as much as for the pupils in school. In other words, this approach could be seen as meeting the need to address division at two different educational levels.

The Epartners project also differed from Dissolving Boundaries in that it provided the majority of participating schools with explicit content to work on together; the focus was on nutrition and enterprise, with children exploring the market for cupcakes, designing their own cakes, and working in mixed teams on issues related to cost and nutritional value. The university students created lesson plans with the help of their tutors and their partner teachers.

In the first year, 2013–2014, limited funding meant that it was extremely difficult for schools to be able to run a face-to-face event as part of the program (Austin, Hunter, & Hollywood, 2015). Nevertheless, evaluation of that year's work showed that in a case study of two academic secondary schools, teachers' understanding of the use of ICT for cross-community work increased substantially with the help of their university-student mentors. The university students noted the benefits for the pupils they were working with, ranging from access to a Virtual Learning Environment (VLE) 24/7, greater autonomy in learning, and, as one put it, "It boosted the pupils' self-confidence and also enabled them to meet others… from a different background and made them more open minded" (p. 5).

However, the vast majority of comments related to getting the coursework completed and mastering the technology to do this; relatively little reference was made to the different religious composition of the pupils in the linked schools. University students saw the experience as an opportunity to learn about the reality of the classroom. Any inter-cultural learning that took place was more of a by-product of the main focus of the link. The authors' conclusion from that work was as follows:

> We think that this example serves as a useful point to reflect on what the purposes of inter-school contact should be. While it can be argued that a fundamental purpose is to encourage children to become tolerant and respect diversity, which are core principles of the citizenship element of the curriculum, there is also a need to prepare young people to be able to deal with this in the type of contexts where they are most likely to encounter difference and diversity. Some research indicates that this is much more likely to occur in the workplace rather than in the neighborhood or in social settings. Eyben, Morrow, Wilson, and Robinson's work (2002) on creating work spaces that are respectful of diversity notes that Northern Ireland is characterized by a culture of "separation, avoidance and politeness" (p. 13) and that the workplace is "one of the few places where people meet across lines of division" (p. 12). In effect, the case study might suggest that enabling young people to deal with the kind of challenge they could face at work is an entirely appropriate goal for schools. (Austin et al., 2015, p. 514)

In the work carried out on Epartners in its second year, 2014–2015, while retaining the focus on trust-building through agreed areas of the curriculum, two important changes were made. The first was that funding was found to expand the number of schools from 16 to 28 and recruitment concentrated on schools that had a measured level of social and economic disadvantage. This led to 28 primary schools being recruited in 14 cross-community partnerships and funds made available for them all to have a face-to-face meeting. Further, to give schools the additional ICT support they said was needed, an intern was recruited with a background in computer science. Evaluation findings, published here for the first time, concentrated on five key areas.

Teachers' Use of and Confidence in ICT

Data showed that there was a marked increase in teacher confidence and use of both the VLE, a platform called "Fronter" and the video-conferencing tool "Collaborate," comparing responses at the start of the program and at the end. For example, before Epartners, 66.7% of teachers who responded had not used the VLE Fronter. At the end of the program, 73.4% of teachers believed that their skills in Fronter had improved to the point where 66.7% felt confident in helping another teacher use it. Similarly, in terms of their use of the video-conferencing tool, before Epartners, 73.3% of teachers said they had never used Collaborate, but by the end, 80% of teachers felt their skills had improved, and 64.3% said they would be confident in helping another teacher in their school with this. One typical teacher comment was:

> We've found our eLearning link hugely enjoyable. Getting familiar with the construction of Fronter rooms, and being able to discuss the benefits with colleagues in school, has meant that I am able to give concrete examples of how collaboration online can be used in school." (Epartner teacher)

Strong Support for Mix of Face-to-Face Contact and Online Interaction

Over three quarters of teachers had a face-to-face event held in a range of venues, including university campuses, the Nerve Centre Belfast, W5, The Walls of Derry, and Parkanaur forest park.

Nearly all, some 90%, rated their event "Very Valuable" or "Valuable," and 80% found that the face to face was very valuable for stimulating online interaction; 70% found it very valuable for building trust between the pupils. One of the teachers described how he and the teacher from the other school had planned their face to face event:

> The schools ... started the morning of Friday the 27th with video conference. On this the children discussed their online contributions and what their expectations were for the tour of Derry's Walls later on in the day. The bus

left .... The children from each school then had to sit beside a pupil not from their own school and find out five pieces of information regarding the person sitting beside them. For the tour, children were then put into their five groups consisting of pupils from each school, and together they walked the Walls with the guide getting the history of the city in which they live. Not only was this informative; it proved very enjoyable with both sets of pupils mixing very easily, so much you were nearly afraid to stop the conversations so the guide could give his information. The collaboration that we had online helped with this as the children were not strangers to each other and were excited to meet the person in real life as opposed to a face on screen.

Embedding Shared Education in the Curriculum

Most teachers supported the Epartner focus on team-building and working together on a non-contentious topic. Two of the teachers in separate parts of the city of Derry/Londonderry carried out work on a local history topic; one of them commented later on the learning benefits for the pupils of having another audience and the way that the link had enabled the teacher to fulfill one of the required elements of the ICT accreditation scheme:

> For the past two weeks, my pupils have been working on their PowerPoints that arose out of a visit to the Walls of Derry. Normally when this is done within the classroom environment, it is only shared with their peers. Due to our participation within this project, it has enabled us to share our work with another school online, thus contributing to us covering one of the five E's. It has made our learning more meaningful in that the audience the pupils were writing for were not themselves.

Another, who had agreed at a planning session with his partner teacher to work on Fair Trade as the focus for their work, highlighted the importance of ensuring that this kind of work fits neatly into what is already required:

> We found that agreeing to work jointly on a topic both schools already studied was a super start to our project. Both Primary Seven classes do work on Fairtrade, and drawing activities from our existing plans, and providing a forum for display and discussion was of great benefit. We discussed the importance of being fair, uploaded our Fairtrade posters, and shared our research on organizations working to make the world a fairer place. Because we had already planned these, there was no additional workload involved, and I felt we were much more likely to get them done! The pupils really enjoyed seeing their work in the Fronter room and liked sharing ideas and thoughts.

Key Role Played by University Student Tutors

University students were placed in 65% of the schools, the majority doing their placement as part of a degree in B.Sc. Honors Consumer Management & Food Innovation or as one of their modules in education. Ninety percent of teachers found these students useful, particularly in supporting the ICT work and running the face-to-face event. One of the teachers commented,

> The cupcake challenge day was a great day out; it was well organized; all activities proved to be educational and enjoyable for both myself and the children. The students were fantastic. My pupils commented on how enthusiastic they were and how well they had baked their buns. As a young teacher, I feel I have learned a lot from being involved in this project, and hopefully I will be involved in similar things in the future.

Pupil Benefits in ICT, Communication, and Understanding Others

In a summary comment at the end of the program, one of the teachers referred to the range of learning benefits she felt her pupils had gained:

> The children have developed their ICT skills further and writing for an audience, even in a discussion forum, has given us a lot of food for thought. As a result, I have really noticed the quality of their contributions improve. As in a previous post, when the children are sharing with a wider audience, it sometimes makes them focus more. The children have also had to think about how to talk effectively when video conferencing via Collaborate.

One of the university students commented on the way that the age of these children, most around 11 years old, meant that they entered into this kind of work with a relatively open mind:

> The beauty of working with younger school children is that they are less aware of the difference in backgrounds and cultures than older children may be. To children aged 10 or 11, friendship is friendship; it is this pure and simple nature that makes the E-Partnership so easy! The children are being exposed to other backgrounds in a natural way, using learning and fun as the primary focus. The children are engaging with their partner school well on the discussion boards and are freely sharing their ideas and coming up with compromises to ensure that everyone is pleased. I believe this helps the children to develop key negotiation skills as well as teamwork abilities.

In summarizing the benefits of the project, it is clear that there was a range of impressive educational outcomes for the pupils as well as substantial up-skilling for teachers in terms of the use of blended learning for cross-community engagement, precisely what the shared education policy aspires to.

CONCLUSION

There is a sense that Northern Ireland in 2016 has reached a potential "tipping point," where policy around shared education could provide valuable and sustainable experiences for *all* children in their diverse schools. If implemented well, with appropriate training for teachers, this could make a significant contribution to the process of cross-community trust-building, especially if paramilitary activities remain at a marginal level. But there is an important caveat here: while it is true that schools can apply for funding for this work, there is as yet no requirement that they should make any use of ICT. Given the widely dispersed location of the majority of schools, it is difficult to see how the stated ambitions of the government can be achieved without moving blended contact to the center of what schools do. It is ironic that all schools already have the ICT infrastructure to do this.

In terms of links between Northern Ireland and the Republic of Ireland, it remains to be seen whether the investment in the European Studies and the Dissolving Boundaries programs will be built on in the future. The evidence is there to show how such links can be managed effectively, but is there sufficient political will after 16 years of uneasy peace to follow this through with funding?

In the summer of 2016, the body responsible for implementing "shared education"–in Northern Ireland the Education and Skills Authority–began to draw up plans for the professional development of teachers who had started to work together on a cross-community basis within Northern Ireland. Some funding will be provided to support this work, which may also at a later date include some cross-border work with teachers in the Republic of Ireland. One important point to note is that the basis of funding support in Northern Ireland is around local geographical clusters of schools. While there are clear advantages in this for easier face-to-face contact, it remains to be seen how well blended contact fits into this strategy.

REFERENCES

Allport, G. W. (1954). *The nature of prejudice*. Reading, MA: Addison Wesley.

Assistant Chief Inspector (2012). *The education and training inspectorate, Northern Ireland, The dissolving boundaries programme*. Retrieved from http://www.etini. gov.uk/index/surveys-evaluations/surveys-evaluations-post-primary/surveys-evaluations-post-primary-2012/joint-evaluation-report-dissolving-boundaries-programme-2010-2011.htm

Austin, R. (Ed.). (1986). Values education in history teaching. In R. Austin (Ed.), *History in school: Studies in teaching history in Northern Ireland.* (pp. 46–54). Coleraine, NI: University of Ulster.

Austin, R. (2006). The role of ICT in bridge-building and social inclusion; Theory, policy and practice issues. *European Journal of Teacher Education, 29*(2), 145–161.

Austin, R. (2011). ICT, Enterprise education and intercultural learning. *International Journal of Information and Communication Technology Education, 7*(4), 60–71.

Austin, R., & Anderson, J. (2008). *E-schooling: Global messages from a small island*. London and New York, NY: Routledge.

Austin, R., & Hunter, W. (2012). Whatever you say, say nothing: Student perceptions of online learning and community in Northern Ireland. *Irish Educational Studies, 31*(4), 451–465.

Austin, R., & Hunter, W. (2013). *Online learning and community cohesion: Linking schools*. New York, NY and London: Routledge.

Austin, R., Hunter, W., & Hollywood, L. (2015). Supporting community cohesion through ICT: The Epartners program in Northern Ireland. *Computers in Human Behavior, 52*, 508–514.

Bew, P., & Gillespie, G. (1999) *Northern Ireland: A chronology of the troubles 1968–99.* Dublin: Gill and Macmillan.

Bonnell, J., Copestake, P., Kerr, D., Passy, R., Reed, C., Salter., R., & Sheikh, S. (2011). *Teaching approaches that help to build resilience to extremism among young people* (DFE Research Report 119). London: DFE.

Council for the Curriculum, Examinations and Assessment. (2015). *Using ICT.* Retrieved from http://ccea.org.uk/curriculum/key_stage_1_2/skills_and_capabilities/cross_curricular_skills/using_ict

Darby, J. (1974). History in the schools; A review article. *Community Forum, 4*(2), 37–42.

Department of Education Northern Ireland. (1982). *The improvement of community relations; The contribution of Schools.* DENI circular 182/21, Bangor, NI: Department of Education.

Department of Education Northern Ireland. (2013). *School omnibus survey–shared education.* Retrieved from https://www.education-ni.gov.uk/sites/default/files/publications/de/2013-school-omnibus-shared-education.pdf

Department of Education Northern Ireland. (2015). *Sharing works—A policy for shared education.* Retrieved from https://www.deni.gov.uk/publications/sharing-works-policy-shared-education

Duffy, G., & Gallagher, T. (2014). Sustaining school partnerships: The context of cross-sectoral collaboration between schools in a separate education system in Northern Ireland. *Review of Education, 2*(2), 189–210.

Education and Training Inspectorate. (2006). *Chief inspector's report 2002–2004,* available from Inspection Services Branch, Department of Education, Northern Ireland, or inspectionservices@deni.gov.uk.

Education and Training Inspectorate. (2012). Joint evaluation report, Department of Education and Skills Inspectorate. Retrieved from http://www.ulster.ac.uk/academicoffice/download/TLC/20%20June%202012/Dissolving%20Boundaries%20-%20Eval%20Report.pdf

Eyben, K., Morrow, D., Wilson, D., & Robinson, B. (2002). *The equity, diversity and interdependence framework: A framework for organisational learning and development.* Coleraine, NI: University of Ulster.

Greer, J. E. (1972). *A questioning generation.* Belfast, NI: Church of Ireland Board of Education.

Hughes, J. (2013). Contact and context: sharing education and building relationships in a divided society. *Research Papers in Education, 29*(2), 193–210. doi:10.1080/0267 1522.2012.754928

Niens, U., Kerr, K., & Connolly, P. (2013). *Evaluation of the effectiveness of the "promoting reconciliation through a shared curriculum experience" program.* Belfast, NI: Center for Effective Education, Queen's University Belfast.

Northern Ireland Assembly, (2015). *Education committee "enquiry into shared and integrated education."* Retrieved from http://www.niassembly.gov.uk/globalassets/documents/reports/education/inquiry-into-shared-and-integrated-education-complete.pdf

O'Connor, U., Beattie, K., & Niens, U. (2008). *An evaluation of the introduction of local and global citizenship to the Northern Ireland curriculum.* Council for the Curriculum, Examinations and Assessment. Coleraine, NI: UNESCO Centre, University of Ulster.

Pollak, A. (2011) *Bringing schools together in Ireland through ICT.* Retrieved fromhttp://sluggerotoole.com/2011/06/30/bringing-schools-together-in-ireland-through-ict/

Rees, R. (1998). *Ireland 1920–25.* Newtownards, NI: Colourpoint Educational.

REF Impact Case Studies (2014). *Dissolving boundaries.* Retrieved from http://impact.ref.ac.uk/CaseStudies/CaseStudy.aspx?Id=1002 and http://results.ref.ac.uk/Results/ByUoa/25#http://results.ref.ac.uk/Results/ByUoa/25

Rickard, A., Grace, A. R., Austin, R. S., & Smyth, J. M. (2014). Assessing impact of ICT Intercultural Work. *International Journal of Information and Communication Technology Education (IJICTE), 10*(3), 1–18.

Robinson, A. (1983). *The schools cultural studies project: A contribution to peace in Northern Ireland.* Coleraine, NI: University of Ulster.

Stewart, A.T (1997) *The narrow ground; Aspects of Ulster, 1609–1969.* Belfast, NI: Blackstaff Press.

CHAPTER 6

ONLINE COLLABORATION BETWEEN ISRAELI AND SLOVAK STUDENTS

Tsafi Timor

The opportunity to create a cross-cultural collaboration project arrived at a lunch table at an international conference on language teaching in Slovakia, where I met a colleague who is a teacher educator just like me, and together we decided to develop a collaboration and offer our students in Israel and Slovakia the opportunity to share their teaching experiences and discuss educational topics. The collaboration turned out to be fruitful and enjoyable and lasted over a full academic year. After a series of email correspondences and Skype/Facebook chats, we agreed on guidelines and topics for collaboration which were sent to our groups. The discussion topics concentrated on three aspects of education: students' motivation, the ideal teacher, and student diversity and inclusion. The guidelines and topics are detailed in the Methodology section (Table 6.1).

The premise of the study was that although people can communicate in various forms of online collaboration, they do not automatically guarantee effective sharing of information or a quality discourse. The present study explores the following aspects of online collaboration:

Collaborative Online Learning in a Global World, pages 75–90.

- Two types of online communication during the collaborative project–dialogical and monological interactions and social interactions.
- The quality of discourse in three layers: (1) Sharing thoughts and feelings; sharing geo-cultural differences; (2) Eliciting reflection and critical thinking; (3) Yielding inferences and new insights on the topic of student diversity and inclusion in the discussions.

THEORETICAL FRAMEWORK

The theoretical framework begins with a definition of collaborative learning and an overview of asynchronous communication, which is the basis for this study, and in turn, narrows down to Internet and e-mail communication and finally to meaningful discourse.

Asynchronous Communication and Collaboration

Despite the continued increase in online learning in higher education, its benefits are still under debate. Kim and Bonk (2006) argue that once the quality of online learning improves, it will contribute to collaboration, case learning, and problem-based learning (PBL). More specifically, in teacher-training programs, opening students' minds to collaborative global learning and developing multicultural understanding is of the utmost importance.

Asynchronous communication is a form of computed-mediated communication (CMC) that supports information exchange and group interaction through a variety of electronic communication tools such as email correspondence, bulletin boards, class list-servs, and online discussion forums (Bodzin & Park, 2000). Gunawardena, Lowe, and Anderson (1997) argue that asynchronous communication is an important pedagogical tool that enables groups to bridge place and time while engaging in learning activities, thus supporting co-construction of knowledge through discourse. Saade and Huang (2009) argue that one of the benefits of online learning networks is that relationships among participants can be formed in culturally diverse global environments across space and time. Cooperative learning in intercultural environments with students of various religious, ethnic, and cultural backgrounds offers the opportunity to view the diversity as a "resource" rather than as a "problem" or "risk" (Portera, 2008). Sharan (2014) argues that cooperative learning based on heterogeneous groups offers all learners the opportunity to contribute to learning by creating a "space" conductive to the exchange of ideas and different viewpoints.

Asynchronous discussions provide opportunities for collaborative learning and dialogue among participants. Singh, Hawkins, and Whymark (2007) argue that electronic discourse and interaction are no less important for classroom interaction than face-to-face interactions. This view supports theories that advocate that the development of thought is mediated by social discourse (e.g. Vygotsky, 1962). The online discussion forum (ODF) is defined as "a web-based application that has been used extensively to bring people together with shared interests and mind-set" (Saadé & Huang, 2009). More specifically, in education, ODFs are used to complement traditional techniques and tutorials (Dube, Bourhis, & Jacob, 2006). Previous studies indicate that online interactions enrich knowledge exchange and improve students' performance (e.g. Zhang, Zhou, Briggs, & Nunamaker, 2006). This is particularly relevant to the educational philosophy in which communication is considered an essential tool for effective learning (Harman & Koohang, 2005). Thus, ODFs can enhance collaborative learning and the formation of new knowledge for students who share interests and goals (Montero, Watts, & Garcia-Carbonell, 2007). Students can engage in authentic learning contexts with others of different backgrounds, and thus, they can reflect individually and collaborative-ly on the same issues and build knowledge in a learning community. One of the benefits of asynchronous communication is that delayed communication allows participants to reflect on their peers' comments and to participate at their own convenience at the right time for them (Hara, Bonk, & Anjeli, 2000; Tiene, 2000).

Garrison, Anderson, and Archer (2001) created the "practical inquiry" model to assess outcomes of collaboration in a higher-education, online course environment. Their model consisted of four phases: the initiation phase with the triggering event that begins the dialogue; the exploration phase in which the learners reflect and exchange information; the integration phase in which the learners begin to propose solutions to the problem; and the resolution phase in which the solution is tested.

One of the issues regarding the effectiveness of online learning is the prevalence of "serial monologues" (Henri, 1991) in which participants express their opinions with little effort made to connect or relate to what others say, thus avoiding dialogues. Good learning, however, is collaborative and social rather than isolated and competitive (Chickering & Ehrmann, 1996). Pawan, Paulus, Yalcin, and Chang (2003) found, too, that interactions were often one-way serial monologues, and although being interesting, they did not end in a resolution of the issue. As for the depth of the online discourse, Hara, Bonk, and Angeli (2000) claimed that 70% of student postings reflected deep cognitive processing, although other studies yielded conflicting findings. For example, Kanuka and Anderson (1998) argued that in asynchronous interactions, information was shared rather than constructed.

Internet-based, e-mail communication, which is sometimes called "technospeak," is considered a conversational form rather than a formal language use (Crystal, 2006). Email has become a dominant, essential and preferred channel of communication in the workplace, with English as the lingua franca (Habil, 2010; Kirkgoz, 2010). Guffey (2010) pointed out four parts in e-mail messages: (1) An informative subject line: Although it is recommended that the subject line be specific, Crystal (2006) argued that in most messages it is quite difficult to see the close relation between the subject line and the function of the message/ topic of discussion. Further, a few emails were observed to be written under the same subject. (2) An opening: The literature suggests a beginning with a proper greeting that indicates friendliness (Guffey, 2010). Roshid (2012) found 17 types of salutations in opening greetings that range from no salutation (8.69%), through more formal (30.43%), to more informal salutations (31.51%). He concludes that the business sector he studied shows the personalized and flexible nature of salutation. (3) A body of the email. (4) An appropriate closing: Roshid (2012) claims that all email messages end either with informal closing (56 cases) or with no closing (31 cases). He explored the features of effective email communication in a specific business sector. Despite being a written text, the features of email language are far from formal language and are deeply influenced by spoken language (Cutting, 2011). Roshid (2012) concludes that the language style of email has shifted from formal to semiformal and informal (personalized), which is demonstrated by contractions, abbreviations, omission of words, personalized opening and closing greetings, and informal expressions and thanks. Nevertheless, this flexibility does not reduce the effectiveness of communication with business counterparts. Rowe (2010) argues for a hybrid language, which consists of written and spoken language and creates a new genre.

Meaningful Discourse

Jonassen et al. (1995) define meaningful discourse as one of the main goals of constructivist learning because it supports knowledge construction through articulation in which participants discuss their positions, reflect and re-evaluate them, and engage in social negotiation. Gilbert and Dabbagh (2005) define meaningful discourse as the ability of learners to demonstrate critical thinking by relating course content to prior knowledge; by interpreting content through analysis, synthesis, and evaluation of others' understanding; and by making inferences by generalizing their understanding and knowledge. Duffy and Cunningham (1996) define meaningful discourse as a process of collaboration and social interaction in which the goal is to share different viewpoints and ideas and collaborate on problem-solving and knowledge-building activities. Naturally, while students are engaged in collaboration, they articulate what they know and explain it to others, and at the same time they reflect on what they know; thus, articulation and reflection support knowledge construction.

Content analysis refers to spoken, written, or online texts and allows the researcher to interpret new phenomena (Kupferberg, 2010). Text analysis is subject to multi-disciplinary approaches and modes (Johnstone, 2008). Some approaches explore discourse on the micro level and encourage analysis that brings out the participants' voices: e.g. conversation analysis (Have, 1999). Content analysis can be conducted in varied contexts such as the workplace (Drew & Heritage, 1992). Discourse analysis combines the levels of micro and macro (Holstein & Cubrium, 2000) and explores interactive processes in real time with attention to the changes that occur over time (Blommaert, 2005). Discourse analysis is essential to education because it allows a deep exploration of changes in processes of learning and professional development in education and in teacher education, in the context of multilingualism and multiculturalism (Kupferberg & Olstein, 2005). This exploration can detect when changes occur and dwells on the contribution of the participants in the framework of the educational context.

Structure of Online Discussions

Despite the benefits of online asynchronous communication, there is little research about the impact of protocols and guidelines on meaningful discourse (Gilbert & Dabbagh, 2005). Initial studies demonstrate that the structure of the online discussion has a significant impact on its quality (Hewitt, 2003). Yet, the research literature does not discuss the type or degree of structure that is most effective in promoting meaningful discourse. Gilbert and Dabbagh (2005) argue that it is a major challenge for instructors to structure online discussions in an engaging way. A few models assist instructors with protocols and clear requirements. Brannon and Essex's (2001) combined model suggests that for meaningful discourse to occur, an effective interaction between structure, asynchronous communication methods, and the process of meaning-making must take place. In their model, emphasis on structure consists of online posting protocols, evaluation rubrics, and facilitator guidelines. Asynchronous communication consists of online discussions, email, and listservs. The constructivist process of meaning-making consists of articulation, reflection, and social negotiation.

Gilbert and Dabbagh (2005) examined the impact of three elements of structuring on meaningful discourse in online discussion forums and found that facilitator guidelines and evaluation rubrics had a positive impact on producing meaningful discourse, whereas posting protocols, limiting the length of the postings, and mandating reading citations had a negative impact.

METHODOLOGY

The two cohorts in the study described here were students in a teacher-education college in Tel Aviv, Israel, and a university in Nitra, Slovakia. The 36 participants were divided into 15 pairs and two groups of three students (one Israeli & two Slovaks). Throughout the collaborative process, participants had to study and discuss three different educational topics in writing by e-mail correspondence and via Skype/Facebook chats. Each of the three topics—student motivation, the ideal teacher, student diversity and inclusion—was addressed in a separate correspondence. Before each correspondence the students had to read a relevant academic article. The process was monitored by the two Israeli and Slovak instructors. The "finale" was a video conference at the end of the year where some of the students met face to face for the first time.

Here I present the analysis from the correspondence of a sample of three pairs of students. The sample includes the three sets of correspondence with the highest input in terms of richness of data. Each correspondence comprised at least eight long emails (four from each party). The sets of correspondence pertained to the same pairs for all topics to control personal differences and differences in writing style and to help gain cross-topic insights. For ethical reasons, the participants are not named; where necessary (i.e. geo-cultural issues), they are identified by their initials. Table 6.1 below introduces the topics and guidelines for collaboration:

This chapter examines the third (last) topic in the collaborative process, "student diversity and inclusion," because the richness of data does not permit discussion of more topics given the limited length of this chapter. As this was the last topic in the process, the students were already familiar online with one another, and it was assumed that they would be more open towards each other.

TABLE 6.1. Topics and guidelines for collaboration

The goals of the project:
- To get the opportunity to share teaching experiences and discuss educational topics;
- To create a collaboration between groups of students from different cultures.

The guidelines for the collaboration:
- Each set of correspondence concentrates on a different topic and should include at least four emails by each party;
- Each set of correspondence will be submitted by email to the Israeli and the Slovak instructors;
- Once you get the email address of your counterpart, you can start the correspondence by introducing yourself and providing some background details about yourself.
- Please read the related article before you start the online discussion.
- Please meet the expected deadlines.
We hope you enjoy the project!

The Topic	Deadline for Submission	Background Reading	Guidelines for the Discussion
Students' motivation	January 23	Article on extrinsic and intrinsic motivation	• Provide examples from your class observations and practice teaching;
The ideal teacher	March 28	http://www.ascd.org/publications/educational-leadership/summer10/vol67/num09/The-Best-Teachers-I-Have-Known.aspx	• Write about how the issue is treated in your country; • You may relate to your experience as a learner; • Express your opinion on the topic on the basis of the reading and your personal beliefs; • For topic 3: Which of the following groups are treated differentially: Successful achievers? Underachievers? Learners with learning difficulties?
Student diversity and inclusion	May 31	http://www.hltmag.co.uk/oct09/less02.htm http://www.hltmag.co.uk/oct09/less02.htm http://www.hltmag.co.uk/oct09/less02.htm	http://www.hltmag.co.uk/oct09/less02.htm

Due to the interpretive nature of the study, the qualitative paradigm was adopted. The bottom-up content discourse analysis was applied to the students' style of email/Facebook correspondence on the topic of "student diversity and inclusion." The discourse that emerged in the email and Facebook correspondence provided the data for the analysis. The data were categorized using the qualitative analysis software Narralizer according to the categories and sub-categories that emerged from the correspondence.

FINDINGS AND DISCUSSION

The findings are discussed in two areas: types of interactions (dialogical interactions and social discourse) and the quality of the discourse observed. These are presented below with support from direct quotes of the participants.

Dialogical Interactions

The students had had no previous encounters, so it was important to see if they would produce dialogs or monologues. The participants showed interest in their counterparts' opinions and referred to their ideas in their answers. The analysis yielded three main sub-types of dialogical interactions:

The idea expressed ends in a question, probing the counterpart to tell about one's experience; for example, "In both my classes I have pupils with both learning disabilities (LD), attention deficit hyperactivity disorder (ADHD), and one with pervasive developmental disorder (PDD). Do you have pupils with LD in your class? Does your training include the treatment of an individual student with special needs?"

Phrases that relate to what the counterpart mentioned in a previous email; for example, "I understand it must be difficult for you to approach each and every student individually due to the huge number of pupils in your class."; "I agree with you[,] C[,] that differentiated teaching is a great approach for different levels of pupils, but I think it is very demanding and we don't use it in Slovakia."

Directly asking the counterpart for her opinion or consulting her; for example, "B, I would like to hear your opinion and suggestions (if you have any) regarding how to treat disrupted behavior of a pupil with learning disabilities."; "How do you combine your methods to incorporate audible, visual, oral, kinesthetic and tactile learning styles?"

Another issue arising in the analysis concerned whether any social interactions were formed during the process of online collaboration. These findings are introduced next as social discourse.

Social Discourse

One of the issues about the nature of the collaboration was the observation or lack thereof of a personal tone of writing. The following description of one correspondence between R (Israeli) and K (Slovak) clearly indicates how the relationship became closer over time, with reference to the three topics of correspondence: student motivation, the ideal teacher, and student diversity and inclusion.

The first correspondence, dated December-January, started with a formal opening question by the Slovak student: "How are you?" The reply of the Israeli student was more detailed, yet formal: "Thanks for your email. I'm doing fine, just busy as always at this time for the year, finishing the semester and getting ready for the exams. How are you?" Similarly, the emails ended in a polite, yet formal tone: "I enjoyed reading your email. Take care and have a nice week," or "I hope to hear from you soon."

The second correspondence, dated February-March, reflected a much closer and more friendly tone: "How was your Holiday?"; "Is there any progress with your job search for next year?"; "I'm home alone. My boyfriend is hiking in Argentina and it's raining, so I'm not happy." Similarly, the closure of the emails is more personal: "…[G]oing to make myself some coco [sic] and watch some TV." The response at the other end is equally personal: "Wow, your boyfriend is a really an adventure-loving person. Have you ever thought about going with him?"

The increased personal and friendly tone continues through the third correspondence. K shares personal and family matters which may make her give up on the academic year:

> I don't know what exactly to do. My mind is split, I keep calculating so that's why I don't really focus on anything. I'm glad I was able to pull myself together, to finish this semester, to have time to focus on the things which "recharge" me, and to start the new semester with more enthusiasm.

The personal tone of the emails also features professional comments of appreciation such as "I can't imagine working with 4–5 kids with ADHD in one class. You are amazing. WOW!"

The content analysis of the social aspect of the discourse was conducted via the following categories: "formal opening," "informal opening," and "lacking opening"; "formal closure," "informal closure," and "lacking closure"; and "friendly." It appears that the most frequent categories in this correspondence are the "informal opening sentences" (14 mentions) and "formal closing sentences" (10 mentions). Second was "lacking opening" (7 mentions). Least frequent were "formal opening" (6 mentions), "lacking closure" (4 mentions), and "friendly" sentences (5 mentions).

Examples of informal opening sentences:

A: "We are going to discuss our last topic. I will be missing our weekly emails :-)."

B: "I apologize for answering so late, but I had some health issues because I was stressed and overworked, so I had to slow things down a little bit. Now I'm back and ready to discuss whatever we need to :)."

The *formal opening and closing* sentences were all similar and quite banal; for example:

Opening: "How are you?"; "I hope you are feeling well."; "Thank you for your prompt response."

Closing: "Have a nice day/week/weekend."; "Looking forward to hearing from you."; "All the best."; "Take care."

More of the beginning sentences were informal (14 mentions), and the closing sentences were mostly formal (10). While the formal, usually short, closing sentences might be understood in light of the long emails, the informal opening sentences might be accounted for by the fact that the students found the collaboration delightful and were looking forward to getting responses and proceeding with the correspondence.

In seven emails, the students did not open with any greeting, formal or informal. The lack of an opening usually occurs when the student is eager to share practical teaching experience, such as in in the following from R:

> I have finished my week of practice teaching in school. As I mentioned earlier, part of our training is teaching one day a week, but last week I was there 5 consecutive days. It was hard, especially the early mornings!

Alternatively, the student emphasizes an educational insight she wants to share. A says:

> In the article about heterogeneous classes it is stated that we need to look at our pupils as individuals, while identifying their unique problems, and finding appropriate solutions. I have something important to say regarding this responsibility....

The lack of closure in four emails occurs when the student is curious to know what her counterpart thinks, such as in the first example: A: "What do you think about the article? What do you think about the solutions they offer?" Lack of closure can also occur when she wants to share personal or general insights, which obviate an ending as they already make one, such as in the following example: A: "I feel grateful to be a part of this important role of teaching."

The category of "friendly" sentences included five that picture a close relationship, a feeling of contentment, and motivation to keep in touch even when the formal collaboration is over:

A: "Wow! What a great email! I felt that we think in a similar way :-)."

B: "Thank you very much for this enriching correspondence, I'm happy to have had you as my partner and please, contact me anytime :). We will see each other during our video conference, so I'm not saying goodbye to you yet:)."

As the students came from two different cultures and backgrounds, I was intrigued to see whether cultural issues were embedded in the correspondence. The number of mentions of cultural issues was high (12) and included religious holidays and traditions and demonstrated differences regarding student diversity and inclusion.

QUALITY OF DISCOURSE

This section explores whether the correspondence evoked critical thinking or remained on the surface level of sharing thoughts and feelings, as explained in the methodology.

Sharing knowledge & feelings: The content of the email correspondence consisted of sharing knowledge and feelings on the topic of student diversity and inclusion. This is reflected in the dialogical interactions in the previous section. This section specifies the main issues that were shared by the students, coupled with excerpts.

Ethical issues: "It is argued in the article that a teacher should be familiar with the pupil's profile and family background at the beginning of the year. I'm actually against this, and would rather look at the student as 'a blank sheet.'"

Treatment of special needs: "I noticed that pupils with behavior issues don't respond to traditional discipline. Pupils with learning disabilities like dyslexia struggle with school work regardless of their intellectual abilities. Both groups require specialized learning strategies to meet their potential and avoid self-esteem problems and behavioral difficulties."

Personal aspirations: "My goal is to touch every kid's soul and understand how to meet his/her needs."; "Teaching 'tips' for pupils with special needs."

Lesson plans: "I try to be creative and make the lesson 'colorful' by using diverse activities related to visual, auditory, kinesthetic learning styles."; "It is important to use activities that will make the pupils practice their memory such as small quizzes, or ask the pupils to memorize 5 words each week and during this week use numerous references to these words."

Teaching experience: "I had in my classroom a boy with dyslexia who was not concentrated and he kept disturbing all the time. I knew he likes drawing so I asked him to draw something meaningful for him. He drew a teacher holding his hand :)[.] This made me understand that he needs me as a teacher more than the others do. After the lesson I saw his eyes and I realized that I did something good. My little experience :)."

Sharing Geo-Cultural Differences

Differences in school culture/policy towards student diversity and inclusion. The examples below demonstrate the degree of awareness of pupils with special needs on the school level and in teacher education in Israel. The exchange of emails indicates great curiosity on the part of the participants on how the local school system views the inclusion of pupils with special needs. Indeed, the issue of attitudes towards inclusion is part of school culture (Timor & Burton, 2006).

The excerpts of the Israeli students below indicate awareness on the part of educators about special needs, a regulated policy in schools, and emphasis on special needs in education in teacher-training programs.

R [Israeli]: "In Israel LD is a big issue in teacher training. We take a yearly academic course as well as observe and work with pupils with special needs in our practice teaching."

C [Israeli]: "Which pupils are considered as more important in Slovakia: those who are weak pupils/under-achievers, or those who are gifted and very capable? In Israel there is an ongoing debate about this issue and the emphasis as of today is placed on under-achievers."

In Slovakia, the students attested to lack of training on special needs in teacher education, lack of awareness of individual teachers, and little responsibility on the part of school system towards children with LD.

K [Slovak]: "I have heard about ADD but I don't have an opinion, because of lack of experience and training. I did not receive training in how to deal with these special children. In our university these problems are mentioned in some courses but only theoretically."

B [Slovak]: "During my 2-week[s] of practice teaching the school supervisor told us that there were one or two pupils at school with disorders, but advised us to set the same requirements as for the others."

Differences in religious practices and traditions. In the examples below, the students express enthusiasm about sharing their traditions and teaching each other about the core elements of their traditions and cultures.

A [Israeli]: "Right now I'm on a Passover vacation until Wednesday. Passover is a very important Jewish holiday during which Jews are not supposed to eat flour (only Matzot), and they tell the story of how the Hebrew people [were] set free from King Pharaoh in Egypt."

B [Slovak]: "I love to learn new things about your culture, so thank you very much for sharing. We also had Easter holiday during which we celebrate the resurrection of Jesus. And then we also have Easter Monday when all men and boys go from door to door to visit their relatives or friends and pour water on women and whip them so they stay healthy for the whole year."

Reflection and Critical Thinking

This section focuses on the students' insights and ability to critically reflect on their experience and on their counterpart's experience beyond sheer knowledge or facts.

Reflections: "On the one hand I think that it is important that those kids will be in mainstream education, but on the other hand it is so hard for the teacher to allocate extra time and personal attention to each kid, as each one of them is like 10 kids."; "The practice teaching week made me realize that I do not have a very positive opinion on segregation in education."

The second part of this section introduces the critical thoughts of the students on what they had seen or learned. The ability to critically reflect may indicate the beginning of "reflective inquiry" (Lyons, 2010), which is one of the goals of teacher education.

Critical thinking: The Slovak students demonstrated a level of critical thinking, probably because they understood during the process that the attitudes towards special needs should be changed by the administration and adopted in teacher-training programs.

> "In Slovakia the school system has changed a lot recently, but most of the changes are only 'in the documents' rather than in practice. I wonder what we, as novice teachers can do to implement the changes."

> "There are many kids nowadays diagnosed with LD or ADHD, and at school they get special programs, whereas society is not as informed about learning disorders as it should be. Teachers should become social agents in this respect."

Making inferences: The main inferences revolved around optimal teaching for pupils with special needs, student-teacher relations towards special needs, and ethical issues.

Ethical inferences: "Teachers should not be informed of the pupil's performance in the previous year. They should get only the basic background details and allow the student to turn over a new leaf."

Teaching inferences: "As teachers, we should be aware of the differences between pupils and their needs and use differentiated instruction in order to adjust the form of learning to the level of the pupils in each and every class."

Student-teacher relations inferences: "To work with special needs pupils is really hard. In order to be an effective teacher and build trust with your pupils it is critical to understand the importance of being flexible with your curriculum and understand that the child's needs come … before the curriculum."; "Empathy is one of the most important elements in working with children, especially with children with special needs."

CONCLUSIONS

This study examined two aspects of online communication during a collaborative project: the interactions that took place and the quality of discourse among the participants. The present study did not focus on whether the outcome of the collaboration was effective learning.

The first goal of the study was to explore the types of interactions that took place during the collaborative process. The foci were (1) whether the interactions in the online collaborative project were dialogical or monological, and (2) whether they incorporated social elements. The findings indicated that the students listened to one another and created fruitful dialogues in three modes: probing the counterpart to tell about her experience, relating to an idea expressed in a previous email, and asking direct questions. No "serial monologues" (Henri, 1991) were observed in this correspondence. This means that the students were truly interested in the dialogue with their counterparts. Similarly, the correspondence bore social elements that were characterized by a majority of informal openings to the emails, coupled with friendly notes. This agrees with the definition of meaningful discourse as incorporating social elements (Duffy & Cunningham, 1996; Jonassen et al., 1995). It also agrees with Saadé and Huang (2009), who argue that one of the benefits of online learning networks is that relationships among participants can be formed in culturally diverse global environments across space and time.

The second goal of the study was to analyze the quality of discourse of the online collaborations. The discourse touched on the three layers, indicating that the process contributed to the students on both ends.

1. The level of sharing. The students shared knowledge on the treatment of special needs, their personal aspirations, teaching tips, teaching methods, what they felt about the teaching process, and teaching experience. The interactions showed enthusiasm and curiosity about the exploration of cultural and traditional differences, particularly on the issue of student diversity and inclusion.
2. The level of reflection and critical thinking. The students managed to critically reflect on their experience and their counterparts' experience beyond sheer knowledge or facts. They demonstrated the ability to seek change, to criticize the existing system, and at the same time to come up with new ideas.
3. The level of making inferences. Although novice teachers, the students managed to make inferences about ethical issues, teacher-student relationships, and attitudes towards special needs and inclusion that were developed during this year of collaboration.

The evidence suggests that students reached the highest level, which agrees with theories attesting that the development of thought is mediated by social discourse (e.g. Vygotsky, 1962).

The discourse in this study meets the criteria of meaningful discourse: the online collaboration enabled the students to elaborate on an important topic in education, to share viewpoints and ideas, and to create a synergy of different views and experiences. They demonstrated critical thinking by relating the newly acquired knowledge on student diversity and inclusion to prior knowledge or lack thereof, by enhancing understanding, making inferences, and generalizing their understanding and knowledge (Gilbert & Dabbagh, 2005). The study provided a social context via email and Facebook to acquire experience and practice (Bruffee, 1984). This collaborative project turned out to have opened social and cultural boundaries on top of the collaborative learning around a certain topic, thus providing a framework for teachers from different cultures to collaborate in the future.

The success of the collaboration can also be attributed to the emphasis on structure and facilitating guidelines that were offered to the students (Gilbert & Dabbagh, 2005; Hewitt, 2003). At this point, almost a year and a half after the end of the online collaboration, some of the students are still in contact with their counterparts on both a professional and social level.

REFERENCES

Blommaert, J. (2005). *Discourse: Key topics in sociolinguistics*. Cambridge, UK: Cambridge University Press.

Bodzin, A. M.,, & Park, J. C. (2000). Dialogue patterns of preservice science teachers using asynchronous computer-mediated communications on the world wide web. *Journal of Computers in Mathematics and Science Teaching, 19*(2), 161–194.

Brannon, R. F., & Essex, C. (2001). Synchronous and asynchronous communication tools in distance education. *TechTrends, 4*(1), 36–42.

Bruffee, K. A. (1984). Collaborative learning and the "conversation of mankind." *College English, 46*(7), 635–652.

Chickering, A. W., & Ehrmann, S. C. (1996). Implementing the seven principles: Technology as lever. *AAHE Bulletin,* 3–6. Retrieved from http://www.tltgroup.org/programs/seven.html

Crystal, D. (2006). *Language and the Internet*. Cambridge: Cambridge University Press.

Cutting, J. (2011). Spoken discourse. In K. Hyland & B. Paltridge (Eds.), *The continuum companion to discourse analysis* (pp. 155–170). New York, NY: Continuum International Publishing Group.

Drew, P., & Heritage, J. (1992). Analyzing talk at work. In P. Drew & J. Heritage (Eds.), *Talk at work: Interaction in institutional settings* (pp. 1–65). New York, NY: Cambridge University Press.

Dube, L., Bourhis, L., & Jacob, R. (2006). Towards a typology of virtual communities of practice. *Interdisciplinary Journal of Information, Knowledge and Management, 1*, 69–93. Retrieved from http://ijikm.org/Volume1/IJIKMv1p069-093Dube.pdf

Duffy, T. M., & Cunningham, D. J. (1996). Constructivism: Implications for the design and delivery of instruction. In D. H. Jonassen (Ed.), *Handbook of research for educational communications and technology. A project of the association for educational communications and technology* (pp. 170–198). New York, NY: Simon & Schuster Macmillan.

Garrison, D. R., Anderson, T., & Archer, W. (2001). Critical thinking, cognitive presence and computer conferencing in distance education. *American Journal of Distance Education, 15*(1), 7–23. Retrieved from http://www.atl.ualberta.ca/cmc/CTinTextEnvFinal.pdf

Gilbert, P. K., & Dabbagh, N. (2005). How to structure online discussions for meaningful discourse: A case study. *British Journal of Educational Technology, 36*(1), 5–18.

Guffey, M. E. (2010). *Essentials of business communication* (8th ed.). Mason, OH: South-Western Cengage Learning.

Gunawardena, C. N., Lowe, C. A., & Anderson, T. (1997). Analysis of a global online debate and the development of an interaction analysis model for examining social construction of knowledge in computer conferencing. *Journal of Educational Computing Research, 17,* 397–431.

Habil, H. (2010). Functions and strategies of email communication at the workplace. In R. Taiwo (Ed.), *Handbook of research on discourse behavior and digital communication: Language structures and social interaction* (pp. 479–489). Hershey, PA: IGI Global.

Hara, N., Bonk, C. J., & Anjeli, C. (2000). Content analysis of online discussions in an applied educational psychology course. *Instructional Science, 28,* 115–152.

Harman, K., & Koohang, A. (2005). Discussion board: A learning object. *Interdisciplinary Journal of Knowledge and Learning Objects, 1,* 67–77.

Henri, F. (1991). Distance learning and computer-mediated communication: Interactive, quasi-interactive or monologue? In C. O'Malley (Ed.), *Computer supported collaborative learning.* (pp. 145–161). Berlin: Springer-Verlag.

Have, P. T. (1999). *Doing conversation analysis: A practical guide.* London: Sage.

Hewitt, J. (2003). How habitual online practices affect the development of asynchronous discussion threads. *Journal of Educational Computing Research, 28,* 31–45.

Holstein, J. A., & Gubrium, J. F. (2000). *The self we live by: Narrative identity in a postmodern world.* New York, NY: Oxford University Press.

Jonassen, D., Davidson, M., Collins, A., Campbell, J., & Bannan-Haag, B. (1995). Constructivism and computer-mediated communication in distance education. *The American Journal of Distance Education, 9*(2), 7–26.

Johnstone, B. (2008). *Discourse analysis.* (2nd ed.). Malden, MA: Blackwell.

Kanuka, H., & Anderson, T. (1998). Online social interchange, discord and knowledge construction. *Journal of Distance Education, 13*(1), 57–74.

Kim, K. J., & Bonk, C. J. (2006). The future of online teaching and learning in higher education. *Educause Quarterly, 29*(4), 22–30.

Kirkgoz, Y. (2010). Analyzing the discourse of e-mail communication. In R. Taiwo (Ed.), *Handbook of research on discourse behavior and digital communication: Language structures and social interaction* (pp. 335–348). Hershey, PA: IGI Global Publishers.

Kupferberg, I. (2010). *Text and discourse research: Viewpoints of research methods.* Beer-Sheva, Israel: Ben Gurion University. [Hebrew].

Kupferberg, I., & Olstein, E. (Eds.) (2005). *Discourse in education: Educational events as research field.* Tel-Aviv: Mofet Institute. [Hebrew].

Lyons, N. (Ed.) (2010). *Handbook of reflection and reflective inquiry: Mapping a way of knowing for professional reflective inquiry.* New-York: Springer Science and Business Media, LLC.

Montero, B., Watts, F., & Garcia-Carbonell, A. (2007). Discussion forum interactions: Text and context. *System, 35,* 566–582.

Pawan, F., Paulus, T. M., Yalcin, S., & Chang, C. F. (2003). Online learning: patterns of engagement and interaction among in-service teachers. *Language Learning & Technology, 7*(3), 119–140.

Portera, A. (2008). Intercultural education in Europe: Epistemological and semantic aspects. *Intercultural Education, 19*(6) 481–492.

Roshid, M. M. (2012). What makes e-mail communication effective? A discourse analysis in an international business sector. *International Conference: ICT for Language Learning* (5th ed,). Florence, Italy.

Rowe, C. (2010). Status and email construction in three Hong Kong workplaces. In R. Taiwo (Ed.), *Handbook of research on discourse behavior and digital communication: Language structures and social interaction* (pp. 18–38). Hershey, Pa: IGI Global Publishers.

Saadé, R. G., & Huang, Q. (2009). Meaningful learning in discussion forums: Towards discourse analysis, *Issues in Informing Science and Information Technology, 6,* 87–99.

Sharan, Y. (2014). Learning to cooperate for cooperative learning. *Anales de psicología, 30*(3), 802–807. Retrieved from http://dx.doi.org/10.6018/analesps.30.3.201211

Singh, G., Hawkins, L., & Whymark, G. (2007). An integrated model of collaborative knowledge building. *Interdisciplinary Journal of E-Learning and Learning Objects, 3,* 85–105. Retrieved from http://ijello.org/Volume3/IJKLOv3p085-105Singh385.pd

Tiene, D. (2000). Online discussions: A survey of advantages and disadvantages compared to face-to-face discussions, *Journal of Educational Multimedia and Hypermedia, 9*(4), 371–384.

Timor, T., & Burton, N. (2006) School culture and climate in the context of inclusion of students with learning disabilities in mainstream secondary schools in Tel-Aviv, Israel. *International Journal of Inclusive Education, 10*(6), 495–510.

Vygotsky, L. S. (1962). Thought and language. New York, NY/London: Wiley/MIT Press.

Zhang, D., Zhou, L., Briggs, R. O., & Nunamaker, J. F. (2006). Instructional video in e-learning: Assessing the impact of interactive video on learning effectiveness. *Information and Management, 43*(1), 15–27.

CHAPTER 7

COMPETITIVE GAME EFFECT ON COLLABORATIVE LEARNING IN A VIRTUAL WORLD

Miri Shonfeld and Paul Resta

This chapter discusses the learning experiences of university students who engaged in a competitive-game-like activity as part of working collaboratively in cross-cultural, cross-national, virtual learning teams in a 3D virtual world. This study is the latest of a series designed to explore the potential usefulness of 3D virtual worlds supporting cross-cultural learning teams and to understand the student experience.

It was assumed that integrating a game-based activity as part of a CSCL course could help motivate the students to seek to enhance the performance of their teams in the competition. It might increase their feeling of belonging and sense of community and responsibility to the group. The preparation of the task by the students, as well as the competitive-game activity (*Amazing Race*), challenged the team members to show responsibility and flexibility in order to be in the group that won the race by being the first to upload their group pictures as they completed the game tasks in different VW situations and contexts (Figure 7.1).

The goal of the series of tasks was to explore the benefits and limitations of virtual worlds in collaborative learning. In addition, the project explored the chal-

Collaborative Online Learning in a Global World, pages 91–109.
Copyright © 2019 by Information Age Publishing

FIGURE 7.1.   A transnational group visiting the art museum

lenges transnational learning teams encountered in working together across continents, similar to what global corporations face when teams are composed of members who live in different time zones. The project also incorporated intercultural
education methods often used by teachers in online meetings with classrooms in
schools all over the world.

LITERATURE REVIEW

Virtual worlds offer new opportunities for cross-cultural and cross-national collaboration. Games such as *World of Warcraft*, in which over 11 million participants
from different countries collaborate in guilds and quests, have demonstrated the
power of cross-national collaboration (Jarmon, Lim, & Carpenter, 2009). In these
multiplayer games, collaboration is essential to accomplish the various tasks.

Virtual worlds also offer the potential of cross-cultural collaboration in higher
education because they provide conditions for experiential, embodied, and so-
cial-reality spaces (Gonzáleza et al., 2013; Jermon, 2009; Radford et al., 2011).
In a virtual-world environment, students can see and hear each other's avatars,

teleport themselves, or meet with the group on an island to help create the feeling of being together. The virtual world offers a stronger sense of place and of the presence of others than text-based environments such as online forums and bulletin boards (Bulu, 2012). Even in other synchronous environments, such as Blackboard Collaborate, in which students can speak with peers and see them using a web-camera, there is still the feeling that they are in different places. In virtual worlds, characteristics of the real world such as topography, movement, and physics all contribute to the sense of being in a virtual place and together (Smart, Cascio, & Paffendof, 2007). Virtual worlds such as *Second Life* (*SL*) provide opportunities including performative, experiential, collaborative, and game-based learning (Warburton, 2009). These environments also provide opportunities for students to explore their own identities or to take on new ones (Mayrath et al., 2009). Thus, the experience may be much more than the immersion in a new context, but rather, the adoption of new and different roles within it.

Virtual worlds also provide a unique approach to cross-national collaborative activities to better understand the effects of cognitive, social, and teaching presence and how a 3D environment affects the engagement and motivation of transnational students. Previous studies have indicated that virtual environments enhance student motivation and engagement, facilitate collaboration, and provide immersive, experiential learning opportunities unavailable in asynchronous and synchronous learning environments offered by traditional learning management systems (Aldrich, 2009; Dede et al., 2005; Gee 2003; Kirriemuir & McFarlane, 2004; Prensky 2006; Shonfeld, Resta, & Yaniv, 2011). Students can teach each other language in a relevant space requiring a specific vocabulary (Shonfeld & Raz, 2011). The avatar environments also act as a powerful communication medium for students to display knowledge and understanding and engage in the development of higher-order thinking skills such as interpreting, analyzing, evaluating, synthesizing, and solving complex problems (Falloon, 2010).

It is important to understand the meaning of learning with avatars. Students find that the virtual representations which they choose are important to their learning experience and strengthen collaboration. Usually, students choose and design avatars that are similar to themselves. Students of all creeds, cultures, and religions found significance in the likeness of the virtual representations to themselves (Figure 7.2). Thus, it is important for some learners to implement virtual worlds in a friendly environment where they can easily change and shape their avatars (Shonfeld & Kritz, 2013).

Competition is sometimes viewed as an obstacle to achieving success in collaborative learning. Competition often produces social issues and constraints that can distract the group from focusing on the real problem (Stevens, 2000). However, it might also be a motivational force since it enhances group identity. Processes of collaborative learning in a competitive environment are similar to collaborative-learning processes observed in cooperative contexts (Hutchins, 1995; Ladd & Harcourt, 2005). Moreover, the cognitive processes of computer-supported col-

FIGURE 7.2.   Students chose different avatars according to their own appearance

laborative learning appear similar whether students are working toward shared or more competing goals (Shafer, 2004).

Di Blas, Poggi, and Torrebruno (2006), who used a virtual world for team competition, revealed that the mix of collaboration and, competition both in the "physical" and the "cultural" components of the games and team activities was highly engaging and effectively motivated participants to study. They claimed that competition can be a powerful source of engagement and a motivator for academic achievement when it occurs in a collaborative environment where the teams compete. In contrast, individual competition in a teacher-education course caused decreased levels of solidarity in the online environment (Peters, Hewitt, & Brett, 2006).

Previous studies by the authors of this study have focused on understanding: (1) the student experience of working collaboratively in a team with students from another culture and country in a virtual-world environment (Resta & Shonfeld, 2016); (2) the strategies, benefits, and challenges of planning and implementing transnational collaborative-learning activities in such environments (Resta & Shonfeld, 2014); and (3) student perceptions of social, cognitive, and teaching presence (Shonfeld, Resta, & Yaniv, 2011). In each of the previous studies, the activities were designed to foster collaboration by having the cross-national learning teams design a collaborative-learning task in the virtual world to accomplish a specific educational objective. These tasks ranged from learning about another culture and its language, traditions, or history to learning about a particular place, such as how to navigate the Metro in Paris or dive into the Red Sea to understand the impact of environmental changes (Figure 7.3).

FIGURE 7.3. The Western Wall in Jerusalem and the Annex Galleries in California

Previous research has demonstrated that team-based collaboration in game-based learning may be beneficial because it leads to higher engagement levels and encourages teammates to motivate and support each other. The present study was intended to further explore the effects of incorporating a competitive game into a collaborative learning process.

CONTEXT

Graduate education students from the University of Texas at Austin and Kibbutzim College in Tel Aviv were organized into groups of five to work in online collaboration in the *Second Life* (*SL*) environment. They were asked to create tasks for a game-like learning activity designed to help learners develop their navigation skills in *SL* while learning about places and cultures across the virtual globe by participating in a competitive game *Amazing Race*.

The groups met at the virtual auditorium of Kibbutzim College in order to develop the *SL* activity for the final game. They learned how to work in VW by undertaking tasks from the previous year's game and then sending pictures of their group at the place, such as "placing a note in the Western Wall in Jerusalem."

The team discussed the places they were interested in exploring for their activity in the class's Moodle site. After visiting the VW sites, they then selected the place in *SL* in which to design their learning-task activity. They developed a description of the task with the instructions needed to enable other teams to teleport to the desired location and to complete the activity. The team provided photos, preparing the activity to help others understand both the location and the nature of the task to be completed (Figures 7.1–7.5). Examples of 3D learning environments that show interactions of student avatars engaged in collaborative learning activity in the 3D environment are presented in Figures 3 and 5.

METHOD

Participants

The participants in the *Amazing Race* competition during the study year 2015 consisted of graduate students (11) in a Computer-Supported Collaborative Learning class at the University of Texas and graduate students (18) in a Collaborative Learning seminar class at Kibbutzim College in Israel. Nine were males and 20 were females. Most of them worked in the schools or elsewhere in the education field. Both classes were offered by the respective education departments.

Learning Environment

The Kibbutzim students met at the College Island in *SL* after an introductory lesson about the theory of 3D environments in education and the practice in *SL*. They built their avatars and met with their groups after discussing their ideas in an online forum of the class.

The competitive game was based on the model of the *Amazing Race* TV program, in which teams of people race to complete a task. The concept was modified to have the learning teams competing to complete the learning tasks designed by the other teams. All of the teams met at the same place in *SL* and started the race at the same time. They had one hour to successfully complete the learning tasks designed by the other teams, and all teams had to return to the starting point at the end of the hour (Figure 7.4). The team that completed all of the tasks in the shortest time would win. If no team completed all of the tasks within the one-hour period, the one completing the most would be declared the winner.

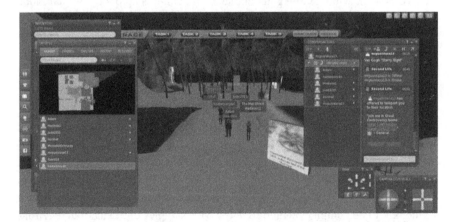

FIGURE 7.4. The Amazing Race hood at the top of the screen (Tasks 1–5) and the open menus in SL (participants list, chat, moving menu, and camera control)

Design Constraints

A major constraint in designing the 3D world collaborative-learning activities was the offset in the calendars between the schools in the two countries. The authors had to overlay the academic calendars of the two institutions to find a common time period of four weeks that would fit both class schedules. The common time occurred during the last four weeks of the U.S. course and the first four of the Israel course.

Selecting the virtual World Collaborative-Learning Activity

The collaborative-learning activity to be accomplished and the sites in the virtual world were selected to be consistent with the objectives of both courses. At the beginning, the teams explored the VW learning tasks developed in previous offerings of the courses. This was helpful for students considering the wide range of learning tasks and settings in the virtual world that might work for the task they would design. The design activity involved both asynchronous and synchronous work by the teams. Some of the groups met four times and some only twice.

Avatar Identity

Students were able to choose their avatars. Examples of diversity of avatar identities used by students in the study can be seen in Figures 1–5. Some chose a casual look (jeans and shorts), while others chose a more official appearance (jackets and dresses).

Interactions in virtual worlds are based on real-life interactions, including movements, gestures, and conversations. Figures 1–5 show some of the interac-

FIGURE 7.5.   Students' avatars on a gondola in Venice

tions possible with avatars engaged in the collaborative learning activities in the 3D environment (e.g. role playing, visiting a museum or an archeological place, sailing).

PROCEDURE

Assigning Students to Virtual Teams

Since some students work or have other regular commitments during the week, or there may be periods when they are not available, it is useful to obtain this information to help the faculty members to assign students to the virtual-learning teams. A survey used by the authors provided the information used in forming teams. Other factors included the level of English-speaking skills of the team members from non-English-speaking countries and their computer-science skills. An important criterion in forming the teams was assuring that at least one member from the non-English-speaking country had strong English-speaking skills to help translate for the other team members.

Introducing Students to Virtual World

The first activity for students was to register, create their avatars, and learn the basics in navigating in the virtual world. Virtual worlds such as *SL* offer video tutorials that can help them accomplish these tasks. Beginning in the virtual world is not easy, and the learning curve is steep. Thus, it is very helpful to have students explore and become familiar with the virtual-world environment and the avatar capabilities prior to the start of the collaborative activity between the two classes.

Initiating the Virtual World Collaborative-Learning Activity

The first synchronous meeting in the virtual world took place with the instructors from both countries participating. The instructors and students introduced themselves and briefly shared some information about their backgrounds and interests (one minute each). The instructors discussed the collaborative-learning task and the schedule of activities. They also described the resources available and how to get help if the students encountered difficulties.

Monitoring and Mentoring the Collaborative-Learning Activities

The instructors observed the team meetings and activities in the virtual world to assist if the students were encountering difficulties and also to observe the level of participation and contribution of the individual team members. If a team member was absent or appeared not to participate in the discussions and activities, the instructor met with the student in the virtual world to offer assistance.

Student Reflections

An important component of the collaborative-learning activity was the reflections of students throughout the process. This was not required of the students in Texas. However, they were encouraged to share their experiences to help both the other students and the instructors. It was part of the Israeli students' seminar work.

Self and Peer Assessment

At the end of the project, the team members completed a self and peer assessment designed to help them compare their assessments of their own contributions to the team tasks with the assessments made by their teammates. The assessment included both positive comments as well as suggestions to improve their performance as members of global virtual teams.

RESULTS

This section provides a summary of student perceptions from student surveys, transcripts of student interactions, and reflections related to the perceived challenges, benefits, and limitations of cross-cultural collaboration in the 3D virtual environment. The perceptions, noted by initialed quotes of the participants, include problems posed by technology, time differences, English-language fluency, and/or differing cultural views and norms, as well as how they were addressed and resolved.

The reflections clearly show that introducing competition among the groups increased the motivation and intensity of collaboration within each group. As a result of introducing the element of competition, the following factors emerged:

- Preparation and organization
- Togetherness in collaboration
- Challenges
- Mutual responsibility
- Decision-making process.
- Flexibility, patience
- Communication approach
- Responsibility within the team
- Group support

Preparation and Organization

Following the completion of the design of their collaborative-learning activity, some teams turned their attention to preparing for the race. D wrote: "Tonight we sat polishing the work for the upcoming marathon in two days. It is just great to see the motivation and collaboration so that our exact instructions and the overall assignment will be done inside of five minutes and not deviate from it." Other teams did not focus as well on planning for the race. One team member from Group A complained about the lack of advance planning in the group: "My feeling, at least, was of some sense of chaos and lack of early expectations at the planning level ... but lack of planning mainly caused by the fact that we hadn't practiced."

Togetherness in Collaboration

The reflections also demonstrated the recognition that each participant is important and has a role to play on the team. N indicated that:

> there is no doubt that the characteristics of the members of the group stood out—who is meticulous, who is creative, those who tend to become frustrated and who takes advantage of someone else's efforts. With all this, I think this is not a group if even one is missing—every human being has something to contribute and everyone can learn from a peer.

S added, "I truly believe in collaborative learning. I think collaborative learning is more effective and promotes learning much more than individual learning. Even with our unpleasant experience, it was easier to cope with the problems together."

While the competition took place during the one-hour game, Y was looking for the group: "The first thing I looked for was if there was anyone I knew. For me, it gives me confidence that I am not alone." A also noted the need to work together to complete the competitive task and wrote,

> In the beginning it took us a long time to meet at the right place and be photographed but already during the task and with the use of chat we began to understand that if we don't divide the work we will fail ... and also the fact we did it together from the very first moment we entered and communicated through chat was very helpful to experience together the uncertainty, challenges and technical difficulties.

H also stressed the importance of "togetherness" in the competitive task by indicating that "some read the task and explained it to the other members, some checked that everyone 'was' together, some took pictures, etc.... I enjoyed working together as a team, after we felt already solidified following the activities we had done together beforehand." Others expressed concern when there was a perceived lack of togetherness in the team, such as SH's comment: "Was there an atmosphere of competition in the air? The combination of competition and being asked to stay home alone bothered me. I did not want to sit alone and do the tasks."

In addition, SH asked whether this was collaborative learning when there was competition. "Where there is no mutual help or support, I'm not sure that there is collaborative learning. To me it's the first and main point in learning of this kind and which was very lacking in this task." But in another post, she wrote, "The last two weeks our team built the game 'The Amazing Race' in SL. Collaboration in the group was excellent, beyond what I expected. We created strong and relevant ties through the WhatsApp group and planned our strategies."

In contrast, H explained how collaboration was achieved and said,

> I see that collaboration is achieved in every new meeting, towards the final goal—unifying the group. Sometimes there is difficulty in learning and collaboration from afar, but this time they were not felt, on the contrary, the work was actually really good and fruitful.

Based on the different academic calendars, all of the students agreed to hold the *Amazing Race* at the very beginning of the vacation for the U.S. students. N said, "I was surprised to find the commitment of our members to the group that despite the holiday they continued to conduct a dialogue with us."

Challenges

The students' reflections indicated that the *Amazing Race* competition was both a challenging and interesting task that enhanced their motivation. K wrote,

> Creating a video was an amazing collaborative experience with Julia, who made the movie. H. who was in charge of the production and me doing the voice recording.... Even though we met at 10 o'clock at night and we were very tired, we were able to encourage each other to redo the work when we were not satisfied. We had the patience to talk to each other into trying once more even though it was hard for me to persevere since I had a lot of things on my mind. J. took care of the summary and Al. had disappeared.

Z also claimed that "it was a more interesting experience than virtual experiences which I had done till now."

E, on the other hand, said,

> Just the competition task alone put pressure and the need to go out and look elsewhere just pressured us more, after we managed to understand each task, we faced the task of uploading pictures to the site, we inadvertently put it all up in the wrong group.

Mutual Responsibility

K wrote about mutual responsibility within the team and the problems that arose when team members did not fulfill their commitments. He indicated:

> The question is whether in a collaborative group the members have to take responsibility for the other members who do not show interest in participating? Do we have to put pressure on the inactive members to collaborate or should we just go ahead with the task so we can meet the deadline and get satisfactory work done on time? We volunteered to make the video, but Al. never offered to help or showed

he cared about it. In collaborative work, there must be, in my opinion, common motivation to do the work. You can't force participants to make time unless they are motivated to do it.

The *Amazing Race* competition also demonstrated a number of instances in which team members assumed roles and responsibilities to support others. For example, N stated,

> Due to language differences and technological difficulties with some of the group members I became the "bridge" between the group members and translated what was said into English and Hebrew, which promoted and contributed to collaboration. In addition, we have also used the group WhatsApp to coordinate locations.

Y, despite technical difficulties, thought of ways to contribute to the group. "I did both tasks without showing my Avatar (I was transparent). I thought that if I photographed, at least I would be able to help the team." Y assumed full responsibility:

> Technical issues were difficult for me.... I myself felt less in the competition because I was busy with Avatar, and I felt I really hindered the rest of the group. At the end, I felt guilty that we haven't won. It was an unpleasant feeling.

K, despite being abroad, felt a sense of group responsibility to participate:

> Since I was in Canada for personal reasons at the time of the competition, I prepared to wake up at 5:30 to participate in the competition. I felt it was important for me to accomplish the goal we had set beforehand and not to let down the members of the group. I was there on time and so were the other members of my group.

Decision-Making Process

The reflections noted both the importance and difficulty of a shared decision-making process. Y thought that everyone should know how to contribute ideas and opinions, while SH said,

> Fast collaboration led us all to rethink our thoughts where we all are partners. Our joint thinking and discussion between us yielded very interesting ideas. I think that without the group, it would not have been possible to reach all these ideas.

H said that she noticed diversity among the group members and an attempt to form one opinion: "I think the main task of this collaboration is consolidating the various factors into one cohesive product, containing all segments." To do so requires flexibility and patience. However, it was difficult to distribute the tasks. "It makes it very difficult to plan the implementation of the task and divide the work between us towards various tasks awaiting us in the competition."

Flexibility and Patience

Y thought that everyone should contribute ideas and opinions yet also know how to be flexible with others. SH said she learned that sometimes plans can change at the last minute:

> In collaborative learning one needs to have patience and build trust in order to develop relationships that allow productive work together and to be lenient on the subject of time, as well. One of the challenges of joint collaborative working in sync is to find a time that is suitable for all members of the group [to] meet.

Flexibility includes being open and respectful of the ideas generated by other members of the group. Y indicated: "Most of the group members liked the 'Venice' of H., including me, and although I really wanted us to take my 'Rome' I went with the group and agreed."

On the other hand, failure to be flexible and open to the contributions of other members in the team can create problems. As noted by A, "Al. doesn't allow us to put up the model images, only he does it. Al. only trusts himself and is unable to make room for others."

Communication Within the Team

Of course, communication is also important. A discussed the problems that arose through lack of communication:

> One student on the other end was not really active so far and it feels quite in the air and doesn't really allow for progress, in order to construct knowledge together there must be interaction in the process to create something new.

S wrote, "We experienced quite a bit of frustration along the way, but perhaps due to the fact that all four of us were together, and not dependent on the Internet, we were able to overcome problems and to communicate." Z claimed that the communication was also fun. "We finished last. But the task itself was enjoyable, communication with members of my group, and cracking tasks created a unique shared experience."

R referred to the communication during the competition and said, "We connected through the Internet and we managed to be on time. The pressure was very nice, because missing a meeting was not an option."

Group Support

The sense of support from other members of the team was expressed in the reflections. V wondered,

> There is a pride... but why? It's a virtual game and the prize is virtually…. So what is this great excitement I feel? When I got home I put up the things that need fixing on our WhatsApp group, I was happy and cheered up by my teammates who saw things

less "tragic" than I did, I felt that I had support from my group members and they all tried to figure out what needs to be improved and came up with amazing ideas.

DISCUSSION

3D learning environments such as *SL* have been used in education for nearly a decade (Jarmon et al., 2009). There has been significant interest in the use of 3D environments as learning tools because of technological development (Burton & Martin, 2017). Kibbutzim College, like many other academic institutions, has invested resources in that area, including the purchase of an island in *SL*, upon which the virtual Kibbutzim College was constructed. Graduate students from the Kibbutzim College and the University of Texas had previously met in these environments while participating in joint courses (Resta & Shonfeld, 2014). They were trained to use 3D virtual environments such as *SL*. They collaborated in groups, creating educational activities such as role-playing or touring and exploring different countries, museums, and archeological sites. In the *Amazing Race* experience, the entire collaborative project took place in *SL*. Students were tasked with designing a learning activity that used a 3D virtual environment. They met their partners in the other country in virtual worlds and were exposed to the potential benefits and limitations of virtual worlds in supporting collaborative learning.

For several years, during the final whole class meeting, the teams made a presentation of their collaborative learning projects in the virtual world. In the years 2015 and 2016, a game-like competition was introduced as the culminating activity. As noted earlier, it was based on the *Amazing Race* concept. All the teams started and ended at the same time with the goal of being the first to complete all of the learning activities. Each team worked to complete all of the collaborative-learning activities created by the other teams. The observations by the instructors, as well as the reflections of the students, indicated that this was an exciting and engaging activity.

As noted in the results, most students reported a positive experience and a sense of community and group cohesion that grew over the time that they worked together. The study revealed the following factors that must be carefully considered in the design and implementation of transnational collaborative-learning activities and the effective use of competition among the teams as a culminating activity.

Acceptance and Use of SL in a Collaborative Activity

The student perceptions indicated a willingness to accept the challenges of engaging in cross-cultural collaboration in a virtual world. The comments expressed openness and excitement at the opportunity to collaborate with teammates from another country. They noted that their communications during team meetings in the virtual world helped contribute to their sense of being with their teammates in the same virtual space. This, in turn, helped them to become more familiar and comfortable with the other members of their team. These responses are congruent with the suggestion of Fetscherin and Lattermann (2008) that student acceptance of *SL* is dependent upon the perceived value of the communication.

Immersive Experiential Learning

Similar to previous studies, the study results indicated that the virtual environment enhanced student motivation and engagement and provided immersive, experiential learning opportunities unavailable in traditional learning-management systems (Aldrich, 2009; Burton, & Martin, 2017; Dede et al., 2005; Gee, 2003; Kirriemuir & McFarlane, 2004; Shonfeld, Resta, & Yaniv, 2011). In addition, students indicated that the immersive 3D environment contributed to their sense of their being together in the same virtual place at the same time. This, in turn, increased their sense of social presence. Social presence is the degree to which a person is perceived as a "real person" in mediated communication and is essential for creating a trusting environment for interpersonal communication and collaboration. The sense of being in the same virtual place at the same time helps to contribute to social presence and sense of group cohesion of learning teams in the virtual world (Traphagan et al., 2010).

Although most students in the classes chose or designed avatars that were similar to them, some commented that the feeling of taking on a different virtual representation had an impact on the roles they tended to assume in interacting with other team members. This aligns with what Mayrath et al. (2009) found about how the context and the selected avatar representation led to the adoption of new and different roles in the immersive virtual environment.

Mixing Competition with collaborative Learning

Similar to other virtual worlds (Warburton, 2009), the *Second Life* environment provided the students with the opportunity to engage in performative, collaborative, and game-based activities. It also supported both the collaborative and competitive activities of the virtual teams. Stevens (2000) noted that competition is often viewed as a barrier to effective use of collaborative learning; however, the results of our study are aligned with those of DiBlas, Poggi, and Torrebruno (2006), who found that the mix of collaboration and competition in games and team activities in their study was highly engaging and motivating to the participants. In our study, the student responses related to the *Amazing Race* competition between the teams resulted in high levels of motivation and engagement. In addition, a number of comments from students indicated that the support they experienced from their team members during the race greatly heightened their sense of community and positive interdependence with their team members.

Addressing Technical Problems

One of the challenges is that the use of *SL* requires both broadband access to the Internet and a relatively new computer. *SL* requires computer speed of at least

800 MHZ and 512 MB of memory. Failure to meet these requirements has during this and previous studies resulted in a student experiencing slow download time of the *SL* software and software freezing up and crashing, all of which impact the student's *SL* experience. Prior to initiating the collaborative activity, the students were provided with the technical requirements for the activity. Options were available for those who were not able to meet them by having them use computers and/or gain broadband access to the Internet at the university, a friend's home, or an Internet café.

Although the collaborative-learning activities did not require advanced skills in accomplishing complex tasks, such as building objects, the collaborative activities required that the students acquire the basic skills of how to move, sit, fly, teleport, navigate, speak, and write, etc., in the virtual world. These functions and the *SL* interface take time to learn, and this represented more of a challenge for the Israeli students who did not have time in advance to explore *SL* prior to initiating the cross-cultural collaboration.

Collaboration and Trust

Forming transnational collaborative teams and helping them be successful in the collaborative activities required both initial planning and scaffolding to help the teams develop their skills in online collaboration. The team members had to trust each other initially and later verify and adjust accordingly (swift trust). As noted by Crisp and Jarvenpaa (2013), cognitive components of swift trust render it fragile and in need of reinforcement and calibration based upon the actions of the team members. As the individual members make positive contributions in the early stages of working together, they develop confidence and move to deeper levels of trust as they are successful in accomplishing tasks together.

Challenges

Although an effort was made by the instructors to form teams based on their stated availability to meet during specific times and days of the week, problems still arose in levels of attendance during the collaborative activities. Teams that experienced absences, particularly those that were not explained in advance by the team member, displayed a sense of frustration and a sense of lowered trust and sense of community. It might be that competition produces social issues (Stevens, 2000). However, others claim that collaborative learning in a competitive environment is similar to other collaborative-learning processes (Hutchins, 1995; Ladd & Harcourt, 2005). Thus, collaborative projects must emphasize individual and mutual responsibility and group support.

Competition

Most students positively commented on their experience of the *Amazing Race*'s culminating activity. Several indicated that during this competition among the teams they felt the greatest support from their team members and had the greatest sense of being a team. This result raises the possibility of the potential value of introducing some type of competition between the teams earlier in the process.

In summary, the *Amazing Race* identified the benefits as well as the challenges of designing and conducting transnational collaborative-learning activities in *SL*. The reflections by the participants and authors have led to some guidelines for consideration in the design of such experiences.

The major challenges of differences in time zone, culture, and facility in English must be carefully considered in designing transnational collaborative-learning activities. It is also important to provide scaffolding and support for the collaborative teams in the early stages. Although we were surprised by how quickly the transnational teams solidified, developed trust, and demonstrated elements of becoming high-performance virtual teams, the technical challenge remains, and it is likely that future efforts will also require alternatives since the technology continues to change exponentially. An important finding of this study is that it is possible to carry out a transnational collaborative activity in *SL* during a 4–6-week period.

Finally, the positive responses to introducing the game-like *Amazing Race* competition as a culminating activity and its effects on cohesion and support within the teams suggests that future research should be done to explore possible effects of introducing game-like competitions on the development of team, sense of community, and trust.

REFERENCES

Aldrich, C. (2009). *Learning online with games, simulations, and virtual worlds: Strategies for online instruction.* San Francisco, CA: Jossey-Bass.

Bulu, S. T. (2012). Place presence, social presence, co-presence, and satisfaction in virtual worlds. *Computers & Education, 58*(1), 154–161.

Burton, B. G., & Martin, B. (2017). Knowledge creation and student engagement within 3D virtual worlds. *International Journal of Virtual and Augmented Reality (IJVAR), 1*(1), 43–59.

Crisp, C., & Jarvenpaa, S. (2013). Swift trust in global virtual teams: Trusting beliefs and normative actions. *Journal of Personnel Psychology, 12*(1), 45–56.

Dede, C., Clarke, J., Ketelhut, D., Nelson, B., & Bowman, C. (2005). *Fostering motivation, learning, and transfer in multi-user virtual environments.* Paper presented at the American Educational Research Association Conference, Montreal, Canada.

Di Blas, N., Poggi, C., & Torrebruno, A. (2006). Collaboration and playful competition in a 3d educational virtual world: The Learning@Europe experience. In E. Pearson & P. Bohman (Eds.), *Proceedings of EdMedia: World Conference on Educational Media and Technology 2006* (pp. 1191–1198). Association for the Advancement of Computing in Education (AACE).

Falloon, G. (2010). Using avatars and virtual environments in learning: What do they have to offer? *British Journal of Educational Technology, 41*(1), 108–122.

Fetscherin, M., & Lattemann, C. (2008). User acceptance of virtual worlds. *Journal of Electronic Commerce Research, 9*(3), 231–242.

Gee, J. P. (2003). *What videogames have to teach us about learning and literacy.* New York, NY: Palgrave Macmillan.

Gonzáleza, M. A., Santosb, B. S. N., Vargasb, A. R., Martin-Gutiérreza , J. M., & Orihuela, A. R. (2013). Virtual worlds opportunities and challenges in the 21st century. *Procedia Computer Science, 25,* 330–337.

Hutchins, E. (1995). *Cognition in the wild.* Cambridge, MA: MIT Press.

Jarmon, L., Lim, K. Y. T., & Carpenter, B. S. (2009). Pedagogy, education and innovation in virtual worlds. *Journal of virtual Worlds, 2*(1). Retrieved from https://journals.tdl.org/jvwr/article/view/639/470

Kirriemuir, J., & McFarlane, A. (2004). *Literature review in games and learning.* Retrieved from https://www.nfer.ac.uk/publications/FUTL27/FUTL27literaturereview.pdf

Ladd, B., and Harcourt, E. (2005). Student competitions and bots in an introductory programming course. *Journal of Computing Sciences in Colleges, 20,* 274–284.

Mayrath, M., Traphagan, T., Jarmon, L., Trivedi, A., & Resta, P. (2009). *Teaching with virtual worlds: Factors to consider for instructional use of Second Life.* Paper presented to 2009 Annual Convention of the American Educational Research Association. San Diego, CA.

Peters, V., Hewitt, J., & Brett, C. (2006). Competition and collaboration in a computer-mediated teacher education course. In C. Crawford, R. Carlsen, K. McFerrin, J. Price, R. Weber, & D. Willis (Eds.), *Proceedings of Society for Information Technology & Teacher Education International Conference 2006* (pp. 487–501). Chesapeake, VA: Association for the Advancement of Computing in Education (AACE).

Prensky, M. (2006). *Don't bother me, Mom, I'm learning!: How computer and video games are preparing your kids for 21st century success and how you can help!* St. Paul, MN: Paragon House.

Radford, M., Vlachantoni, A., Evandrou, M., & Schröder-Butterfill, E. (2011). *A literature review on the usefulness of Second Life as a pedagogic tool in the postgraduate teaching of gerontology and other policy relevant social sciences in the UK.* Retrieved from http://eprints.soton.ac.uk/207437/1/CRA_DP_1102.pdf

Resta, P., & Shonfeld, M. (2014). Challenges and strategies in designing transnational learning team projects in virtual worlds. In M. Searson & M. Ochoa (Eds.), *Proceedings of Society for Information Technology & Teacher Education International Conference* (pp. 403–409). Chesapeake, VA: Association for the Advancement of Computing in Education (AACE).

Resta, P., & Shonfeld, M. (2016). Challenges and strategies in designing cross-national learning team projects in virtual worlds. In T. Anderson, (Ed.). *Virtual worlds in online and distance education* (pp. 262–275). Edmonton, Canada: Athabasca University Press.

Shafer, D. W. (2004). When computer-supported collaboration means computer-supported competition: Professional mediation as a model for collaborative learning. *Journal of Interactive Learning Research, 15*(2), 101–115.

Shonfeld, M., & Kritz, M. (2013). Virtual representations in 3D learning environments. *Interdisciplinary Journal of E-Learning and Learning Objects, 9,* 249–266.

Shonfeld, M., & Raz, A. (2011). *Using Second Life in the language classroom.* In press.

Shonfeld, M., Resta, P., &Yaniv, H. (2011). Engagement and social presence in a virtual world (Second Life) learning environment. *Proceedings of SITE*. Nashville, TN.

Smart, J., Cascio, J., & Paffendof, J. (2007). *Metaverse roadmap: Pathways to the 3D web.* Retrieved from http://www.metaverseroadmap.org/overview

Stevens, R. R. (2000). Divisions of labor in school and in the workplace: Comparing computer and paper-supported activities across settings. *Journal of the Learning Sciences, 9*(4), 373–401.

Traphagan, T., Chiang, Y., Hyeseung M., Wattanawaha, B., Lee, H., Mayrath, M., Woo, J., & Resta, P. (2010). Cognitive, social and teaching presence in a virtual world and a regular text chat. *Computers & Education, 55*(3), 923–936.

Warburton, S. (2009). Second Life in higher education: Assessing the potential for and the barriers to deploying virtual worlds in learning and teaching. *British Journal of Educational Technology, 40*(3), 414–426.

CHAPTER 8

TEC

An Online Collaborative Learning Model in a Multicultural Environment

Miki Kritz, Efrat Bachar, and Miri Shonfeld

Innovative teaching and learning on the Internet enables practical connections in a safe environment without reference to stereotypes and external appearance, concentrating on the process of learning and mutual enrichment through meaningful dialogue. In a multicultural society such as Israel, which is characterized by tensions between Arab and Jewish cultures, there is a need for a special model of online collaborative learning based on successful knowledge and experience in order to lead educational communities to a more enlightened future. The Technology, Education and Cultural Diversity (TEC) model combines collaborative and meaningful teaching and learning with education in values and multiculturalism in an advanced teaching environment.

The TEC model ensures gradual progress in several educational and academic dimensions: collaborative and individual teaching and learning; innovative, significant pedagogy; recognition and openness to other cultures while presenting one's personal culture; deepening human values; mutual respect; and advanced information and communication skills. In the TEC program for pupils, a hundred classes from different schools participate—Jews and Arabs, religious and

Collaborative Online Learning in a Global World, pages 111–124.
Copyright © 2019 by Information Age Publishing
111

secular—from different sectors and cultures. They study together in the social network called TECS which is supported in three languages (Hebrew, Arabic, and English). Pupils develop digital content collaboratively on different issues related to culture, values, and heritage.

This chapter reviews the model, the various aspects of the TEC pupils program, and the results of the assessment conducted through questionnaires and interviews with the educational staff and pupils.

THEORETICAL BACKGROUND

Schools in Israel belong to different cultures and denominations. Their aim is to train the young to deal with data-intensive environments, with rapid changes and transitions in a pluralistic society, while highlighting the cultural uniqueness of each community. Acknowledgement of others' cultures and intercultural dialogue are essential to deepen mutual knowledge and respect for the sake of a more enlightened human future.

The technological reality of the 21st century allows for communication between different cultures. People can use the Internet to deepen their familiarity with the other's culture, find common universal values along with each culture's unique values, and develop a dialogue characterized by openness, understanding, and mutual respect (Shonfeld, Hoter, & Ganayem, 2013). The multi-cultural project reported here promoted a study of the impacts of advanced technologies on cultural shifts through fruitful discussion and dialogue with people from other cultures. This activity was used as a place of exposure and use of innovative learning technologies similar to online conferences in teacher education (Shonfeld, 2005).

The TEC Model

The TEC model offers a link between members of different cultures through learning technologies. The rationale of the TEC model is based on online teaching and learning that allows for relevant interaction without reference to stereotypes and external appearance. Online virtuality allows members to connect more easily, but connecting is not enough to resolve more complex conflicts. Following Allport's hypothesis (Allport, 1954), Pettigrew and Tropp (2008) listed the supporting conditions that create connection between cultures in what is referred to as the *Contact Hypothesis*: equality of participants, collaboration rather than competition, institutional support, and a long period of dialogue and partnership between groups rather than individuals.

The TEC model, based on the Contact Hypothesis and the conditions that support creating connections between cultures, offers an additional level based on the gradual development of online communications, media tools, various degrees of participation, and the strengthening of trust between the groups during the development of the group work. The model's uniqueness is expressed in its suitabil-

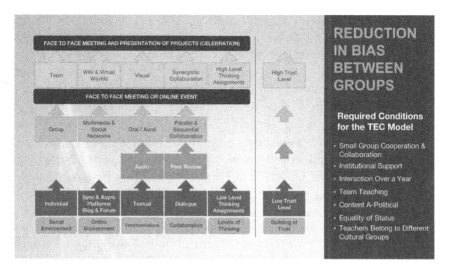

FIGURE 8.1. The TEC model

ity for developing skills for the 21st-century reality through innovative software based on collaboration via the Internet.

Online Collaborative Learning

Collaborative learning is of educational importance because its essence lies in the interaction between the learner and a learning environment. It enables personal expression within a group while at the same time creating social ties. Collaborative learning promotes thinking (Gerdy, 1998; Harasim, 2012), contributes to the group's as well as the individual's achievements, and produces a variety of products. Moreover, it prepares students for real life and integration into the modern labor market (MOE, 2011). The organization and management of collaborative learning are complex and require much effort from both the teacher and the student. It is desirable that the teaching also be collaborative so that the teachers themselves demonstrate the method to the students. Demonstrating collaborative teaching is particularly important, especially in teacher-training colleges, as this will affect the teaching and collaborative learning in schools during their training and after (Shonfeld, 2017).

Collaborative learning in online environments is more effective than in traditional environments (Swan, Shen, & Hiltz, 2006; Tsuei, 2011) because the skills of teamwork in the Internet environment are more visible than in a F2F environment and are measurable and comparable (Levy, 2007). The development of technology in the field of learning analytics enables charting and assessing the individual contribution of each user to the joint product. This tracking option is one of the major advantages of an online system as it allows the group advisor and participants to monitor the work process (Tal & Tal, 2006). In fact, this has become the basis for the theoretical foundation for online collaborative learning in educational frameworks (Johnson & Johnson, 2013).

Online collaborative learning theory (OCL) has developed with the spread of online learning in the education system (Harasim, 2012). In online courses, collaborative learning is of great value because it eliminates the feeling of loneliness in the student and creates interaction between the learners and a sense of social presence (Resta & Shonfeld, 2013). Two factors make up the social presence—group cohesion and awareness of others—and these contribute to improved learning and the ability to integrate different teaching methods and increases in student interest and satisfaction (Abedin, 2012; Palloff & Patt, 2005).

Learning communities are a part of the school experience, and now every student can be a part of the processes and the products through online discussion groups. Students from one institution can study in a course given by another institution. Education conducted in this way is not easy to manage, but it prepares students for the realities of the 21st century (Yang, 2014).

The digital age offers solutions to difficulties in organizing collaborative learning environments (Harasim, 2012; Sharan, 2010) using collaborative technological tools and virtual environments, enabling the creation of heterogeneous groups that were not previously possible due to physical limitations. Google tools that allow shared writing from a distance or synchronous platforms for online meetings are examples of how to bridge the distance, since they provide a suitable venue for productive teamwork.

Technological tools can enhance various stages of collaborative learning, from the presentation of the rules, demonstrations, creating tasks, and individual or group assessment. Choosing collaborative learning tools will be based on understanding of the cognitive and social processes of learning (Sharples et al., 1993). When choosing the technological environment, one must examine the potential activities and the possible outcomes (Meishar-Tal & Tal-Elhasid, 2008).

Common tools are forums, wikis, blogs, social and educational networks, and Google tools. In recent years, with the development of WEB2 tools that allow writing shared documents and uploading images and multimedia files to a network (Picasa, YouTube, etc.), options for collaborative learning have expanded via the Internet and include local, national, and international projects. Examples of collaborative projects for children around the world are IEARN for elementary schools; KIDLINK for intermediate schools, which are a platform for collaborative learning for teachers and students around the world; and FaTe2, which deals with digital stories in 3D worlds (Garzotto & Forfori, 2006). TEC programs permit collaboration among students from different cultures using online environments (Shonfeld et. al, 2013).

THE CONTEXT

The TEC Center in Israel acts in teacher-training colleges and in schools to strengthen trust among online collaborative learning groups from different cultures (Arabs and Jews, religious and secular) through the TEC model and develops collaborative online learning (Shonfeld, Hoter, & Ganayem, 2013).

The TEC program for pupils has been operating since 2009. Fifth- and sixth-grade students work online together all year divided into three groups, one from each of three cultural groups: the secular sector, the religious sector, and the Arab sector. The students work in mixed groups of six students, two from each culture, and join to perform collaborative tasks. Their relationship develops gradually, to assuage the likelihood of prejudice: textual at the beginning, then oral and then visual. The TEC activity, it is assumed, produces a connection and mutual trust among the students of different cultures and prepares them for an experiential F2F meeting at the end of the program. The goal is to reduce prejudice and increase the trust among students of different cultures.

The program opens with a training experience of three days for all the teachers in the program. Each group of three teachers, one from each culture, prepares a program that includes tasks for the students. The training experience is conducted in a unique, online social network that includes the use of information and communication technologies such as network sharing, synchronous and asynchronous communication, online discussion, use of Web 2.0 for the production of a collaborative product, podcasts, and building digital games and videos. These various technologies are utilized while implementing online learning activities that require thinking and higher-order collaboration skills (e.g. choosing a subject, deciding about division of labor, exchanging materials and products, and assembling the final product).

The research question is: What is the contribution of the TEC program to teachers and students participating in the program?

METHODOLOGY

The study utilized a mixed methodology that included quantitative and qualitative aspects. It included online questionnaires with open and closed questions. Intervention groups and control groups (pupils of the same school and the same age who had not participated in the program) answered the questionnaire. The questions sought general information such as meetings with children of other religions before the program and conceptions of other religions, hobbies and interests, declared knowledge about Israel and cities with mixed populations, information about the school and ICT, collaboration and understanding others, readiness to interact with children of other religions, and summarizing the project. The optional answers were: Yes, No, and I do not know. The comparison between the intervention group and the control group was conducted using a Chi-square test. The comparisons were made on each question of the questionnaire separately.

The qualitative section included interviews with the participating teachers and students. The teacher interviews included questions about their personal attitudes and their students' work on the project. The teachers' interview started with an open question: "Tell me about the program and your role in it." During the conversation, additional questions explored the different aspects studied in this work. Also, discussions with groups of students who participated in the program took place at the end of the year. The researchers tried to understand the views of the children, the challenges they encountered, and the contribution of the program and its impact on the children.

FINDINGS

Comparison between the intervention group (TEC program participants, N=108) and the control group (N=112) showed no significant difference in personal attitudes toward issues which did not relate to the program goals, like love of sports, of reading books, and of music and declared knowledge about Israel. In addition, a comparison between boys and girls in the intervention group found no significant differences. The test also compared the students in religious and secular schools. Here, too, no significant differences were found toward issues which did not relate to the program goals. Only one item showed significantly higher scores for students who did not participate in the program: playing a musical instrument.

In the answers to questions that had an affinity or connection to issues which the TEC program deals with, such as those dealing with collaboration through the Internet at various levels, it was found that 92% of the project's participants liked the idea of communicating with children from other schools; however, only about 44% of the control group participants from all cultures (those who hadn't

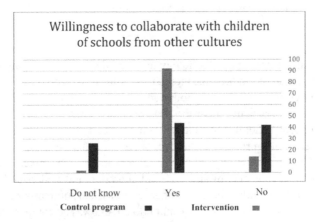

FIGURE 8.2. Division of willingness to collaborate with children of schools from other cultures

participated in the project) liked the idea. Figure 8.2 presents the distribution of the pupils' answers.

On the issue of using the Internet to learn with students from other schools, there was a big difference: 52% of the participants in the project used the Internet to study with students from other schools; however, only about 27% of the control group did so. Also, significant differences were found between the two groups in using the Internet for learning. Participants in the program (78%) enjoyed learning in this manner (via a synchronous online lesson), much more than those who did not participate (about 30%), and the difference was significant: $\chi^2(2, N=126) = 28.41, p<.001$.

The possibility of learning something new by virtue of doing so with students from another school also revealed a clear benefit of the program participants: $\chi^2(2, N=126) = 19.64, p<.001$, the most significant one. It was found that about 82% of the participants believed that they could learn something new when collaborating with those from another school. In contrast, only 59% from the control group felt that way.

Asking what students thought about those in other schools and the similarities and differences among them produced an interesting result. Fifty percent of the participants, compared with 45.5% from the control group, believed that there were differences between themselves and students from other schools, but at the same time, approximately 49% of participants in the program and only about 35% of the control group thought that there was no difference. It should be noted that about 20% of the control group answered "do not know" as opposed to only 1% of the program participants.

The issue of equality of educational opportunity of pupils from schools educating different sectors found that 90% of the participants believed that the answer was "yes," as did 75% in the control group. Over 70% of the participants did not agree with the statement that they were different than students from other sectors. In contrast, about 55% of the control group believed so. This position was consistent with the previous findings and reinforced it.

On the issue of students' degree of opportunity to communicate safely with members of different religions or nationalities, the program participants felt that their ability to communicate with members of another nationality or religion was relatively high. About 66% answered "safe" or "very safe," while only about 47% of the control group agreed. Program participants showed more interest in working with other children on the Internet. Some 84% replied "interesting" or "very interesting" to the question, "Is working with other children on the Internet interesting?" In contrast, only about 30% of the control group had the same level of interest.

The findings also indicated that the program's participants believed that the quality of their work with other students online was "good" or "very good" (87%); on the other hand, only 27% from the control group believed that it would be. OCL was highly appreciated by the participants at the intervention program.

The questionnaires also reflected these results: the respondents felt that the work with others was very interesting (74%), interesting (25%); very good (77%), good (13%); very easy (40%), easy (29%), okay (31%). The last question dealt with the desire to participate in a similar project the following year. About 83% of the participants wanted to continue, while only 60% of the control group expressed a desire to participate in this kind of program.

QUALITATIVE FINDINGS

The interviews with the principals, parents, and children produced the following findings:

Students' Attitudes Toward Participation in the Program

The interviews showed that children enjoyed taking part in the program. They noted a number of benefits: new friends, familiarity with children from a different culture, and new technological tools. In addition, Hebrew language skills improved in the Arab sector. One of the teachers said that she was surprised to find an increase in the level of interest of her students. Furthermore, she proudly noted that the creativity of her students increased when using technological tools that they had mastered. She noted that the students exhibited confidence when making the presentations they had prepared and when they introduced their school to students from other schools. The principal said that the students who had taken part in the program exhibited "leadership skills" and a greater degree of trust in the other sectors. Although students and teachers suggested ways to improve the program, which are discussed later in this paper, the overall impression was that the students enjoyed taking part in the program and wanted more interaction with the other schools and more frequent meetings. In interviews with the students, most mentioned the use of technology and online collaborative work as motivational. The reference was to their immense enjoyment of a different way of learning, without books and notebooks. The use of technology was not a hindrance; on the contrary, the ability of students to quickly adopt technology became a motivating factor to participate in the program.

Learning Gains

Many teachers described how children internalized the technological knowledge and transferred it to other lessons. In some cases, they did so on their own initiative and in others with the support of the teachers who accompanied them. One of the teachers described the students in the program as technological leaders in their school.

The children had usually had little contact with or knowledge about children in other localities and noted that participation in the program led them to a better appreciation of the others' festivals, traditions, language, and food. One student noted that "they are like us, but different." In one Arab school, some students said that they had prior knowledge about Jews but had not had a close relationship with them. The ongoing contact in the program over the year allowed them to gain a better understanding of the "other."

At one of the Jewish schools, one teacher said that he was pleasantly surprised by his students, who had started out with a feeling of superiority toward Arab students and discovered that Arab children were just as good at teleprocessing as them. Interesting to note, various delays in the program due to technical problems did not affect the motivation of the students because there were always other activities available. Some children mentioned that they had not learned enough about other students and that they would like to continue the program to have more opportunities to meet with them (these data were collected before the children had met face to face at the conclusion of the program in May). In one Arab school, some children had difficulties in Hebrew, but the principal noted that this was related to their lack of self-confidence with the language. After they overcame their initial trepidation, they improved steadily. And as the weeks went by, their language skills indeed improved. These children, and Jewish children as well, found ways to use the Google translator to bolster their communication.

Collaborative Learning

In response to the question about what they enjoyed most, the students spoke about collaborative learning activities, where children from one school sent a written description of a picture of a clown which later was the basis of a drawing by the other students in the group and was compared with the original drawing. This is a good example of an educational activity at the appropriate level: challenging but achievable collaboratively.

The Children's Personal Development

All of the teachers mentioned the contribution of the program as a real change maker in their students' lives. In all the interviews, teachers described in detail the significant changes they saw in the way the students conducted themselves, the increase in their level of tolerance and acceptance of others, and the development of their behavior and attitudes. They described friendship and contacts which were built gradually, some of which have continued even beyond the official activity hours. The students also reported the contribution to their attitudes generated by the program. One student described how early in the course he objected meeting with Arabs, but he got to know them at the meetings and saw that they were like everyone else. He added: "One mustn't be judged by religion." Students elaborated on the extensive knowledge they acquired on the "other" and the friendships that developed between them.

Teachers' Professional Development

Many teachers mentioned that participation in the program was a significant factor in their personal technology development. They spoke of regeneration and a sense of progress even though they had a steep learning curve in terms of control and feeling comfortable with the new software. Their professional development was reflected in an improved ability to use ICT in the classroom, a significant enhancement of the technological toolbox of an online collaborative environment. Some of the teachers were able to apply these new skills in other areas of teaching as well.

A science teacher said that she learned the necessary ICT skills along with the children and enjoyed the new style of teaching where she was more a guide and escort than a teacher. She also noted that she had been involved in the program for two years. The first year she had studied the ICT applications and therefore in the second year she was more successful.

Multicultural collaborative learning contributed significantly to the personal worlds of the program participants as reflected in their emotional development, changed attitudes, reduced barriers and prejudices, and greater desire to get to know the other. Some even saw their participation as their mission to develop a more just and tolerant society.

Principals, Parents, and the School

Concurrent with the direct contribution of the program to its participants, wider circles were affected: other students, the participants' friends, all the schools' teachers, and even members of the entire community. Students' stories at home about their experiences in the program also contributed to raising parents' awareness of the importance of the program. Many teachers had not mentioned that the very existence of the program at their school impacted students who hadn't participated: through direct exposure in school forums, to stories of experiences and challenges told by students in the program, and in other cases through conversations and sharing experiences directly. This exposure aroused curiosity about the program and contributed to an awareness of its basic ideas.

Some of the schools participating in the program started promoting multiculturalism programs. In other schools, where the idea of multiculturalism was not obvious, the very existence of the program and its success provided a lever to a moral statement for the entire community. Further to the findings of this study, we should examine the possibility of advertising the program and distributing its products and the experiences of participants formally and institutionally within the participating schools and to the wider community.

Data from the interviews clearly showed that some parents, mainly those with strong religious views, were anxious at the beginning of the program, and a concentrated effort by the principals was required to reassure them. Nevertheless, one of the teachers found it valuable to emphasize that the program was part of a broader vision of connecting the school to the outside world, both in Israel and abroad. For her, it was "part of preparing children for life" and coping with the challenges of an isolated school.

In conclusion, the results pointed out the contribution of the program to the students, teachers, principals, parents, and the entire community. The contribution was related to pedagogy (collaborative learning) as well as to attitudes (multiculturalism).

DISCUSSION

In response to the study question: "What is the contribution of the TEC program for teachers and students participating in it?" it was found that the aspects of the program that were designed to reduce prejudice and increase trust among students of different cultures were successful. This is in line with the TEC model's aim (Shonfeld et al., 2013) to increase trust among groups from different cultures.

Analysis of teacher and student interviews showed a substantial contribution to the field of technology and to the personal multi-cultural and pedagogical fields. In the technology field, the contribution was primarily significant for teachers who had not been familiar with current technology. In addition, schools that were not at a high ICT level gained the most in terms of infrastructure and their ICT skills. This is a great contribution to the national and international goals of preparing children for the 21st century (Hine, 2011; MOE, 2011).

In the personal field, the emphasis was on increased openness and establishing connections among teachers in various sectors. Most teachers reported that the main contribution in this area was evident among the students. The students themselves also reported significant personal emotional and attitudinal changes. From a pedagogical perspective, many students considered the unique, collaborative learning program as motivational, fun, and enriching. Collaborative learning adds a sense of social presence and increases engagement (Harasim, 2012; Resta & Shonfeld, 2013). The students in the program changed their attitudes just by knowing that their friends were also participating in such a program. These data support previous studies (Zoubi, 2011) which found an influence on three social affinity circles of multicultural group participants: the parents' circle, the sibling circle, and the circle of close friends of the participants.

As for learning something new from collaborating with students from another culture, the program participants had a clear advantage. The experience enhanced their willingness to study with students from other schools. In terms of the ability and desire to have contact with the "other," program participants showed a relatively high degree of confidence in their ability to communicate with members of another nationality or religion. The program also contributed to the language skills of the Arab students since Hebrew was the required language of communication during the year-long project. It seems that the long duration of the program was one of the important factors responsible for these results. One of the supporting conditions that create connection between cultures is a long period of dialogue and partnership among groups rather than individuals. This is based on

Allport's contact theory (1954), which the TEC model follows (Shonfeld, Hoter, & Ganayem, 2013).

One of the challenges of the program, as with other collaborative programs, is adapting educational materials to the different levels of the students (Shonfeld, 2017), especially when learning takes place among schools with diverse populations. A good example of an educational activity at the appropriate level was the written description of a picture of a clown which later became a drawing by the other students in the group and was compared to the original drawing, challenging but achievable through collaboration because it has the possibility to work on different levels. This program might serve as an example to those who find it difficult to implement collaborative learning in schools. Collaborative learning is of educational importance, mainly because of the interaction between the learner and the environment. Collaborative learning allows students to learn effectively, to express themselves within the group, and at the same time to create social ties (Tsuei, 2011).

Interview findings emphasize the significant role of the principal in supporting the program. The program in some schools was part of a broader vision of connecting the school to the outside world, in Israel and abroad, and as a part of preparing children for life. Education conducted in this way is not easy to manage, but it prepares students for the realities of the 21st century (Yang, 2014). This compatibility between the vision of the program and the values and aspirations of schools which participate is crucial for its continuation. The program's innovative pedagogy of collaborative learning online (Harasim, 2012) helps educational leaders to cope with environments which otherwise oppose this approach and influences similar programs elsewhere. One example is the "Dissolving Boundaries" that connect the schools in Northern Ireland and the Republic of Ireland (Austin et al., 2009).

These findings are compatible with subsequent studies on the TEC model, which is based on the gradual adoption of telecommunications, media tools, varying degrees of collaboration, and the strengthening of trust between the groups during the development of the collaborative learning that serves as a connecting platform for group work (Hoter, Shonfeld, & Ganayem, 2009; Shonfeld, Hoter, & Ganayem, 2013; Walther et al., 2015). The TEC experience led most participants to indicate a stronger desire than those in the control group to continue learning in a program with online collaborative learning in a multi-cultural environment. Yet, one can limit and assume that these findings are also affected by the "experimental stage effect"—the effect of the prestige of participation in the experiment on its results.

Given the ongoing tension in Israel and its borders and the difficulties of face-to-face meetings, the program focuses on online collaborative learning to achieve its goals. However, it is likely that this model is suitable for adoption elsewhere around the world and can be used as a way to link children from different countries. Future research into online collaborative learning using the TEC model may help promote this goal.

REFERENCES

Abedin, B. (2012). *Sense of community and learning outcomes in computer supported collaborative learning (CSCL) environments*. Sapporo, Japan: Business and Information, Academy of Taiwan Information Systems Research.

Allport, G. W. (1954). *The nature of prejudice*. Cambridge, MA: Addison-Wesley.

Austin.R., Smyth.J., Rickard, A., Mallon, M., Flynn, P., & Metcalfe, N. (2009). *Cross-border digital school partnerships. Dissolving boundaries 1999–2009*. The Department of Education, Northern Ireland and the Department for Education and Science, Dublin. University of Ulster.

Garzotto, F., & Forfori, M. (2006). *FaTe2: Storytelling edutainment experiences in 2D and 3D collaborative spaces*. In Proceedings of the Conference on Interaction Design and Children, Tampere, Finland. Retrieved from http://playpen.icomtek.csir.co.za/~acdc/education/IDC2006%20conference/proceedings/IDC-ConferenceProceedings/p113-garzotto.pdf

Gerdy, K. (1998). *If Socrates only knew: Expanding law class discourse*. CALI Conference on Law School Computing, Chicago, Illinois.

Harasim, L. (2012). *Learning theory and online technology: How new technologies are transforming learning opportunities*. New York, NY: Routledge Press.

Hine, P. (Ed.) (2011). *UNESCO report: ICT competency framework for teachers* (pp. 3–10). Paris, France: United Nations Educational, Scientific and Cultural Organization.

Hoter, E., Shonfeld, M., & Ganayim, A. (2009). Information and communication Technology (ICT) in the service of multiculturalism. *International Review of Research in Open and Distance Learning, 10*(2). Retrieved from http://www.irrodl.org/index.php/irrodl/article/view/601/1207

Johnson, D. W., & Johnson, F. P. (2013*). Joining together: Group theory and group skills*. Boston, MA: Pearson.

Levy, L. (2007). *Isum kishurey avodat zevet belmida besvivat internet.* [Application in team work skills in internet environment]. Retrieved from http://telem-pub.openu.ac.il/users/chais/2007/noon/N_2.pdf

Meishar-Tal, H., & Tal-Elhasid, E. (2008). Measuring collaboration in educational wikis—A methodological discussion. *International Journal of Emerging Technologies in Learning (iJET), 3*, Kassel, Germany: International Association of Online Engineering.

MOE. (2011). *Adapting the educational system to the 21st century*. Retrieved from http://cms.education.gov.il/EducationCMS/Units/MadaTech/englishsifria/AdaptingtheEducationSystemtothe21Century/Vision_and_rationale.htm

Palloff, R. M., & Pratt, K. (2005). *Collaborating online: Learning together in communities*. San Francisco, CA: Jossey-Bass.

Pettigrew, T. F., & Tropp, L. R. (2008). How does intergroup contact reduce prejudice? Meta-analytic tests of three mediators. *European Journal of Social Psychology, 38*, 922–934.

Resta, P., & Shonfeld, M. (2013). A study of trans-national learning teams in a virtual world. In R. McBride & M. Searson (Eds.), *Proceedings of Society for Information Technology & Teacher Education International Conference 2013* (pp. 2932–2940). Chesapeake, VA: Association for the Advancement of Computing in Education (AACE).

Sharan, Y. (2010). Cooperative learning for academic and social gains: Valued pedagogy, problematic practice. *European Journal of Education, 45*(2), 300–310.

Sharples, M., Goodlet, J. S., Beck, E.E., Wood, C.C., Easterbrook, S.M., & Plowman, L. (1993). Research issues in the study of computer supported collaborative writing. In M. Sharples (Ed.), *Computer supported collaborative work,* (pp. 9–28). Berlin, Heidelberg, New York, NY: Springer-Verlag.

Shonfeld, M. (2005). *The impact of an online conference in education: A case study.* (Unpublished doctoral dissertation). Nova Southeastern University, Fort Lauderdale, Florida.

Shonfeld, M., Hoter, E., & Ganayem, A. (2013). Connecting cultures in conflict through ICT in Israel. In R. S. P. Austin & W. J. Hunter (Eds.), *Online learning and community cohesion: Linking schools* (pp. 42–58). New York, NY:Routledge.

Shonfeld, M. (2017). Collaboration in Learning. In O. Goldsten & U. Melamed (Eds.) *Pedagogy at the digital age* (pp. 187–216). Tel Aviv: Kalil, Mofet. [Hebrew].

Swan, K., Shen, J., & Hiltz, S. R. (2006). Assessment and collaboration in online learning. *Journal of Asynchronous Learning Networks, 10*(1), 45–62.

Tal, H., & Tal, A. (2006). Collaborative task in a WIKI environment. [Hebrew]. In Y. Eshet-Alkalai, A. Caspi, & Y. Yair. (Eds.). *Proceeding of the 1st Chais Conference for the study of innovation and Learning Technologies: Learning in the Technological Era* (pp. 43–54), Raana, Israel: The Open University of Israel.

Tsuei, M. (2011). Development of a peer-assisted learning strategy in computer-supported collaborative learning environments for elementary school students. *British Journal of Educational Technology, 42*(2), 214–232.

Walther, J. B., Elaine, H., Ganayem, A., & Shonfeld, M. (2015). Computer-mediated communication and the reduction of prejudice: A controlled longitudinal field experiment among Jews and Arabs in Israel. *Computers in Human Behavior, 52,* 550–558.

Yang, H. (2014). Infusing ICT into K–12 teacher education: From China's perspective. In M. Searson & M. Ochoa (Eds.), *Proceedings Figure 8.2 Division of willingness to collaborate with children of schools from other cultures of Society for Information Technology & Teacher Education International Conference 2014* (p. 65). Chesapeake, VA: Association for the Advancement of Computing in Education (AACE).

Zoubi, B. (2011). *The direct and indirect influence of Jewish and Arab participation in bi-national soccer clubs on the attitudes and perceptions of their family members and friends toward the other side.* (Unpublished doctoral dissertation). University of Haifa, Israel. [Hebrew].

CHAPTER 9

COOPERATIVE ONLINE RESEARCH MEETINGS OF CEREBRAL PALSY AND GRADUATE STUDENTS TO PROMOTE WEB ACCESSIBILITY

Betty Shrieber and Rachel Peled

This chapter presents a collaboration between postgraduate students, many already employed as teachers in schools in Israel while also studying in an Educational Technology M.Ed. program, and young adult pupils (aged 19–21) with cerebral palsy (CP) studying in a special-education school. The initiative began in 2011 as an "Assistive Technologies for Students with Special Needs" postgraduate course, which included cooperative-learning groups (postgraduate students and pupils with CP) centered on the issue of web accessibility. Most of the contact between students and pupils was conducted online via Facebook, with two additional face-to-face meetings. One meeting was held at the Kibbutzim College of Education in Tel Aviv, Israel, and the second at the special-education school.

The initiative was primarily a collaborative and online study to examine the issue of web accessibility, including defining accessibility, reviewing web

Collaborative Online Learning in a Global World, pages 125–138.
Copyright © 2019 by Information Age Publishing

accessibility in Israel and the world, assessing measures of accessibility of public and private websites, and analyzing them according to specific accessibility criteria. Letters were sent to website managers after the analysis was completed requesting some changes and recommending what could be changed on their sites to improve accessibility for people with special needs. The postgraduate students were exposed to the unique needs of pupils with disabilities and their use of diverse assistive technologies to utilize their communicative and scholastic skills. Pupils were given the opportunity to participate in online meetings and discussions while tackling academic tasks. They were exposed to a new world of content relevant to their daily lives, learned self-advocacy by writing letters to site managers, and gained a better understanding of their power as consumers.

LITERATURE REVIEW

This literature review deals with the advantages of cooperative online learning among heterogeneous groups for improving social environments and interaction and the impact of the collaborative process on changing opinions and stances regarding people with special needs. The review outlines the issue of web accessibility that was used in this project as the shared learning field for the two groups. It describes the web accessibility law in Israel and the World Wide Web Consortium's (W3C) accessibility guidelines that were drawn up in the U.S.A.

Online Cooperative Learning

Cooperation is defined as the ability to work with others to achieve common goals. In cooperative activities, the individual looks for outcomes beneficial to him/her and to the group as a whole. Cooperative learning is a teaching approach that entails dividing students into small groups to increase their individual learning potential (Johnson & Johnson, 1989, 1993; Johnson, Johnson, & Smith, 2014).

The cooperative teaching approach is based on the idea that learning is as interpersonal as it is intrapersonal (Salomon, 2000). Intrapersonal skills enable learners to employ their academic, emotional, and social abilities, while interpersonal skills allow learners to function within a group, with their personal contributions based on an exchange of opinions, examining alternatives while confronting the views of others, none of which exists in self-learning. Gardner defines interpersonal intelligence as "the ability to understand other people: what motivates them, how they work, how to work cooperatively with them" (Gardner, 1993, p. 9).

Studies have consistently shown that cooperative learning improves social interaction, even among university students from different ethnic, cultural, language, social class, ability, and gender groups (Johnson, Johnson, & Smith, 2014), and promotes mutual responsibility among learners, often helping them develop interpersonal ties outside school (Johnson & Johnson, 1989, 1993; Sharan, 2010).

Studies also indicate that cooperative learning promotes significant and substantial increases in achievement (Johnson, Johnson, & Smith, 2014).

The last decade has been typified by a significant increase in the use of computers in the education system and particularly at teacher-training colleges (Goldstein, 2009). The research literature review conducted by Swan and Shea (2005) points to the many advantages of online learning environments in higher-education-institution teaching. The role of moderators in online activities is significant, nurturing learners to be self-motivated, able to initiate, and take responsibility. Students appreciate a technology-rich learning environment and achieve higher learning outcomes in such environments. Moderators guide and direct the group by asking questions, offering alternatives, and encouraging participants to develop criteria for consideration, thus making their own decisions (Goldstein, 2009).

Familiarization, Attitudes, and Prejudice

The ability to change attitudes and address the understanding of minority groups is one of the most important issues in a multicultural society. Changing opinions and stances of professionals working in the rehabilitation and education of people with special needs is a core topic of interest for policy makers and researchers, yet just a handful of studies have focused on this field (Shen, 2010). Social perception is formed in a spiral process, beginning with an immediate reaction of attraction or rejection, then evolving to form impressions, positions based on categories and labels, and finally consolidating into a stance or attitude that influences thought processes and more complex addresses toward the other. Theories regarding the change of stance indicate that the initial phase, that of first impressions, is the easiest to alter (Visser & Cooper, 2007).

Literature examining the social attitudes of the people with special needs shows that people with disabilities are often perceived as at one of two extremes, either as superhuman (extraordinarily successful handicapped) or conversely poor and pitiful. Seldom if ever does public opinion manage to see them as just "regular" people, doing "regular" activities. The media also contribute greatly to this stereotype of the disabled as helpless and misfortunate people, destined to live a miserable existence (Kama, 2004).

Web Accessibility Laws and Regulations

The Internet is an important and vital information source in the world and can serve to address many needs. It provides a rich and varied source of information, a (distance education) learning environment, a platform for finding employment, an access to consumer information, and a means of communication for service provision for education, business, culture, leisure, and more.

Millions of people around the world suffer from disabilities that prevent their access to the Internet, but accessible Internet service would allow such people to conveniently perform a range of activities such as searching libraries, databases and knowledge bases; completing schooling; working, engaging in commerce and culture; enjoying entertainment; and could serve as an efficient platform to promote their civic involvement in society. For people with disabilities, the Internet can be a vital and incredibly significant tool, as much as for the rest of the population.

An American initiative calls on public, private, and business institutions to adhere to the World Wide Web Consortium's (W3C) *accessibility guidelines* to make their websites accessible to people with special needs. This set of guidelines provides detailed recommendations for increasing accessibility, including a technical breakdown of various software and tools to manage this process.

An accessible website is one that can be used by people with disabilities, with screen-support software (such as text to speech and/or text descriptions behind each image or link), allowing users to use their TAB key and arrows without a mouse, use of caption links for easier and more effective interaction with the site, emphasizing links, adding captions to video links, and many more (Israel Internet Association, 2010).

In recent years, the State of Israel has passed several new laws and regulations to establish the rights of people with disabilities and/or learning disabilities to enjoy equal opportunities in all aspects of life: leisure, daily activities, employment, and learning (*Equal Rights of Persons with Disabilities Law*, 1998). In 2005, an accessibility section was amended, whereby "all public places and public services must be accessible to people of all disabilities" (*Equal Rights for Persons with Disabilities Law*, 5758–1998, Section 19, p. 14). The regulations regarding accessibility of services (including Internet accessibility) came into effect on October 25, 2013, including a specific and detailed section (Section 35) regarding the accessibility of websites and what is required by law of website owners to meet their obligations (*Regulations for Equal Rights of Persons with Disabilities*, 2013, p. 985).

The "Internet Accessibility" project was launched to promote awareness and make websites more accessible in Israel, a collaboration of "Access Israel" (IAA—Association for the Advancement of Accessibility in Israel) and the Israel Internet Association. Following the new regulations in Israel, as well as international guidelines regarding this issue, a "web accessibility excellence mark" was produced to signify which sites meet standards of accessibility. This constitutes a statement by website owners that their sites are indeed accessible to people with disabilities according to the Web Content Accessibility Guidelines 2.0 (WCAG), published by the W3C.

According to these guidelines, existing websites should be made accessible to the public by October 2016, including all applications or pages that are associated with it from the moment of their launch. Subject to Israeli law, anyone in violation of these regulations may be subject to a class action lawsuit and statutory damages (Israel Internet Association, 2010).

Digital Inclusion

Digital inclusion is defined by the ability of people with disabilities to access and meaningfully participate in the same learning, employment, social, and citizenship activities as others through access to and use of digital technologies. In the context of digital inclusion, "use" is usually understood in relation to the ability of an individual to use, or be able to use, technologies he or she has access to (Seale, 2009; Seale, Draffan, & Wald, 2010).

As a concept, digital inclusion is frequently equated with social inclusion and the "digital divide": "Equality of access, skills and aspirations are essential to ensure that the gap between information rich and poor does not extend to gaps in access to electronically based participatory mechanisms" (Seale, 2009, p. 6).

Inclusive and accessible environments on the Web, using technologies in an innovative manner in terms of their pedagogical and didactic aspects, can advance inclusion processes and enable people with disabilities to enjoy equal opportunities and participate in university matters (de Anna et al., 2014). Findings from online courses, for students with and without disabilities, suggest that an interdisciplinary and informal approach, as well as accessible and usable multimedia tools, are crucial to ensure the active participation of all students–regardless of their health status. Methods and practices of inclusive education have helped strengthen self-esteem, a sense of belonging to a learning community where every student should have the same educational opportunities, and a positive disposition towards dialogue and openness to others (Della Volpe, 2015). To quote Della Volpe,

> It would be desirable to incorporate the activities of online inclusive cooperative learning, to train students on diversity and cooperation, active listening, strategies for inclusive education, sharing of knowledge and skills, as well as to offer them an area of dialogue using an e-learning platform. (Della Volpe, 2015, p. 46)

Therefore, digital inclusion may be broadly conceived as being implemented in educational institutions but may also be more specifically located in curricula, practices, cultures, and communities. However, detailed evidence or examples of how exactly this might happen are currently lacking (Seale, 2009).

DESCRIPTION OF THE INITIATIVE AND RESEARCH PROCESS

This unique model that has been developed with the understanding that cooperative learning should be accomplished "at eye level," meaning with parity, as this approach allows for, and promotes attentiveness and mutual reliance on exchanged knowledge. The technology used in the project–cooperative Facebook platforms–served both as a means to a goal and the goal itself. The collaborative-study objective was to examine web accessibility. Also, students learned about the assistive technologies used by pupils, such as screen readers, use of a head-controlled mouse, and others.

The initiative began in 2011 and has continued on an annual basis since. Each year, the project includes seven academic meetings in which each group works separately (students work at the college or at home, while pupils learn at school with guidance by their teachers) and also together using online discussions via Facebook (a closed account created specifically for the initiative). Additionally, there are two face-to-face meetings, one held in the Kibbutzim College of Education and another in the pupils' school (during which the university students also tour the school).

Joint Meetings

Thirty-five students were divided into seven to 10 groups, with each group assigned to work with one pupil (a ratio of four students to each pupil). Each group had a separate name and section on the Facebook page.

Stage 1: Online introductory meetings. Two online meetings were conducted on Facebook, where students and pupils chatted about where they lived, hobbies, and so forth. These meetings were designed to provide equal ground, without barriers or obstacles that might impede communication. In online discussions, participants' external appearance had yet to be seen (unless they had previously posted their pictures on Facebook), a factor that at times causes some people to recoil when first meeting people with CP.

Stage 2: Face-to-face meetings. Pupils arrived at the college to meet the students personally. The students conducted a tour to present the various college facilities, and everyone convened in the classroom to hold a debate and their first face-to-face introductions.

Most of these initial meetings were also attended by an academic specialist in the field of accessibility, usually a person with a disability, so that both students and pupils had the opportunity to see the strength in disability. These specialists gave a brief lecture on their personal experiences, as children and adults, and described how they managed their situation.

Stage 3: Research into web accessibility. The pupils were asked to search for sites they usually used, checking their level of accessibility, and then submit their remarks to the students, via the Facebook page, regarding websites they chose to investigate (from an accessibility standpoint). The pupils conducted their investigation at school, with the help of their teachers. They examined what elements of the sites helped or hindered their use and updated the university students on their progress.

Concurrently, the graduate students were assigned academic tasks, first to familiarize themselves with the laws and regulations of Internet accessibility in Israel and the U.S. (The W3C Web Accessibility Initiative). Each group of students was required to make an evaluation of website accessibility chosen by its assigned pupil and publish a detailed analysis report on the course's Moodle website. At the same time, the groups published a clear synopsis of their evaluation on the Facebook page to update pupils regarding their findings.

Stage 4: Drafting a letter to website managers. At this point, students and pupils collaborated on writing letters to the managers of the websites that they selected, in which they specified the difficulties they encountered in using the sites and the corrections they proposed. The students provided the initial draft, the pupils reviewed it and added or amended their comments, and the letters were sent to the managers of the websites. The letters were also posted on the Facebook page. If they received responses from the site managers, they were also published.

Stage 5: School meeting. The pupils hosted a meeting in their school for the students, conducting a summary discussion of the meeting. Finally, all attended a lecture by one of the school faculty on a previously chosen subject.

Project Evaluation

Two forms of evaluation were employed to review the project:

1. A formative evaluation was conducted in 2013 using 20 questionnaires given to postgraduate students to understand the significance of the project for them.
2. An analysis of students' reflections (years 2013–2015) was conducted after meeting with them, first in the college, then in the school, and it included reactions of the pupils. Conclusions drawn from these data follow.

Significance of Combining Online and Face-to-Face Meetings

This section will describe the benefits of blended learning: online and face-to-face. Each learning interaction has its own advantage as well as disadvantage. However, the combination of the two within a structured process enables the participants to benefit from the most appropriate interaction for them at every stage of the joint process.

Online Communication as an Effective Platform for Initial Introductions

The students' answers to questions regarding the advantages of online Facebook communications reveal that it did serve as an effective way to begin introductions with pupils. However, some students claimed that they preferred personal, face-to-face meetings over virtual ones.

This project utilized the relative advantages of online learning and discussion. Online platforms allow for both independent and cooperative learning and are effective communication tools as they allow participants to choose locations and times convenient to all. Student reflections as well as Facebook posts reveal that the initial online introductory Facebook meeting allowed equal discourse, particularly relevant to pupils who could authentically introduce themselves, describe their hobbies, likes, dislikes, and families. This unmediated meeting allowed pupils to interact without being "weighed down" or impeded by a physical or speech-related disability. Conversely, during this initial communication, students were not affected by the pupils' appearance, which may often evoke repulsion in those unused to this population. In the following examples, pupils discuss their favorite pastimes, and often add remarks about their manner of communication.

I'm 20-years old, I have CP, I like listening to Middle Eastern music, and love working on the computer. I use a joystick instead of a mouse, which replaces the mouse and allows me to control the screen pointer.

I'm S. I'm 20, and live in.... I use a wheelchair. I am a crazy soccer fan. I like to sing, and write, and every Monday I'm in a singing class. I love Middle Eastern music, and the radio MC Eliko. I'm the youngest in my family, and I love playing on the computer, especially PIPA games. Hope we'll enjoy working together.

The students also introduced themselves. Here is a response to the post by pupil S:

Hey S. I live in ..., and work in ... as a special ed. teacher of a 6th grade class, but most of the drives there aren't so bad, as I'm going against traffic [smile emoticon]. I have two adorable kids... I'm sure we'll enjoy working together.

A review of the ongoing posts between students and pupils reveals that pupils did not choose to hide their disabilities and even presented them naturally as a part of who they were. Evidence of this can be seen in references to the technologies and devices they used: wheelchair, joystick, and others. In cases where pupils found it difficult to write, a few of them communicated via a WhatsApp account, so they could send voice messages in lieu of written posts:

Use of WhatsApp allowed us to send recorded voice messages, so that people could communicate outside the project task, speaking socially, less formally, while on the Facebook page they posted final outcomes, such as decisions regarding certain sites, and the publication of the letter. (Student N)

Synchronization and Balance Between Online and Face-to-Face Meetings

In addition to the online meetings, the project also included two face-to-face meetings. The initial introductions made via Facebook prepared the ground for these personal meetings; the mutual curiosity engendered in the online meetings made both groups eager to actually meet. However, both groups also expressed their apprehensions regarding the meeting. Students' reactions reveal their apprehension and excitement as well as the great curiosity they felt prior to the actual meetings.

I was very curious to know who these people "behind" the computers were, who were writing to us on Facebook. I thought that if they could use Facebook, and write so well, then they must be regular students like us, and there's no need to prepare for the meeting.... [T]he [face-to-face] meetings were an exciting and unique experience, and made me think, and have insights, and feel emotions, like fear and concern. This was the first time in my life that I met students with disabilities.

I didn't think much about it [the meeting] because, as usual, I was so caught up in my life, busy keeping deadlines, functioning as a mother, teacher, daughter, friend and neighbor. And then I saw the visitors. Each student had a different level of impediment as a result of his disability. At first, I wasn't sure how much they understood me but then I decided to "act normally" and talk to them believing that they understood me....

The pupils' reactions also reveal that they enjoyed the meeting, and even those who initially felt some apprehension left in good spirits and a desire to continue work on the project. After the meeting, pupil S posted on Facebook that he was happy to see how impressed the students were with his remarks, adding that the atmosphere was friendly and the meeting was managed in a dignified and heart-warming manner. In the following class discussion, he also remarked that he had approached the meeting with some concern, a fear of being exposed, the possible reactions to his disability and his abilities, and that the students' acceptance and warmth moved him greatly.

One pupil, N, who did not attend the meeting, posted on Facebook that after reading about the wonderful experiences his friends had, he was disappointed he had not attended. He also remarked that after the meeting several people had written to him to say, "We really missed you," and this made him feel very good. He was thrilled to see

that people who don't even know me, and have never met me, still make sure to write and say I was missed. And as to my disability, I don't give it much importance, it's a part of me, and if I address it, it's like I'm ashamed of who I am.

It is clear that the first face-to-face meeting was characterized by a high intensity of students' response to the CP disability, while online meetings showed a balance of reactions. The combination of online and personal meetings allowed for a natural flow and synchronization of communications before, during, and after meetings.

SIGNIFICANCE OF RECIPROCAL INTERACTION

The project stages were designed to structure an equal and balanced process between the two groups. It was therefore important to establish, from the very first, that students would visit the school, where pupils were likely to have felt more comfortable and open to include their visitors in their experiences while on their "home turf." In retrospect, pupils' statements made after this meeting reveal their anxiety before actually meeting and interacting with the students, the importance they attributed to it, and the sense of unease and personal barriers they felt prior to it: "I had more fun in the second meeting with the students, because the first time we just met, but didn't talk enough."; "Last time we really didn't get to know each other. This time, I personally felt more open, and this gave the time to really talk about things relating to the project."

The school meeting exposed the students to the pupils' educational environment and the facilities they used, such as the computer room, therapy pool, and classrooms. They also were shown the assistive technologies used by pupils.

> Seeing their school made me realize the importance of accessibility to people with disabilities, and no doubt technology and progress have created real change with various tools, devices, and software....

> You could see how the school has been adapted to the students' learning there: a parking lot to drop off students right by the door, wheelchairs and doorways wide enough to accommodate them. In the building itself were all the aides necessary for people with special needs.

> It was exciting and moving, particularly in their communications class, where I met pupil B, and she talked to us and her teaching assistant using a tablet.

CHANGE OF ATTITUDES AND CONSOLIDATING PROFESSIONAL IDENTITY

The formative questionnaire evaluation conducted in 2013 revealed that participation in the project increased students' awareness of the special needs of pupils with disabilities. Communication between the groups contributed in a significant and experiential manner to raising their awareness to the range of problems pupils with disabilities struggle with and the technological means that help them cope. The unmediated meetings were an opportunity to develop empathy and understanding of pupils' needs and the assistive technologies they employed.

The attitudes of teachers to pupils with special needs constitute an essential component of their professional identity. Many studies ask whether familiarization of education professionals with people and pupils with special needs has an impact on their attitudes to disability and whether more positive attitudes impact teachers' ability to best incorporate such pupils in a classroom and school setting. Many of these studies have found an important and positive correlation between teachers' attitudes and optimal education practices (Avramidis, Bayliss, & Burden, 2000; Hastings, Hewes, Lock, & Witting, 1996; Hutzler, 2003). Carrington and Brownlee (2001) found an inherent link in preservice teachers who interacted with high-status disabled persons, impacting their knowledge and attitudes towards people with special needs.

After the project's conclusion, students remarked that they had reevaluated their role as educators and came to new insights regarding how they perceived it.

The thoughts running through my mind made me realize things about my role as educator and teacher. During the tour, I kept considering the dilemma of incorporating kids with special needs in regular frameworks, or is it better for them to learn in a place already adapted to their needs [...] The more rooms I saw, and the more I heard the school staff explain how it is working with the pupils, I came to the conclusion that it's better for students with disabilities to learn in special ed. schools like this one [...] but then K told us that at the end of this year he would go on to 11th grade in the regular school near his house. It was then I realized I was wrong, and that special needs kids can do it for sure! They can go to regular schools. I'm sure K will fit in great in his new school.

After the project, it was evident that students felt a need to incorporate insights gleaned from their participation in their future educational endeavors, and they expressed the desire to expose their pupils to special-needs populations:

Today, after the meetings and the course, my attitude to pupils struggling with an assignment because of some disability (hyperactivity, dyslexia, internal disquiet, or others) is different, as is my reaction. I think of some creative solution to help them complete the task. I look for some suitable "scaffolding" that could help him overcome his difficulty. I no longer use phrases like "He's lazy"; "Let him be, he just can't do,"

and remarks like that:

I left the meeting with the motivation to change the small things around me... to present my students with the real significance of accessibility to people with disabilities.

SUMMARY

The literature review and project description shed light on the parallel process of using technology and accessibility for people with special needs and at the same time using the process to review the structural affordances of accessible technology as a means of changing attitudes among people in general and teachers in particular for people with special needs.

Initiative Importance

Positive attitudes towards and perceptions of people with special needs has a great impact on promoting their educational and social inclusion. We believe that gaining a new perspective on people with disabilities will directly and indirectly influence student teachers' future work as educators as they include pupils with special needs in their classrooms.

These adolescent pupils were exposed to research on an academic level and the experience of an equal exchange with "regular" people. This opportunity to participate in cooperative learning provided them with a place to present themselves and the technological needs important to them as people having equal rights.

In this project, we built a bridge to understanding the needs of people with disabilities, while focusing on Internet accessibility and assistive technologies. Exposure to a population of pupils with disabilities, and the technologies they employ, contributed to the university students' awareness as present and future educators. This is substantiated by their post-project remarks, and we hope that this experience will hone their sensitivity to pupils who struggle academically.

As to the efficacy of sending a letter to website managers, answers provided by students in the questionnaires reveal they became aware of the lack of understanding of such managers of the special needs of the disabled and the necessity of making websites accessible to this population, but only half the students felt that they had truly managed to influence the website staffs to actually increase their sites' accessibility.

This was the first exposure of such students to the issue of Internet accessibility, and we hope that research on websites allowed them to better understand the personal needs of all users. The drafting and sending of the letters provided them first-hand experience of self-advocacy, and we hope this helps them refine their ability to articulate their arguments when facing people who refuse to address the legitimate, and legal, requirements of accessibility adaptions.

Advantages of a Blended Course: Online and Face-to-Face Meetings

"Blended" (or "hybrid") instruction entails 30–80% of course content delivered online (Allen & Seaman, 2013). Distance-education courses need to allow students to apply their learning to authentic educational contexts (Correia & Davis, 2008). Blended courses that combine online communication and face-to-face meetings have been found to be the most effective, producing a stronger sense of community among students than either traditional or fully online courses (Rovai & Jordan, 2004; Tayebini & Puteh, 2013).

In this project, we found great advantages in online communication (through Facebook) combined with face-to-face meetings. A preliminary evaluation of Facebook as a learning aid suggests that it has the potential to promote collaborative and cooperative learning. The findings from this study indicate that Facebook may be an appropriate addition to traditional e-learning tools, providing an integration of application that is well received and used by today's students (Irwin, Ball, Desbrow, & Leveritt, 2012).

Nevertheless, despite the effectiveness of online learning, the face-to-face meetings were found to be very powerful. The impact of personal meetings could not have been expected in a purely online platform. Several studies support this experience, with findings that indicate actual, face-to-face meetings, in addition to online communication, are necessary to establish social ties and better understand content. Brady, Holcomb, and Smith (2010) show that more than half of the student-survey participants expressed a preference for face-to-face communication over distance education (Brady, Holcomb, & Smith, 2010).

Also, digital inclusion is relevant to far more non-disabled people than people with disabilities. Thus, the process of digital inclusion has focused on creating gateways, opening doors, and "letting people in" (Seale et al., 2010). Understanding the needs of people with disabilities should be a mutual process, allowing them to express their needs as website users, while education professionals and commercial and private organizations are attentive to their needs.

REFERENCES

Allen, I. E., & Seaman, J. (2013). *Changing course: Ten years of tracking online education in the United States*. Newburyport, MA: Sloan Consortium.

Avramidis, E., Bayliss, P., & Burden, R. (2000). Student teachers' attitudes toward the inclusion of children with special education needs in the ordinary school. *Teacher and Teaching Education, 16*, 277–293.

Brady, K. P., Holcomb, L. B., & Smith, B. V. (2010). The use of alternative social networking sites in higher educational settings: A case study of the e-learning benefits of Ning in education. *Journal of Interactive Online Learning, 9*(2), 151–170.

Carrington, S., & Brownlee, J. (2001). Preparing teachers to support inclusion: The benefits of interaction between a group of preservice teachers and a teaching assistant who is disabled. *Teaching Education, 12*(3), 347–357.

Correia, A., & Davis, N. (2008). Intersecting communities of practice in distance education: The program team and the online course community. *Distance Education, 29*(3), 289–306.

De Anna, L., Canevaro, A., Ghislandi, P., Striano, M., Maragliano, R., & Andrich, R. (2014). Net@accessibility: A research and training project regarding the transition from formal to informal learning for university students who are developing lifelong plans. *ALTER–European Journal of Disability Research/Revue Européenne de Recherche sur le Handicap, 8*(2), 118–134.

Della Volpe, V. (2015). ICT and inclusion in higher education: A comparative approach. *Open Journal of Social Sciences, 3*, 39–47. Retrieved from http://dx.doi.org/10.4236/jss.2015.39007

Equal Rights for Persons with Disabilities Law, 5758–1998, Sefer Hachukim, p. 14. [Hebrew].

Gardner, H. (1993). *Multiple intelligences: The theory in practice*. New York, NY: Basic Books.

Goldstein, O. (2009). *Online course assessment: Group-level event analysis*. Research Task Force to draft the "Pedagogical Manual in the Digital Age." Tel-Aviv, Israel: MOFET Institute. [Hebrew].

Hastings, R.P., Hewes, A., Lock, S., & Witting, A. (1996). Do special educational needs courses have any impact on student teachers' perceptions of children with severe learning difficulties? *British Journal of Special Education, 23*(3), 139–144.

Hutzler, Y. (2003). Attitudes toward the participation of individuals with disabilities in physical activity: A review. *Quest, 55*(4), 347–373.

Irwin, C., Ball, L., Desbrow, B., & Leveritt, M. (2012). Students' perceptions of using Facebook as an interactive learning resource at university. *Australasian Journal of Educational Technology, 28*(7), 1221–1232.

Israel Internet Association (2010). *Web Accessibility in Israel*. Nagish website. Retrieved from https://www.nagish.org.il/?page_id=1035

Johnson, D., & Johnson, R. (1989). *Cooperative learning: Giving at-risk students hopes for a brighter future*. Edina, MN: International Book Company.

Johnson, D. W., & Johnson, R. T. (1993). *Circles of learning: Cooperation in the classroom*. Edina, MN: Interaction Book Company.

Johnson, D.W., Johnson, R.T., & Smith, K.A. (2014). Cooperative learning: Improving university instruction by basing practice on validated theory. *Journal on Excellence in College Teaching 25*, 85–118.

Kama, A. (2004). Supercrips versus the pitiful handicapped: Reception of disabling images by disabled audience members. *Communications, 29*(4), 447–466.

Regulations for equal rights of persons with disabilities (Adjustments for access to service). (2013). *Statute 7240, Section 35–Accessibility Adjustments for Internet Services [Hebrew]*, 985. Retrieved from https://www.isoc.org.il/files/docs/1160_TakHanegishutLeSherut.pdf

Rovai, A. P., & Jordan, H. (2004). Blended learning and sense of community: A comparative analysis with traditional and fully online graduate courses. *The International Review of Research in Open and Distributed Learning, 5*(2), 1–13. Retrieved from http://www.irrodl.org/index.php/irrodl/article/view/192/795

Salomon, G. (2000). *Technology and education in the information age*. Haifa, Israel: Zmora Bitan Publishing. [Hebrew].

Seale, J., Draffan, E. A., & Wald, M. (2010). Digital agility and digital decision-making: Conceptualizing digital inclusion in the context of disabled learners in higher education. *Studies in Higher Education, 35*(4), 445–461.

Seale, J. (2009). *Digital inclusion: A research briefing. Teaching and Learning Research Program*. Southampton, UK: University of Southampton.

Sharan, Y. (2010). Cooperative learning for academic and social gains: Valued pedagogy, problematic practice. *European Journal of Education, 45*(2), 300–313.

Shen, E. (2010). The medium and the message: The personal and the humane. A review of the impact of films depicting people with mental disabilities on student attitudes. *Society and Welfare, 30*(2), 257–287. [Hebrew].

Swan, K., & Shea, P. (2005). The development of virtual learning communities. In. S. R. Hiltz & R. Goldman (Eds.), *Asynchronous learning networks: The research* frontier (pp. 239–260). New York, NY: Hampton Press.

Tayebinik, M., & Puteh, M. (2013). Blended learning or e-learning? *International Magazine on Advances in Computer Science and Telecommunications, 3*(1), 103–110.

Visser, P. S., & Cooper, H. J. (2007). Attitude change. In M. A Hogg & J. Cooper (Eds.), *The SAGE handbook of social psychology: Concise student edition.* (pp. 197–218). London, UK: Sage Publications.

CHAPTER 10

COLLABORATIVE CONCEPTUAL CHANGE IN THE COMPUTER-SCIENCE CLASSROOM

Dalit Levy

Look here [points to the upper level of the fractal in Figure 10.1], so you get pam-pam-pam [waits] tam-tam-tam, bam-bam-bam, now this? [points to the 2nd level of the same fractal] Look, you get tam-tam-tam, tam-tam-tam [lowers voice]. (11th grade student to her classmates)

The above episode was recorded while four students were collaborating on a learning activity aimed at classifying and discussing different recursive phenomena as part of a computer-science course dealing with recursion. Recursion is an interdisciplinary concept with many implications in programming (Hofstadter, 1979), or, as Harvey and Wright (1993) describe it, "recursion is the idea of self-reference applied to computer programs" (p. 168). Snowflakes like those that are presented in four levels of complexity in Figure 10.1 are among the most famous recursive phenomena that can be found outside of computer science. Participating in a collaborative-learning activity, the speaker was trying to draw the attention of her group-mates to a certain characteristic of a recursive phenomenon that she

Collaborative Online Learning in a Global World, pages 139–154.
Copyright © 2019 by Information Age Publishing
139

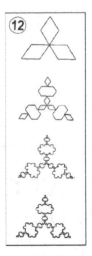

FIGURE 10.1.   An example of a recursive phenomenon

had just recognized. By lowering her voice, she also expressed–without words–a notion of "something getting gradually smaller."

The example utterance was chosen from an abundance of utterances, statements, and non-verbal expressions that were documented during the course of this study focusing on high-school-students' discourse about recursive phenomena, while trying to trace conceptual change with regard to recursion. Much of the research into the conceptualization of recursion has taken place within the framework of learning to program, whereas less emphasis has been placed on understanding how learners construct the concept of recursion as broad, abstract, and interdisciplinary. In addition, in deep contrast to the variety of publications in the field of conceptual change that one can find regarding each of the scientific disciplines being learned in high school (Duit, 2002; Soto & Sanjose, 2002), the focus on conceptual change with regard to computer-science ideas and concepts has been relatively rare. Finally, while many have argued that students' engagement with each other's ideas has benefits for learning (Barron, 2003; Pilkington, 2016; Weinberger, Stegmann, & Fischer, 2007), such engagement has been little studied in the case of learning computer science.

The present chapter sheds light on some of the neglected aspects of the conceptual development of computer-science concepts by discussing recursion as an interdisciplinary idea and by analyzing the class discourse during a collaborative-learning activity. Throughout the inductive analysis of the discourse, the students' expressions were interpreted, refined, and formulated as "preconceptions." The collaborative nature of the learning activity emerged throughout the analysis as a driving force for developing, refining, and changing these preconceptions; therefore, the title of this chapter.

THEORETICAL BACKGROUND

Two themes in the literature set the stage for this chapter's focus on collaborative conceptual change of learners' understanding of recursion. The first is grounded within science education in general, while the second is located within the field of computer-science education.

The Focus on Conceptual Change in Science Education

For more than three decades, conceptual change has been regarded as a most powerful frame for research on teaching and learning science (Duit, 2002; Pilkington, 2016). Throughout these years, the notion became clear that students often enter science classes with prior knowledge, ideas, and beliefs about the phenomena and concepts to be taught. Since this prior knowledge often stands in contrast with what is regarded as "scientific knowledge," the general term "misconceptions" was introduced, and the learners' misconceptions, once thoroughly investigated, were later left aside in favor of the less judgmental term "alternative conceptions." In a paper criticizing the dominance of the focus on misconceptions in the field of science education, the writers recommend moving toward tracing conceptual change instead of locating more and more "wrong" conceptions (Smith, diSessa, & Roschelle, 1993). Tracing conceptual change implies focusing on the cognitive and communicative processes within which conceptual frameworks are constructed, organized, and reorganized.

Conceptual change in science education has become a term denoting "learning science from constructivist perspectives" (Duit, 2002, p. 7). A constructivist belief is that knowledge is necessarily a product of our own cognitive acts and that we construct our understandings through our experiences (Confrey, 1995). In such a view, learning science means that students themselves are constructing and reorganizing their own conceptual frameworks, in a "gradual process during which initial conceptual structures based on … interpretations of everyday experience are continuously enriched and restructured" (Vosniadou & Ioannides, 1998, p. 1213). The constructivist science teacher should encourage a reflective discussion to expose the learners to new conceptions and to different ideas offered by others, in addition to her or his responsibility for offering generalizations and formal terminology. In other words, the teacher's role is to navigate the discussion toward creating a "taken-as-shared" meaning for the scientific concepts being learned in the class (Cobb, Yackel, & Wood, 1992) and thus allowing some conceptual change to occur.

In this chapter, conceptual change denotes pathways from students' existing conceptual frameworks to the computer-science concept to be learned, which in this case is the concept of recursion. To trace conceptual change, the researcher observed and documented students participating in a constructivist and interdisciplinary learning activity. The protocols of that activity shed light both on the private conceptual frameworks students carried with them when entering the class and on a specific kind of conceptual change which will be later described as a *"collaborative conceptual change."* In other words, although the changes occur in one's mind and upon one's conceptual framework, and although each student individually constructs her or his framework, conceptual change can be motivated by taking part in more societal and communicational learning activities (Sfard, 2008).

Recursion as a Powerful Idea in Computer-Science Education

Computer science (CS) is widely perceived nowadays as an educational field that provides the knowledge and skills foundation for contemporary technological advances in K–12 and beyond. Learning CS enhances computational thinking and may contribute to a better understanding of other subjects as well (Wing, 2006). Furthermore, CS educational researchers claim, "Maintaining our ability to meet present and future challenges requires us to acknowledge CS as a core element of all STEM (science, technology, engineering, and mathematics) initiatives" (Stephenson, Gal-Ezer, Haberman, & Verno, 2005, p. 15). However, the increasing complexity and the ever-changing nature of the field has been challenging for curriculum developers, educators, and learners alike: "Despite many years of our trying to broaden our image, computing is still widely perceived as a programmer's field" (Denning, 2004, p. 336).

In order to deal with this challenge, the Israeli CS curriculum for high school introduces CS concepts and problem-solving methods independently of specific computers and programming languages, along with their practical implementation in actual programming languages (Gal-Ezer & Harel, 1999). One of the core concepts in this curriculum is the powerful idea of recursion and the associated method for solving certain computational problems using recursive scripts. Recursive script (RS) is an algorithm that contains itself. In other words, RS is a script that contains a call for a simpler or previous version of itself (Levy, 2002). Recursive scripts allow for formalizing solutions to complex problems in cases when the problem can be broken into simpler but similar sub-problems.

The detailed understanding of recursion is essential for students learning CS. Since it is generally accepted that recursion is one of the most complicated and difficult-to-learn concepts for novice programmers, much of the research into the learning of recursion takes place within the framework of learning to program (Rinderknecht, 2014). Much less emphasis has been put, however, on studying how learners see recursion as an interdisciplinary concept, how they speak about recursive phenomena, how they describe such phenomena using their own language, and how they gradually and collaboratively develop their conceptions regarding recursion. It should be noted though that the ability to interpret general everyday phenomena like trees, rhymes, fractal-like figures, and certain kinds of art as recursive, and the experience of describing such phenomena in a recursive manner, might help in later construction of more formal recursive descriptions using a programming language.

The literature on recursion in computer-science education is wide-ranging. Hofstadter's (1979) book *Gödel, Escher, Bach: An Eternal Golden Braid* gives a comprehensive account. Other books mainly deal with the programming aspects of recursion (for example, Abelson & Sussman, 1996; Roberts, 1986), as does most of the educational literature on recursion. Issues of learning recursion sometimes appear in textbooks together with a warning that it is not going to be easy (Troy & Early, 1992; Wu, Dale, & Bethel, 1998), and the literature suggests methods for overcoming the difficulties. Many writers tend to agree upon one recommendation: "In order to develop a more complete understanding of the topic, it is important for the student to examine recursion from several different perspectives" (Roberts, 1986, p. vii).

In this spirit, Ben-Ari (1997) describes a teaching approach that strongly couples dramatizations of simple, real-world problems with analogous recursive programs. Harvey offers several explanations of recursive programs using different models (Harvey, 1985; Harvey & Wright, 1993). Astrachan (1994) declares that students should be shown as many examples as possible for them to come to "believe" in recursion, and Levy and Lapidot (2000) follow by developing a learning activity in which learners classify recursive examples taken from different disciplines like math, nature, literature, and art. At the same time, George (2000), and Bhuiyan, Greer, and McCalla (1994) earlier, develop a computerized environment designed to help students create different methods of generating recursive programs; later, Morazan (2013) uses video games. Since one of the known difficulties is in differentiating iteration from recursion, some researchers have proposed to teach how to translate an embedded recursive definition into an iteration while remaining in the same programming language (Rinderknecht, 2014; Rubio-Sánchez, 2010). Other researchers have studied the option to introduce recursion at the middle-school level as a way to reduce learners' resistance later on (Gunion, Milford, & Stege, 2009).

All concerned seem to agree on the difficulty of learning and teaching recursion. Some recommendations for teaching have been made. But when trying to find "how it is" in a real class, in a natural educational setting, the research literature in computer-science education is less helpful. The gap is most apparent when looking at computer-science learning through a broader lens. When observing an interdisciplinary and constructivist learning environment, one could also ask, What language do the teacher and the students use? How can one characterize the class discourse? How does this discourse reveal the formal aspects of recursion, and in what ways does it expose the difficulties? What change does the class discourse reflect, and is it a conceptual change? And how is the class discourse shaped by collaborative processes? These questions have guided indepth naturalistic research on learning recursion in Israeli high schools (Levy, 2001, 2002). This chapter summarizes one part of the overall research, namely the nature of the conceptual change in the case of learning recursion via collaborative classroom activities.

METHOD

The overall research goal was to document and analyze learners' discourse of recursive phenomena as a way to look at recursion through the eyes of the learners and to help in understanding the learners' unique ways of speaking and thinking about the general idea of recursion. The focus of this chapter is only on the first phase of the recursion learning process as it naturally evolved during one month of learning in six 11th-grade classes. These classes had just begun the intermediate period of their computer-science course when the learners were first exposed to the idea of recursion.

The documented learning process began when the learners participated in a four-phase learning activity. In the first, introductory, phase, the teacher presented one recursive example and explained the learning activity. During the second phase, each learner received a large sheet of paper with examples of recursive phenomena as in Figure 10.1, and the learners jointly classified these examples while working in groups of three to four learners. In the third phase, usually a week later, each group presented its classification to the whole class, and in the fourth and final phase, the teacher guided a reflective class discussion focused on formulating the general idea of recursion using a more formal language. While the class discourse of the second phase evolved as simultaneous, independent group discussions, during the third and the fourth phases, the discourse took the form of a collaborative whole-class discussion in which students of different groups were negotiating, arguing, and expressing different kinds of understandings. By the time of that collaborative learning activity, the students could indeed program simple functions, but they had never before been exposed to the formalism of recursive functions or to the conceptual framework of recursion.

Accordingly, the students' first experiences with recursion were taking place throughout a learning activity in which recursion was widely viewed as an interdisciplinary concept, rooted in everyday life and experience, not merely as a programming tool or an idea exclusive to computer-science. Such a collaborative and interdisciplinary learning activity indeed stimulated a very rich class discourse concerning both the specific examples of recursive phenomena and the general idea of recursion, when the learners expressed their unique ways of conceiving, thinking, and understanding.

The class discourse during the entire four-phase learning activity in each of the six cases was recorded and documented using observational field notes. The documentation detailed 50 hours of class discourse. The recordings were then fully transcribed, and after excluding utterances not directly connected with the studied learning activity (e.g. two students talking about their driving lessons after school), the gathered "raw data" was transformed into a data record of almost 500 discourse episodes in the form of two or more consecutive utterances expressed by two or more different learners speaking about the same specific issue or theme. The "tam-tam-tam" episode quoted at the beginning of this chapter is an example of an episode documented during the second phase of the learning activity.

The transcriptions of all the discourse episodes, together with field notes, served as the source for an inductive discourse analysis. According to this method of analysis, "As you read through your data, certain words, phrases, patterns of behavior, subjects' ways of thinking, and events repeat and stand out.... These words and phrases are coding categories" (Bogdan & Biklen, 1998, p. 171). For example, the idiosyncratic utterance in the "tam-tam-tam" episode has been interpreted as related to the conceptions of repetition and gradualism. These conceptions have been called "preconceptions" in this study, because they took place in the initiative phase of the learning process. However, the complex network of preconceptions that emerged throughout the analysis reflects an advanced framework of students' thinking about recursion even at that initiative phase. Overall, three analytic perspectives were observed in the students' discourse: content, cognitive, and communicative. They are presented next.

RESULTS

Using the content perspective, the analysis concentrated on what the students talked about and used their words, phrases, drawings, and written productions as coding categories. This section presents these emergent content categories, interprets them as preconceptions, and suggests a model for organizing the preconceptions. As briefly discussed later, the suggested model may reflect a kind of collaborative conceptual change that might have taken place in the observed classes.

Interpretation of Class Episodes

Before listing the key preconceptions that emerged in the course of the discourse analysis, let us look at one class episode in which a student named Hila[1] is talking about the recursive example of a tree (Figure 10.2), trying to realize what happens if she tries to draw more and more levels of the tree, and the others argue with her about her realization.

Hila:	Here we can't see the *end*, but there is an end anyway. It clashes, these leaves will clash. They must clash.
Amos:	Theoretically you can *go on*.
Gil:	It can *go on*, but you won't see it.
Tal:	It is *repeating*. *Periodical*. Everything here is *periodical*.

In the above episode, the students express their ideas concerning the common features of the recursive phenomena they have just classified and also make use of cognitive acts like naming, comparing, classifying, and generalizing (Feuerstein, Rand, Hoffman, & Miller, 1980). The italicized expressions may serve as

[1] All the names are pseudonames.

FIGURE 10.2. The word "Tree" as an example of a recursive phenomenon

indicators, or hints, of the students' unique ways of thinking about the recursive phenomena they have been investigating. When Tal said, "Everything here is periodical," she expressed her own way of perceiving and characterizing the various recursive phenomena she dealt with, using what might be called the periodical preconception. When a student in another case said about the same tree example, "This one is like the other but smaller," he expressed both the preconception of gradualism and the preconception of likeness, which was later reformulated as self-similarity, while comparing it with episodes and preconceptions from other cases. These unique student-made phrases were part of the data gathered, analyzed, and finally entitled as preconceptions representing the students' different ways of thinking about recursion. Here we emphasize that preconceptions are not "misconceptions" and that the different ways of thinking are not "wrong." Considering both the conceptual nature of the discourse and the initial phase of the learning process in which the student had been involved, the label "preconceptions" is most representative.

Emergent Preconceptions When Discussing Recursive Phenomena

Analyzing the discourse, a diverse collection of two dozen content categories came up, with each category including expressions that hint at a similar way of talking and thinking about recursive phenomena. These content categories are regarded as preconceptions, and the entire categorical system is regarded as the network of preconceptions that evolved throughout the study. Table 10.1 presents one third of the categorical system, namely eight categories that are considered key preconceptions. These key preconceptions appeared most often in the students' discourse and were remarkably associated with other preconceptions. Each key preconception in Table 10.1 is illustrated by an utterance expressing it. The representative utterances were selected from among the data gathered at the different classes (titled Case 9...Case 14). For an expanded view, the right column of the table presents the various other preconceptions that tended to be associated with each key pre-conception.

So far, the collection of preconceptions emerging throughout the discourse analysis has been briefly described. Recall that the term "preconception" denotes a specific way of looking at recursive phenomena and of describing certain characteristics of such phenomena. For example, when a student looked at one item from the collection of recursive phenomena and said, "There is a kind of a rule here," (Case 10), his utterance was interpreted as hinting at regularity. In this case, the preconception of regularity denotes that student's specific way of looking for rules in the recursive phenomenon that he was investigating. As stated earlier, preconceptions are not misconceptions; moreover, as the example of regularity

TABLE 10.1. Key Pre-Conceptions Expressed by High-School Students

The Key Pre-Conception	Example of an Utterance Expressing This Pre-Conception	Other Associated Pre-Conceptions
Infinite or Finite (I/F)	"It stops the whole process" (Case 9)	Returning, Sequential, Gradualism, Circular, Periodical, Repetition
Regularity	"There is a kind of a rule here" (Case 10)	Gradualism, Withdrawal, Periodical, Sequential
Gradualism	"From the big one to the little one and vice versa" (Case 10)	I/F, Regularity, Periodical, Sequential, Split, Withdrawal
Periodical	"It is repeating. Periodical" (Case 14)	Circular, Gradualism, Regularity, Repetition, Sequential
Returning	"Here it returns to beginning" (Case 9)	Reflection, I/F, Dependency
Sequential	"There are increasing and decreasing sequences here" (Case 10)	I/F, Gradualism, Regularity, Periodical
Dependency	"There is a kind of ... dependency of the former" (Case 14)	Withdrawal, Sequential, Mutuality
Self-reference	"Things that build themselves" (Case 11)	I/F, Circular, Fractal, Containing

shows, all emergent preconceptions can be thought of as being closely related to recursion by hinting at different characteristics of a variety of recursive phenomena.

Two important findings can be summarized here. First, high-school students indeed expressed a rich and complicated conceptual scheme when they were first exposed to recursion via the classification and discussion of different recursive phenomena. That complex network of preconceptions that emerged throughout the study reflects an advanced framework of students' thinking about recursion even at that initial phase. As the documented learning activity took place mainly as a collaborative discussion involving all students in the class, we claim that the conceptual advancement went hand in hand with the need to negotiate one's conceptions with the others. Within the framework of social constructivism (Confrey, 1995), such a finding might indicate that social interaction can stimulate the elaboration of conceptual knowledge (Van Boxtel, Van der Linden, & Kanselaar, 2000) or, as has been previously claimed, social interaction might motivate conceptual change.

The second finding refers to some key preconceptions like Infinite or Finite, Periodical, and Gradualism (Table 10.1) that were highly linked to others, whereas other preconceptions tended to be more isolated. The more isolated preconceptions are not referred to as "key preconceptions" and therefore can be found listed in Table 10.2 (the non-bolded preconceptions). For example, gradualism was apparent in many discourse episodes as a kind of inherent characteristic of recursive phenomena, which was always jointly expressed with one or more other preconceptions, as is also hinted at in the "tam-tam-tam" episode at the beginning of this chapter. Another example of a highly linked system of preconceptions can be found in several "potentially rich episodes," in which five or more different preconceptions were expressed in the same discourse episode. As has been extensively dealt with elsewhere (Levy, 2001), because of their argumentative nature, those episodes had the most promising potential for conceptual change. The meaning of this second finding is that the students' discourse not only hinted at the components of their conceptual scheme, it also hinted at the process of reconstructing such schemes by expressing linkages and relations (Hiebert & Lefevre, 1986), as well as by differentiating the "stand-alone" components of the conceptual scheme in regard to recursion.

A Suggested Model of Conceptual Change

As a further analytic step, the different phases of the learning activity were considered, and the preconceptions were organized according to the phases in which they appeared. Recall that in Phase 1, the class was first exposed to recursive phenomena, whereas Phase 2 was the classification phase. The students worked in groups of three or four, and in Phase 3, each group presented its classification, categories, and criteria to the other groups. In Phase 4, the teacher guided a

TABLE 10.2. A model for organizing the preconceptions

Preconception	Phase 1	Phase 2	Phase 3	Phase 4
Returning				
Infinite or Finite				
Circularity				
Containing				
Split				
Reflection				
Symmetry				
Sophistry				
Self-reference				
Self-similarity				
Regularity				
Regular gradual recurrence				
Gradualism				
Periodical				
Sequential				
Withdrawal				
Infinite gradual recurrence				
Dependency				
Fractal				
Mutuality				
Function that calls itself				

Consistency of pre-conceptions

Cognitive Potential of collaborative learning

Creating class genre

reflective whole-class discussion. Those four phases lasted between two and four consecutive sessions of two-hour lessons in each case.

Table 10.2 shows the suggested model for organizing the preconceptions, with grey highlighting the phases that were relevant for each preconception. The model includes most recognized preconceptions, and those bolded are the key preconceptions among them.

Two main findings are summarized above: the diversity of the preconceptions that high-school students expressed and the conceptual network that they weaved by expressing linkages and relations among the components of their complicated conceptual scheme. The blue, red, and green boxes that bound three sections of the model (Table 10.2) hint at three additional findings:

1. *The consistency of preconceptions* (blue box). Some preconceptions appeared as early as the exposure in Phase 1 and continued to be expressed all along the learning activity. The most consistent were the pre-conceptions of Infinite or Finite, Circularity, and Containing.

2. *The cognitive potential of group classification and discussion* (red box). The group phases (2 and 3) motivated a rich expression of preconceptions as well as the opportunity for conceptual change. Many of the various preconceptions were rooted in these learning-without-guidance phases. Following Krummheuer (1995) and others, this suggests that the

argumentative nature of the group discussions was responsible for that richness.

3. *The creation and refinement of a class genre appropriate for discussing the idea of recursion* (green box). A terminological shift toward and throughout the final, reflective Phase 4 seemed to occur. In that phase, the students used a slightly more formal language, e.g. their use of Symmetry, Dependency, Fractal, and Mutuality. The linguistic change might also reflect a conceptual change by expressing the process of collaborative reconstruction of ideas and by pointing at the communal dimension of learning (Cobb, 1996; Confrey, 1995). In that sense, the suggested model may reflect a collaborative kind of conceptual change that occurred in the observed classes.

Together with the findings presented earlier, five different results have been discussed, which illuminate the process by which learners construct an abstract concept like recursion. A model for organizing preconceptions and change over time can draw an interesting and unique picture of the ways in which students relate to this interdisciplinary concept, the particular learners' language concerning recursive phenomena, and the nature of the conceptual change that might take place throughout the class discourse—a collaborative conceptual change. When an abstract and interdisciplinary concept like recursion is constructed, the conceptual change is initiated and motivated by taking part in a collaborative and discursive learning environment. Using somewhat metaphoric language, if constructivist educators think about concepts as located in one's mind, change seems to be located somewhere in the contextual/communicative/ discursive space (Roth, 1999; Sfard, 2008; Vygotsky, 1978).

SUMMARY

In analyzing student discourse while engaged in a collaborative classification and generalization activity, one can locate some conceptual processes as they evolve and become expressed in the natural setting, the real classroom. One implication for designing learning environments for conceptual change is obvious because the studied learning activity supports students' construction processes by enabling them to engage actively and reflectively in the learning task, either on the group discourse level or on the whole-class discourse level. This implication may well be extended to other concepts via a similar group activity.

In a sense, the studied context of learning recursion can be thought of as an instructional context that promotes the process of conceptual change (Mason, 2001) in computer-science classes. At the same time, the studied context can be used as an example of a "communicational space" (Sfard, 2008) in a call for investigating other communicational spaces to better understand the collaborative nature of conceptual change. Furthermore, the implications of the findings mentioned above could hold both for understanding how students construct the conceptual scheme of recursion and for understanding more general construction and reconstruction processes.

The preconceptions that emerged in the research hint at the interesting distinction between the more operational kind of conception and the more structural kind of conception. This issue has been raised both by the discourse analysis and by contemporary theories of mathematics education. Following Piaget (1980), some researchers look at the process of constructing abstract mathematical concepts as a gradual process, in which the learner moves from an operational conception towards the more developed structural conception (Breidenbach, Dubinsky, Hawks, & Nichols, 1992; Sfard & Linchevski, 1994). When holding an operational conception, the learners focus on actions and processes, as can be the case for the students who express preconceptions like Infinite or Finite, Gradualism, and Periodical.

On the other hand, focusing and expressing the preconceptions of Containing, Fractal, and Self-reference could be interpreted as representing a more structural conception of recursion. Discovering that all the different kinds of conceptions were jointly present in the same class was interesting. Moreover, they often harmoniously existed within a single utterance expressed by the same student. Such harmony contradicts former findings concerning the superiority of the operational conception of recursion, even when the students expressing that kind of conception were not novices (Aharoni, 1999). The operational conception of recursion might be a consequence of a programming-oriented thinking, constructed by overemphasizing computing and algorithmic aspects of recursion throughout a programming-oriented curriculum. The implication for teaching computer-science concepts in general—and for teaching recursion especially—is obvious: the learners should be exposed to a broader view, to various ways of thinking about the basic concepts of computer science, and to a larger variety of programming as well as non-programming learning activities.

In an even more general sense, we emphasize that the recognition of the role of the class discourse in the process of constructing scientific concepts "has been one of the most important conditions in making possible changes in teaching practice" (Mortimer & Machado, 2000, p. 440). Within the young and growing research community of computer-science education, such recognition is a must.

REFERENCES

Abelson, H., & Sussman, G. S., with Sussman, J. (1996). *Structure and interpretation of computer programs* (2nd ed.). Cambridge, MA: MIT press.

Aharoni, D. (1999). *Undergraduate students' perception of data structures* (Doctoral dissertation) [Hebrew]. Technion—Israel Institute of Technology, Haifa.

Astrachan, O. (1994). Self-reference is an illustrative essential. *Proceedings of the 25th SIGCSE Technical Symposium on Computer Science Education* (pp. 238–242). Phoenix, AZ.

Barron, B. (2003). When smart groups fail. *The Journal of the Learning Sciences, 12*(3), 307–359.

Ben-Ari, M. (1997). Recursion: From drama to program. *Journal of Computer Science Education, 113*, 9–12.

Bhuiyan, S., Greer, J. E., & McCalla, G. I. (1994). Supporting the learning of recursive problem solving. *Interactive Learning Environments, 42*, 115–139.

Bogdan, R. C., & Biklen, S. K. (1998). *Qualitative research for education: An introduction to theory and methods* (3rd ed.). Boston, MA: Allyn & Bacon.

Breidenbach, D., Dubinsky, E., Hawks, J., & Nichols, D. (1992). Development of the process conception of function. *Educational Studies in Mathematics, 23*, 247–285.

Cobb, P. (1996). Accounting for mathematical learning in the social context of the classroom. *Eighth International Congress on Mathematics Education ICME 8*. Seville, Spain.

Cobb P., Yackel, E., & Wood, T. (1992). Interaction and learning in mathematics classroom situations. *Educational Studies in Mathematics Education, 23*, 99–122.

Confrey J. (1995). How compatible are radical constructivism, sociocultural approaches, and social constructivism? In L. P. Steffe & J. Gale (Eds.), *Constructivism in education* (pp. 185–225). Hillsdale, NJ: Lawrence Erlbaum Associates.

Denning, P. J. (2004). Great principles in computing curricula. *Proceedings of SIGCSE'04* (pp. 336–341). Norfolk, VA: ACM.

Duit, R. (2002). Conceptual change–Still a powerful frame for improving science teaching and learning? *Proceedings of the Third European Symposium on Conceptual Change* (pp. 5–16). Turku, Finland.

Feuerstein, R., Rand, Y., Hoffman, M. B., & Miller, R. (1980). *Instrumental Enrichment—An Intervention Program for Cognitive Modifiability*. Baltimore, MD: University Park Press.

Gal-Ezer, J., & Harel, D. (1999). Curriculum and course syllabi for a high school CS program. *Computer Science Education, 9*(2), 114–147.

George, C. E. (2000). EROSI–Visualizing recursion and discovering new errors, *Proceedings of the 31st SIGCSE Technical Symposium on Computer-Science Education* (pp. 305–309). Austin, TX.

Gunion, K., Milford, T., & Stege, U. (2009). The paradigm recursion: Is it more accessible when introduced in middle school? *Journal of Problem Solving, 2*(2), 142–172.

Harvey, B. (1985). *Computer science Logo style: Intermediate programming* (Vol. 1). Cambridge, MA: MIT Press.

Harvey, B., & Wright, M. (1993). *Simply scheme–Introducing computer-science*. Cambridge, MA: MIT Press.

Hiebert, J., & Lefevre, P. (1986). Conceptual and procedural knowledge in mathematics: An introductory analysis. In J. Hiebert (Ed.), *Conceptual and procedural knowledge: The case of mathematics* (pp. 1–27). Hillsdale, NJ: Lawrence Erlbaum.

Hofstadter, D. (1979) *Gödel, Escher, Bach: An eternal golden braid*, New York, NY: Basic Books.

Krummheuer, G. (1995). The ethnography of argumentation. In P. Cobb & H. Beauersfeld (Eds.), *The emergence of mathematical meaning–Interactions in classroom culture*. (pp. 229–270) Hillsdale, NJ: Erlbaum.

Levy, D. (2001). Insights and conflicts in discussing recursion: A case study. *Computer-Science Education, 114*, 305–322.

Levy, D. (2002). Shared terminology, private syntax: The case of recursive descriptions. *The 7th Annual Conference on Innovations and Technology in Computer Science Education (ITiCSE02)*. Arhus, Denmark.

Levy D., & Lapidot, T. (2000). Recursively speaking: Analyzing students' discourse of recursive phenomena. *Proceedings of the Thirty-First SIGCSE Technical Symposium on Computer Science Education (SIGCSE 2000),* Austin, TX.

Mason, L. (2001). Introduction: Instructional practices for conceptual change in science domains. *Learning and Instruction, 114*(5), 259–263.

Morazán, M. T. (2013). Functional video games in CS1 II–Distributed programming for beginners. In McCarthy J. (Ed.), Trends in Functional Programming–14th International Symposium, TFP2013. Provo, UT, USA. *Lecture Notes in Computer Science*, (Vol. 8322) (pp. 149–67). Berlin, Germany: Springer.

Mortimer, F. M., & Machado, A. H. (2000). Anomalies and conflicts in class-room discourse. *Science Education, 84*, 429–444.

Pilkington, R. (2016). *Discourse, dialogue and technology enhanced learning*. New York, NY: Routledge.

Piaget, J. (1980). *Adaptation and intelligence: Organic selection and phenocopy* (3rd ed.) Chicago, IL: University of Chicago Press.

Rinderknecht, C. (2014). A survey on teaching and learning recursive programming. *Informatics in Education, 13*(1), 87–119.

Roberts, E. S. (1986). *Thinking recursively*. New York, NY: John Wiley & Sons.

Roth, W. M. (1999). Discourse and agency in school science laboratories, *Discourse Processes, 28*, 27–60.

Rubio-Sánchez, M. (2010). *Tail recursive programming by applying generalization.* Proceedings of the 15th Annual Conference on Innovation and Technology in Computer Science Education ITiCSE10 (pp. 98–102). Bilkent, Ankara, Turkey.

Sfard, A. (2008). *Thinking as communicating: Human development, the growth of discourses, and mathematizing*. Cambridge, UK: Cambridge University Press.

Sfard, A., & Linchevski, L. (1994). The gains and pitfalls of reification–The case of algebra. *Educational Studies in Mathematics, 26*, 191–228.

Soto, C., & Sanjose, V. (2002). Research on conceptual change: A review in science education. *Third European Symposium on Conceptual Change*. Turku, Finland.

Smith, J. P., diSessa, A. A., & Roschelle, J. (1993). Misconceptions reconceived: A Constructivist analysis of knowledge in transition, *The Journal of the Learning Sciences, 32*, 115–163.

Stephenson, C., Gal-Ezer, J., Haberman, B., & Verno, A. (2005). *The new educational imperative: Improving high school computer science education*. Final report of the CSTA Curriculum Improvement Task Force, February 2005. Retrieved from http://csta.acm.org/Publications/White_Paper07_06.pdf

Troy, M. E., & Early, G. (1992). Unraveling recursion, Part II. *The Computing Teacher, 19*(7), 21–25.

Van Boxtel, C., Van der Linden, J., & Kanselaar, G. (2000). Collaborative learning tasks and the elaboration of conceptual knowledge. *Learning and Instruction, 104,* 311–330.

Vosniadou, S., & Ioannides, C. (1998). From conceptual change to science education: A psychological point of view. *International Journal of Science Education, 20*, 1213–1230.

Vygotsky, L. S. (1978). *Mind in society: The development of higher psychological processes*. Cambridge, MA: Harvard University Press.

Weinberger, A., Stegnmann, K., & Fischer, F. (2007). Knowledge convergence in collaborative learning: Concepts and assessment. *Learning and Instruction, 17*, 416–426.

Wing, J. M. (2006). Computational thinking. *Communications of the ACM, 49*(3), 33–35.

Wu, C., Dale, N. B., & Bethel, L. J. (1998). Conceptual models and cognitive learning styles in teaching recursion. *SIGCSE Bulletin, 30*, 292–296.

CHAPTER 11

WHAT INFLUENCES TEACHER EDUCATORS' USE OF COLLABORATIVE LEARNING?

Miri Shonfeld and Yehudith Weinberger

An entirely new approach to thinking and learning has started to emerge in the 21st century as a result of the invention of the Internet (Harasim, 2012). Technology and social media have led to changes in all areas of life. Daily online communication has become commonplace, and information systems and networks offer a new model for sharing (Blau, 2011). Thus, distances between cultures and continents have been shortened, and learning activities and work have become common among workers from different countries (Resta & Carol, 2010; Shonfeld, 2017). Learning methodologies have been similarly impacted by these rapid technological changes (Harasim, 2012; Warschauer & Grimes, 2007). For example, Harasim (2012) introduced Online Collaborative Learning (henceforth OCL) as a new learning theory, far beyond the concept of collaboration as a teaching and learning methodology.

In spite of the availability of web-based tools, the use of collaborative learning (henceforth CL) tools is limited in education, particularly in teacher-education programs. Since change in the education system depends on teacher preparation (Melamed et al., 2011), teacher-education colleges should provide their students

Collaborative Online Learning in a Global World, pages 155–174.

155

with collaborative skills as part of preparing them to be teachers in the information age (Resta & Laferrière, 2007; Resta et al., 2011). Consequently, instructors at teacher-education institutions are expected to renew their teaching methods while integrating appropriate new learning environments (Hine, 2011). More research into CL in teacher-education colleges, along with its integration and practice, can enrich knowledge of this important approach to learning and expand its use in a variety of disciplines (Shonfeld, 2017).

The study reported in this chapter explored teacher-educators' conceptions and knowledge about the use of CL methods in a teacher-education college in Israel to understand how their attitudes and willingness can influence the integration of CL into their teaching. The following section provides a theoretical background of CL and its use in teacher-education programs. Subsequent sections present the methodology and the results that emerged from the study. The paper ends with a discussion of CL as a teaching method and recommendations on the ways it might be integrated into the curricula of teacher-education colleges.

COLLABORATIVE LEARNING: DEFINITION AND PEDAGOGICAL BENEFITS

As a pedagogical approach, CL involves organizing students into learning groups, regardless of age or grade level, to achieve a common goal, such as solving a problem, completing a task, or collaborating on a project (Brody & Davidson, 1998). Instructors commonly view CL as students working together in creative ways to deepen the learning experience. CL also places an emphasis on active learning, peer assessment, and the development of social and cognitive skills. It is a general pedagogical approach that includes a variety of methods and models for implementation.

In CL, the mechanism of the group's common goal is theoretically based on positive interdependence and at the same time on each individual's responsibility for his or her personal contribution to the group. Kirschner (2001) notes how mounting a stage play is an example of CL–each role (lighting, costumes, direction, etc.) is crucial to the final production, but those responsible for each role do not need to learn what the others do. True collaborative learning requires significant interdependence between learners (Hung & Chen, 2001) and relies on dialogue and other interactions between them. The degree of collaboration relies on the shared ownership of the outcome and the quality of interaction during the process (Slavin, 2010).

The literature discusses collaboration and cooperation as dependent on time, place, and research group. In their work on cooperation, Johnson and Johnson (2013) distinguished between formal and informal cooperative learning. The former consists of students working together for one class period to several weeks to achieve shared learning goals and jointly complete specific tasks and assignments. In contrast, informal cooperative learning consists of having students work together to achieve a joint learning goal in temporary, ad-hoc groups that last from a few minutes to one class period. Davidson and Major (2014) propose distinguishing between "cooperation" and "collaboration." In cooperative learning, the focus is on working together interdependently; in collaborative learning, the focus is on learners working toward a common goal but not necessarily interdependently. In the collaborative approach, the clear definition of each participant's share in the project is less important in relation to the final accomplishment of the joint mission. Researchers focusing on online learning more often use the term collaboration.

Salmons's (2006) taxonomy for online collaboration is based on five steps. The first step is a dialogue between learners, and the second is based on peer review; both steps require mutual help and provide the basis for collaborative work. The third step is parallel collaboration, in which every member of the group works independently, and at the end they combine their individual work. This step is similar to many definitions of cooperative work. At the fourth step, there is a deeper collaboration, in which everyone's work is based on the earlier contributions of all the members of the group. Only after completing all these steps can groups create a synergistic collaboration in which solving a problem or doing the task is a real effort of all members of the group. Since the advent of the Internet and particularly the invention of the browser in 1993, new opportunities for collaboration in education have appeared (Bonk, 2009). CL in its online form has been described not just as an approach to learning but, according to Harasim (2012), as a new learning theory called "Online OCL."

In many cases, CL has been underpinned by educational theory, particularly the constructivist approach to learning (Vygotsky, 1978). Proponents of the constructivist approach claim that construction of knowledge is a key process in learning and it occurs as a result of social interaction. That is, learning occurs through the active involvement of learners, who build the mental structures that connect segmented units of information to provide meaningful knowledge. According to this approach, transferring ready-made knowledge does not allow the students to connect information units and to actively create meaning cognitively. Thus, knowledge is created while groups of students discuss issues (Barkley, Cross, & Major, 2005; Harasim, 2012).

Learning in disparate social groups increases academic achievement, encourages creative thinking, and intensifies and develops social skills (Jehn, Northcraft, & Neale, 1999). But without direction and guidance, negative relationships between learners may develop, with the risk of stereotyping and diminished academic achievement (Johnson & Johnson, 2013). In school settings, CL has a great potential to promote meaningful interactions and empathy between students and teachers and among students themselves. Empathetic culture in the classroom can create a sense of worth, competence, and belonging and is likely to assist teachers not only in establishing a productive atmosphere in their classes but also in promoting meaningful learning by creating profound insights. Additionally, an empathetic classroom environment encourages all parties concerned to think, initiate, create, learn, and develop (Weinberger, 2017).

Collaborative learning is not only active but also interactive. Each student interacts with other learners, and when exchanging ideas and knowledge, each student builds his/her own world of knowledge. A link was found between collaborative projects, student involvement in learning, and knowledge construction (Brett, 2004; Stahl, 2006). Additionally, collaborative learning provides learners with skills needed in the working world, where working groups are common (Palloff & Pratt, 2005). However, the amount of research on collaborative learning in schools is greater than in higher-education institutions and teacher-education colleges (Barkley et al., 2005; Tsuei, 2011).

Collaborative Learning in Teacher Education

Since the 1970s, the use of CL has expanded gradually in the education system in general and in teacher-education institutions in particular. Collaborative projects in teacher-education programs have been found to increase student engagement (Chen, Gonyea, & Kuh, 2008; Shonfeld, Resta, & Yaniv, 2011) and learning motivation. Nonetheless, they are not common in these settings in the 21st century despite the availability of digitally enabled collaborative environments. This may be due to the limited amount of CL in these institutions or the reluctance of lecturers to change their teaching methods (Schrire, Shonfeld, & Zelkovitz, 2014). In addition, it might result from concerns about technical problems and the difficulty of resolving them and that CL preparation is time-consuming and lengthy. Sometimes, rather than devoting time and thought to the organization and preparation of structured communication processes for effective CL, lecturers mistake the interaction between learners as coincidental (Kreijns, Kirschner, & Jochems, 2002). Therefore, it is essential that teacher-education instructors devote time to understanding the theory of CL and its teaching methods.

In the digital age, because of the development of communication and the many opportunities to distribute information on the Internet, greater collaborative learning is possible. Creating CL environments is an integral part of work in the global world, and the education system should prepare learners to achieve this skill. In schools used as learning centers, learners can connect with others around the world as well as with other schools and academic institutions. Such activities enable collaboration, heterogeneous teamwork, and more diverse products than those coming from homogeneous groups. Therefore, teacher-training institutions' management and teaching staff need to keep abreast of what is being done in CL and prepare their students for teaching in CL environments in schools (Bonk, 2009; Shonfeld, 2017).

Integrating CL in teaching and learning is part of the Israeli national education program (Melamed et al., 2011). One example of online collaborative learning in teacher training in Israel is the Technology, Education, and Cultural Diversity (TEC) program. All students from colleges of education are invited to attend courses in an online, collaborative-learning program. In the Israeli educational system, most Arabic students study in different colleges from Jewish students, and separate provision is also made for Orthodox and non-Orthodox Jewish students. However, at the TEC program, students from all types of education colleges participate (secular Jewish, religious, and Arabic) and are taught collaboratively by a team of instructors representative of the different sectors. At the beginning of the course, the medium is text-based, through forums; but as the course progresses, audio, media, and visual communication are introduced. The course has online units, some asynchronous and some synchronous, including discussion forums. After a few months of learning collaboratively in small groups via virtual meetings, students meet each other "face to face" to work on a joint project and present it. Teamwork is an essential element in the course, and before an assignment, it is explained to the participants that teamwork and collaboration are of great importance and are taken into account in the final grade. At the end of the course, participants receive both a personal grade and a team grade. The team grade takes into account the collaboration of the student with the other members of the group and contribution to teamwork. The collaborative learning in the course includes reading an article; creating an educational, online, collaborative multimedia product; participating in discussions; and online teaching (Shonfeld, Hoter, & Ganayem, 2013; Walther, Hoter, Ganayem, & Shonfeld, 2015). Groups that adhere to best practices by virtual groups, such as starting immediately, communicating frequently, overtly acknowledging and replying to one another's messages, and being clear about expectations and progress (Walther & Bunz, 2005) are more likely to create greater trust in the group and succeed in the CL experience (Shonfeld, Ganayem, Hoter, & Walther, 2015). Learning these principles of good practice is important because learning without experience might lead to frustration in collaborative learning (Brown, 2008).

Changing the educational system in Israel and making it suitable for the 21st century by using innovative pedagogy depends upon the training of teachers, most of whom come from teachers' colleges (Melamed et al., 2011). Although it is important to explore CL in teacher-training colleges and to incorporate collaborative projects with students from various countries (Resta & Shonfeld, 2014), such projects have challenges. This is primarily because of time differences between various locations around the world and language difficulties. Additionally, the technology used, whether LMS (Learning Management System) or virtual worlds, might be difficult to use. It must be taken into consideration that such challenges may also induce frustration (Brown, 2008; Harasim, 2012; Resta & Shonfeld, 2014).

Additional experiences, models, and studies of CL in higher education may enrich our understanding of the field, lead teacher trainees to experience global collaboration, and promote its use in teacher education. Given its present and future importance, the research question in this study focused on the factors that may affect lecturers' readiness to integrate CL in teacher-education settings.

METHODOLOGY

The current study took place at the largest teachers' college in Israel, founded in 1939 at the initiative of the kibbutzim movement. The college sought to establish a seminary for teacher education (K–10) in the spirit of the pedagogical concepts that had been forged in the kibbutzim (e.g., Yogev & Michaeli, 2009). The main campus is located in the center of Tel Aviv, and its 5,500 students come from all sectors of Israeli society. The study utilized both quantitative and qualitative methods.

Sample

A questionnaire was sent to all faculty members who taught in the college. Of these, 86 responded. The analysis of the demographic questions of the questionnaire characterizes the sample, which includes six variables: Gender, Age, Years of Experience, Program, and Function in the college (such as Lecturer or Pedagogical Advisor[1]). Table 11.1 presents the demographic variables.

As can be seen, most of the respondents were women, the majority aged between 40 and 60, and there were more lecturers than PAs. Most respondents taught in the undergraduate programs, and a majority had taught for more than 10 years. The sample represents the actual distribution of the faculty members in the college who participated in this research.

Tools

The data were collected by an online questionnaire in Google form that was sent to the faculty members by e-mail and by an internal message system, once at the beginning of the school year and a second time three weeks later.

The CL questionnaire was based on three other questionnaires–"Collaborative Learning" (Brown, 2008), "The Collaborative Learning, Social Presence, and Satisfaction" (Spears, 2012), and "Leading a System-wide Pedagogical Change" (Weinberger, 2018). It was modified to suit the population and the context of the study and was translated into Hebrew. The questionnaire included one multiple-choice question, one open question, and 27 statements to be rated on a five-point Likert scale (ranging from 1=strongly disagree to 5=strongly agree). The questionnaire consisted of four parts addressing the themes of the research: Knowledge and conceptions about CL, attitudes towards CL, previous experience with CL, and willingness to use CL.

Knowledge and conceptions were addressed with an open question about the characteristics of CL and 12 statements about its advantages and disadvantages. The first six statements dealt with advantages of CL, such as better understanding of the subject, sharing knowledge and experience development of higher-order thinking, a relaxed atmosphere, strengthening communication skills, and gaining new friends. Reliability for this section of the questionnaire was Cronbach's alpha

---

[1] A Pedagogical Advisor is a faculty member who teaches pedagogical subjects in the teacher education program and instructs the student based on his/her practical experience in the field.

TABLE 11.1. Distribution of study subjects according to individual characteristics (n = 86)

Variables	Values	N	%
Gender	Male	10	11.6
	Female	76	88.4
Age	30-39	8	9.3
	40-49	24	37.2
	50-59	34	39.5
	60+	20	23.3
Program	Undergraduate	59	67.9
	Graduate	27	32.1
Function	PA	33	38.4
	Lecturer	51	59.3
Years of experience	1–3	12	14.1
	4–9	11	12.9
	10–19	19	22.4
	20–29	21	24.7
	30+	22	25.9

=.82. The other six statements dealt with disadvantages of CL, such as waste of time, difficulties in participation, not suitable to all subjects and students. Reliability for this section was α =.79.

The attitude section consisted of four statements addressing students' preferences and the importance of this kind of experience to their future role. Reliability of this section was α =.67.

The previous-experience section of the questionnaire consisted of one multiple-choice question about the amount of CL use (this was treated as the dependent variable) and six statements. Based on factor analysis, the statements were divided into two variables representing two different subjects (see Table 11.2). One of them dealt with CL organizational complexity, and the other dealt with CL evaluation complexity. The factor analysis (Principal Component Analysis) explained 52% of the variance. The first variable, Organization Complexity, consisted of four statements ("Working in the group takes more time than working alone."; "It is hard to maintain contact in the team."; "It is easy to organize CL."; "It is easy to reach consensus in the group."). The second variable, Evaluation Complexity, consisted of two statements ("Members with limited contribution get the same credit."; "Unfair evaluation."). The last section, Willingness, included five statements dealing with students' and lecturers' competence with CL. This section's reliability was α =.78.

TABLE 11.2. Factor Loading for the Experience Items on Two Factors (N=86)

Item	Factor Loadings	
	Factor 1 Organization Complexity	Factor 2 Evaluation Complexity
Hard to maintain contact	.75	.03
More time than working alone	.67	–.10
Easy to organize	.62	.23
Easy to reach consensus	.54	.00
Members with limited contribution	.04	.85
Unfair evaluation	.02	.83
Percentage of explained variance	29.49%	23.34%

The validity of the questionnaire was strengthened by sending it to 10 faculty members as a pilot and amending it as a result of their comments.

Data Analysis

Data were analyzed using two methods according to the type of question in the questionnaire: quantitative for closed questions and qualitative for open questions. The quantitative analysis was done using SPSS. The analysis was based on descriptive statistics. Reliability was found for all variables, and factor analysis was used when reliability was missing and two subjects were addressed in the same question. Pearson correlations were examined for continuous research variables, and Chi-Square tests were used for discrete variables. ANOVA and hierarchical regression were conducted to predict the variables that explained the variance in CL use.

In the qualitative analysis, the focus of inquiry was a lecturer's answers to the open question about collaborative learning. An interpretive content analysis of the statements was conducted in three stages. First, an intuitive process of bottom-up coding (Bowen, 2009) was applied using an emic approach (subject's point of view). On the basis of this coding, major themes were formulated (Denzin & Lincoln, 2002). In the second stage, the themes were mapped by finding the connections between them, and categories of the analysis were determined (Denzin & Lincoln, 2008). Finally, the analytic process of grouping all the statements in their respective categories was carried out from the top down, according to the etic approach (researcher's point of view). An analysis of this type offers a broad interpretation and a variety of meanings for the research topic. A system of conceptualizations was developed, which expressed the lecturers' response-patterns to the research questions, and the study's narrative line was then constructed (Strauss & Corbin, 1997).

Ethical Aspects

Information was gathered anonymously and indirectly to reduce any interference with respect to the respondents' statements. No personal identification of the respondents was required, either during the information-gathering phase or in the presentations made in this article. Qualitative analysis involves ethical considerations and judgment; therefore, it was conducted by one author and validated by the other.

FINDINGS

This study examined lecturers' knowledge and conceptions of CL and attitudes towards it as well as their previous experience with and willingness to use CL in their instruction. Statistical analyses of these data were designed to identify the factors that might influence lecturers' readiness and contribute to their willingness to incorporate CL in their teacher-preparation courses.

Differences in Use of Collaborative Learning

Descriptive statistics from the questionnaire results indicated that respondents' use of CL was at a reasonably high level (Range 1–4, $M=3.2$, $SD=.82$). To more closely examine CL use, t-tests were conducted. Results showed that, on average, female instructors used CL significantly more than male instructors ($t=7.92$, $p<.01$). This was not surprising given the much greater percentage of female instructors in this sample. Results also showed a significant different of CL use by program, with lecturers in the undergraduate program using CL significantly more than those in the graduate program ($t=5.14$, $p<.05$). Last, average CL use by pedagogic advisers was significantly greater than by subject-specialist lecturers ($t=4.69$, $p<.05$).

The Characteristics of Collaborative Learning

Of the 86 faculty members who responded to the questionnaire, 60 answered the open-ended question, "What are the characteristics of collaborative learning?" Analysis of the responses revealed three major categories:

- Practices embedded in collaborative learning
- Educational ideologies at the heart of collaborative learning
- Theoretical characteristics of the approach

"Practices embedded in collaborative learning" includes examples of what happens during this type of learning activity. Most of the lecturers' answers were grouped into this category. They were mainly related to the learners' activities, their involvement in the learning process, and cooperation in the community of thinking through the different stages of learning. One typical comment was, "Learning together, in groups, in teams, in community learning; learning from each other, defining a common goal and creating a common product, everyone brings to the table their view, life experience and insights into the joint work of the team." In addition, the lecturers described a variety of learning methods which were used in CL:

"Tours, conferences, shared experiences outside the college, seminars, museums, plays, guided tours, visiting special schools, dialogues, brainstorming." It should be noted that these activities are not exclusive to CL. Some lecturers referred to other aspects, such as "rational division of roles (from personal choice), so everyone relies on his/her abilities," or "the possibility of joint learning of students from different institutions as well as from different countries."

The "educational ideologies" category included the pedagogical rationale for CL, such as the reference to the pedagogical benefits of this strategy, the educational goals one can achieve through it, or justifying its use. One of the pedagogical benefits was the reference to the individual's contribution to another student's learning, while underlining specific areas in which the individual excels, expressing those specific areas, learning which relies on each participant adding his or her knowledge to that being learned. This type of process also enables, as one respondent emphasized,

> Wide and deep activity of the subject following the collaboration process...to be a partner from an open place, which enables observation from a new perspective... encouraging learning out of the box, out of fixation, allowing creativity and boldness.

Some of the lecturers referred to the role of the CL teacher and claimed "not to mediate but as a guide, to connect the knowledge of the participants."

Among pedagogical objectives that CL promotes, the cultivation of good relations with others by promoting collaboration among students of different knowledge and backgrounds was prominent. As one of the respondents noted:

> Creating communication brings participants closer and even friendships. A sense of belonging we all need...partnerships are formed not only in common thinking, but also in actual experiences...the opportunity to meet other people and work with them as a team...mutual assistance–psychological and cognitive; mutual responsibility.

This strategy is seen as strengthening social and interpersonal ties in the group and contributes to improving motivation and enjoyment of learning.

CL is also seen by respondents as a way to promote multi-cultural perspectives in educational interactions:

> Encouraging multiculturalism...building relationships with others in order to set and solve problems and share information collaboratively and culturally; the ability to communicate, to share, to have a dialogue and even a critical dialogue; to resolve confrontations.

Some lecturers also mentioned the issue of developing competencies and learning skills among students: "The student's responsibility for his own learning process and as part of a group...nurtures skills required for the 21st century such as communication, teamwork, and problem-solving."

Further insights into the values that lecturers ascribed to CL were found in the ways they justified it by including a variety of ideas that examine the role of knowledge in the educational process, for example,

> Use of the wisdom of the masses, even in a limited way…the whole is greater than its parts…[recognition] that knowledge is not exclusively for the lecturer…[beyond] hierarchical structure and power relations–where the collaborative structure is aware of power relations…fostering skills required for the 21st century.

The category of "characteristics of CL" refers to processes that occur during learning and teaching and includes the conceptualization of what goes on during collaborative learning and teaching. Several ideas appeared in the lecturers' answers in this respect. One was the partnership in the learning process and the product:

> What characterizes collaborative learning is the joint work of several individuals to one, uniform product with the agreement of the group…encouraging peer learning, sharing in the broadest sense–the contribution of each individual according to abilities and talent to a general product.

Another emphasis was the relationship between the individual and the group during the process:

> The two main components of collaborative learning are the individual–who conveys something of himself to the group[–]…and group responsibility for learning and for the work of all the individuals in the group…learning with a partner, mutual aid, joint investigation and cross-fertilization…attempts to find strengths and weaknesses of each participant.

Further characterization of CL included the active involvement of learners in the learning process: "Learning in which students take an active part in shaping the content and learning objectives as well as relaying the content." It was also an opportunity to develop skills, such as learning skills and competencies, such as "the ability to listen and share. Modesty–downplaying one's ego…." Some of the respondents' answers put a spotlight on the unique interaction that takes place between teacher and students in collaborative learning: "Fruitful dialogue between teacher and student, closer and democratic human relations. Joint uncertainty [of both teachers and students] in the process of finding knowledge." Notably absent from the lecturers' answers on collaborative learning characteristics were any disadvantages of CL.

Factors That Predict Use of Collaborative Learning

In order to examine the relationship between research variables (CL Use, Willingness, Attitude, Advantages, Disadvantages, Evaluation Complexity, Organization Complexity) Pearson correlations were examined, and the findings are presented in Table 11.3.

TABLE 11.3. Pearson Correlations Between Research Variables (n = 86)

Measures	Willingness	Attitude	Advantages	Disadvantages	Evaluation	Organization	CL Use
Willingness							
Attitude	.26*						
Advantages	.29**	.36**					
Disadvantages	-.43***	-.33**	-.56***				
Evaluation	-.21	-.14	-.06	.15			
Organization	-.11	.00	-.13	.14	-.04		
CL Use	.55***	.36**	.27*	-.44***	-.08	-.16	
M	3.87	3.89	4.14	2.89	3.47	2.79	3.16
SD	.56	.62	.54	.66	.81	.65	.82

Table 11.3 presents significant correlations between research variables and the dependent variable of CL use. The correlations are positive for Willingness, Attitude, and Advantages and Disadvantages; hence, the higher the level of Willingness, Attitude, and Advantages and Disadvantages, the greater the CL use.

Significant positive correlations were found between Willingness and Attitude and between Willingness and Advantages. The more the respondents' attitude to CL was positive and the more they saw its advantages, the more willing they were to use it in class. Significant negative correlations were found between Willingness and Disadvantages. The fewer disadvantages faculty members found in CL, the greater their willingness to use it. Significant positive correlations were found between Attitude and Advantages. That is, the more advantages they could see in CL, the more positive their attitude toward it. Significant negative correlations were found between Disadvantages and Advantages, which means that if participants found greater advantages in CL, they would see fewer disadvantages in it. A significant positive correlation was found between Advantages and Evaluation, meaning that the fewer disadvantages of CL seen by staff, the less complexity they found in its evaluation.

To find the contribution of the variables to CL use, a hierarchical regression analysis was conducted. The predictors were entered as four steps: (1) Personal details (Gender, Function, and Program); (2) Attitudes and Conceptions regarding CL (Attitude, Advantages, and Disadvantages); (3) Experience with CL (Organization Complexity and Evaluation Complexity); and (4) Willingness. An interaction between the demographic details and research variables was entered as a fifth step. In the regression analysis, the entry of the first four steps was forced, while that of the interaction was entered according to its significant contribution to the explained variance. The demographic variables were chosen as predictors because the researchers assumed that they were relevant, and an interaction was also found between demographic details and willingness. Table 11.4 presents the standardized and unstandardized coefficients of the hierarchical regression of respondents' CL use.

The regression explained 43% of variance in respondents' use of CL. Of the demographic variables, Gender, Function, and Program contributed significantly by adding 13% to the explained variance in CL use. The beta coefficient of the Function variable was negative and significant. Thus, if the respondent was a pedagogic advisor, he or she would be more likely to integrate more CL into his or her classes.

The second step introduced the Attitude, Advantages, and Disadvantages of CL. Only Disadvantages contributed significantly by adding 10% to the explained variance in CL use. The β coefficient of Disadvantages was negative, indicating that instructors who saw fewer disadvantages were more likely to use CL. The third step introduced the conception of Evaluation Complexity and Organization Complexity of CL, which added only 1% to the explained variance. In effect, Evaluation Complexity and Organization Complexity didn't affect CL use.

TABLE 11.4.   Hierarchical Regression Coefficients of Respondents' CL Use (n =86)

Step	Predictors	B	b	R²	ΔR²
1	Gender	−.30	−.12	.13*	.13*
	Function	−.40	−.25*		
	Program	−.28	−.17		
2	Attitude	.20	.15	.23***	.10*
	Advantages	−.15	−.09		
	Disadvantages	−.38	−.31*		
3	Advantages	−.15	−.09	.24***	.01
	Disadvantages	−.38	−.30*		
	Evaluation	.05	.05		
	Organization	.13	.10		
4	Willingness	.57	.40***	.35***	.11**
5	Function× Willingness	.25	.29	.43***	.08**

*p < .05. **p < .01. ***p < .001.

The fourth step introduced Willingness to use CL, which contributed signifi-cantly by adding 11% to the explained variance in CL use. Based on the change in the β coefficient for this variable between steps three (β=−.31, $p<.05$) and four (β=−.16, $p>.05$), it seems that Willingness was a mediator. Indeed, in the Sobel analysis to test mediation, the result was significant (Z=3.09, $p<.01$).

In the last step, researchers added the interaction between Function × Will-ingness, which added 11% to the explained variance of CL use. To explain the

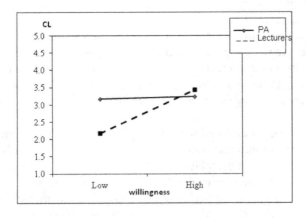

FIGURE 11.1.   Interaction of Function × Willingness

interaction, the regression method of Aiken and West (1991) was used. The inter-action Willingness × Function in lecturers' and pedagogic advisors' use of CL is presented in Figure 11.1.

This figure reveals that there was a significant correlation between Willingness and CL use for lecturers (β=.47, p<.001) but no significant correlation (β=.03, p<.05) for pedagogic advisors. Hence, the Willingness variable influenced CL use only for lecturers but not pedagogic advisors.

DISCUSSION

Collaborative learning is considered to be an important skill in the 21st century; it is therefore crucial that future teachers should experience these practices dur-ing their educational preparation, both as learners and as teachers. Since teachers tend to teach in the way they were taught (Goldstein et al., 2012), such successful experiences may encourage them to implement CL with the pupils in their classes (Harasim, 2012; Shonfeld, 2016). As such, teacher educators should design and implement collaborative learning and thereby create a community of learners (Zygouris-Coe, 2012).

The findings of this study indicate that faculty members in general, according to their own expressed views, tend to apply CL to a moderate or moderately high degree. This statistic is surprising given the low use of CL in teacher-education programs reported by others (Shonfeld & Goldstein, 2014; Schrire, Shonfeld, & Zelkovitz, 2014). One possible way to explain this disparity is the fact that in the current research the source of the data is lecturers' self-reports, which reflects their subjective conceptions in the field of CL. Yet, significant differences were found in relation to this aspect between male and female staff, lecturers, and peda-gogical advisors and those who teach in undergraduate and in graduate programs. Those most likely to use CL are female lecturers, faculty members who teach undergraduate programs, and pedagogical advisors. Similar gender differences have been found in other research, showing that males are more competitive and less cooperative (Molina et al., 2013). However, the small number of males in the sample who were lecturers and not PAs might have caused this difference. The differences that were found amongst the teaching staff could be explained by the dissimilar aims of each program, depending on the level of the degree programs and their different target audiences. For example, the undergraduate program that results in the bachelor's degree is focused on teacher education, which includes exploring various teaching methods. CL may be perceived by these lecturers as a core element of their work. However, the graduate program that is directed to the master's degree is focused on teachers' professional development in a specific domain, and CL may not be perceived as central to this purpose.

The data analysis also points to an interaction between the role of the faculty member and willingness to use CL. The willingness amongst PAs to use CL seems to be more extensive than among lecturers. One possible explanation could be lecturers' perception of their expertise. Most lecturers see their role in teacher-education programs as expanding students' knowledge in the relevant discipline. In contrast, PAs recognize that in addition to their responsibility to present the body of the relevant knowledge in education, their duty is also to instruct student teachers in how to teach. CL is one of the strategies that PAs introduce. The willingness to use CL is already built into their perception of their role in the education program. They may consider using CL as one of the mandatory methods they must expose their students to as part of their job, regardless of their willingness to do so. Thus, the willingness was found to be affecting lecturers' more than PAs' practices.

It is important to explain and present the recent research on CL in teacher-education programs showing that CL increases student engagement (Chen, Gonyea, & Kuh, 2008; Shonfeld, Resta, & Yaniv, 2011), learning motivation, and student knowledge construction (Brett, 2004; Stahl, 2006). The positive correlations that were found between the use of CL and lecturers' knowledge about this strategy and their positive attitudes towards it and willingness to implement it indicate the strong affinity between these variables. That is to say, lecturers' familiarity with the advantages and the disadvantages of CL influenced their attitudes and willingness to use it and actually their readiness to practice it in their classes. These findings can be explained by the model that was proposed by the philosopher De Shalit (2004) in the context of promoting systemic change in environmental policy. He argued that, as in any policy change, attaining an essential change among lecturers' patterns of teaching requires an action in three dimensions: knowledge, awareness, and consciousness. In this instance, the first dimension is the expansion of faculty members' knowledge about CL, which includes their familiarity with the ideas, principles, and practices of the domain. The second dimension is faculty members' awareness of the relevance of CL to their professional challenges and pedagogical rationale. The third dimension is the awareness of the need for practical actions to complete the desirable change and the capability to achieve it.

Since the use of CL varies between low levels to higher levels of collaboration and appears in many different ways (Salmons, 2006), it was important to analyze the participants' descriptions and definitions of CL. The qualitative analysis of faculty members' answers indicates that they are familiar with some practices of CL, especially those that involve the students cooperating in the learning process. Additionally, they grasp the educational rationale for collaborative learning, including the pedagogical benefits of this strategy and the ideas that justify its use. Addressing the theoretical characteristics of the approach, they tend to focus on the advantages of CL without even mentioning the challenges of implementing it. This was supported further by the quantitative results detailed above. This is a kind of naïve approach that highlights the need for more in-depth study and inquiry. Furthermore, the regression results point out the importance of knowing the disadvantages of CL as a predictor of its increased integration in class. Evidence from experienced staff like those in the TEC program has shown that extended use of CL increases the chances of its success (Shonfeld, Hoter, & Ganayem, 2013). Knowing the rules of CL and increasing trust between groups (Shonfeld, Ganayem, Hoter, & Walther, 2015) is very important to reduce the risk of frustration in collaborative learning (Brown, 2013).

IMPLICATIONS

Based on these findings and discussion, perhaps the first step toward promoting the use of CL in an education college should be initiating a program of faculty members' professional development focusing on CL, aimed especially at lecturers, those who teach in the disciplines, and in graduate programs. This program should be carefully planned to address both theoretical and practical knowledge, including the benefits and the challenges of CL. Inter alia, it should cope with some complex issues, such as the evaluation of students' knowledge and proficiencies and the organization and monitoring of learning. Since this study found that the most influential factor on lecturers' use of CL was their willingness to incorporate it in their classes, which was based on their competency and readiness, it is crucial to raise their consciousness of CL (De Shalit, 2004). It would be a good idea to recruit the pedagogical advisors to do this in learning sessions using the fan method: faculty members share their teaching knowledge and best practices in the subject of collaborative learning and teaching with their colleagues.

LIMITATIONS

This research was limited to 86 faculty members in one college in Israel, and, therefore, further research at other colleges in more countries should be undertaken. A comparison between findings will promote a deeper understanding of these results and the ways that teacher-education colleges adapt CL in teaching. It is important to look at the levels of CL (Salmons, 2006), the various definitions of it (Johnson & Johnson, 2013), and the ways faculty members are trained to use CL for the future of the teachers and for the development of new pedagogies (Barkley, Cross, & Major, 2005; Bonk, 2009; Harasim, 2012; Hine, 2011). Thus, this research is a first call to other researchers in this field to collaborate and explore ways of including CL and OCL in teacher-preparation programs.

REFERENCES

Aiken, L. S., & West, S. G. (1991). *Multiple regression: Testing and interpreting interactions*. Newbury Park, CA: Sage.

Barkley, E., Cross, K., & Major, C. (2005). *Collaborative learning techniques: A handbook for college faculty*. San Francisco, CA: Jossey-Bass.

Blau, I. (2011). E-collaboration within, between, and without institutions. *International Journal of E-Collaboration, 7*(4), 22–36.

Bonk, C. J. (2009). *The world is open: How web technology is revolutionizing education*. San Francisco, CA: Jossey-Bass.

Bowen, G. A. (2009). Document analysis as a qualitative research method. *Qualitative Research Journal, 9*(2), 27–40.

Brett, C. (2004). Off-line factors contributing to online engagement. *Technology, Pedagogy and Education, 13*(1), 83–95.

Brody, C., & Davidson, N. (1998). Introduction: Professional development and cooperative learning. In C. Brody & N. Davidson (Eds.), *Professional development for cooperative learning: Issues and approaches* (pp. 3–24). Albany, NY: SUNY.

Brown, F. A. (2008). Collaborative learning in the EAP classroom: Students' perceptions. *ESP World, 17*(7), 1–18.

Chen, P., Gonyea, R., & Kuh, G. (2008). Learning at a distance: Engaged or not? *Innovate, 4*(3). Retrieved from http://www.innovateonline.info/index.php?view=article&id=438&action=article

Davidson, N., & Major, C. H. (2014). Boundary crossings: Cooperative learning, collaborative learning, and problem-based learning. *Journal on Excellence in College Teaching, 25*(3&4), 7–55.

De Shalit, A. (2004). *Red and green: Democracy, justice and environmentalism*. Tel Aviv, Israel: Bavel Publication. [Hebrew].

Denzin, N. K., & Lincoln, Y. S. (2002). *The qualitative inquiry reader*. Thousand Oaks, CA: Sage.

Denzin, N. K., & Lincoln, Y. S. (2008). Introduction: The discipline and practice of qualitative research–Strategies of qualitative inquiry. In N. K. Denzin & Y. S. Lincoln (Eds.), *Strategies of qualitative inquiry,* (pp. 3–7). Thousand Oaks, CA: Sage.

Goldstein, O., Waldman, N., Tesler, B., Shonfeld, M., Forkosh-Baruch, A., Zelkovitz., Z., Mor, N., Heilweil, I., Kozminsky, L., & Zidan, W. (2012). Preparing student teachers for computer-supported teaching and the integration of information and communication technologies in colleges of education: The state in the 2008–2009 academic year. *Dapim, 54*, 20–67 [Hebrew].

Harasim, L. (2012). *Learning theory and online technology: How new technologies are transforming learning opportunities*. New York, NY: Routledge Press.

Hine, P. (Ed.) (2011). *ICT Competency Framework for Teacher* (pp. 3–10). Paris, France: United Nations Educational, Scientific and Cultural Organization.

Hung, D. W. L., & Chen, D. (2001). Situated cognition, Vygotskian thought and learning from the communities of practice perspective: Implications for the design of web-based e-learning. *Educational Media International, 38*(1), 3–12.

Jehn, K., Northcraft, G., & Neale, M. (1999). Why differences make a difference: A field study of diversity, conflict, and performance in workgroups. *Administrative Science Quarterly, 44*, 741–763.

Johnson, D. W., & Johnson, F. P. (2013). *Joining together: Group theory and group skills*. Boston, MA: Pearson.

Kirschner, P. A. (2001). Using integrated electronic environments for collaborative teaching/learning. *Research Dialog in Learning and Instruction, 2*, 1–9.

Kreijns, K., Kirschner, P. A., & Jochems, W., (2002). The sociability of computer-supported collaborative learning environments. *Educational Technology & Society, 5*(1), 8–22.

Melamed, U., Peled, R., Mor, N., Shonfeld, M., Harel, S., & Ben Shimon, I. (2011). *Tohnit Lehasharat Hamihlalot Lmea Ha21. [A Program for Adjusting Teacher Education Colleges to the 21st Century]*. Ministry of Education, Israel.

Molina, J. A., Giménez-Nadal, J. I., Cuesta, J. A., Gracia-Lazaro, C., Moreno, Y., & Sanchez, A. (2013). Gender differences in cooperation: Experimental evidence on high school students. *PLOS One, 8*(12), e83700. Retrieved from http://journals.plos.org/plosone/article?id=10.1371/journal.pone.0083700

Palloff, R. M., & Pratt, K. (2005). *Collaborating online: Learning together in communities*. San Francisco, CA: Jossey-Bass.

Resta, P., & Carrol, T. (2010). *Redefining teacher education for digital-age learners: A call to action*. Austin, TX: The University of Texas.

Resta, P., & Laferrière, T. (2007). Technology in support of collaborative learning. *Educational Psychology Review Journal, 19*(1), 65–83.

Resta, P., Searson, M., Patru, M., Knezek, G., & Voogt, J. (2011). *Building a global community of policy-makers, researchers and teachers to move education systems into the digital age*. Edusummit Report, International summit on Education. Paris: UNESCO.

Resta, P., & Shonfeld, M. (2014). Challenges and strategies in designing trans-national learning team projects in virtual worlds. In M. Searson & M. Ochoa (Eds.), *Proceedings of Society for Information Technology & Teacher Education International Conference 2014* (pp. 403–409). Chesapeake, VA: Association for the Advancement of Computing in Education (AACE).

Salmons, J. E. (2006). *Taxonomy of collaborative e-learning*. Cincinnati, OH: Union Institute & University.

Schrire, S., Shonfeld, M., & Zelkovitz, Z. (2014). *Between pedagogy and technology: The pedagogical affordances of online learning environments*. Internal Report. MOFET Institute, Israel, Tel Aviv.

Shonfeld, M. (2017). Collaboration in learning. In O. Goldsten & U. Melamed (Eds.), *Pedagogy at the Digital Age* (pp.187–216). Tel Aviv: Kalil, Mofet.

Shonfeld, M., Ganayem, A., Hoter, E., & Walther, J. B. (2015). Zvatim Mekuvanim, Emun Vedeot Kdumot. [Online teams, trust and prejudice]. *Sugyout Bahevra Haisraelit, 19*, 7–40.

Shonfeld, M., Ganayem, A., Hoter, E. & Walter, J. B. (2015). Online teams, trust and prejudice. *Issues in Israeli Society, 19*, 40-7. [Hebrew]

Shonfeld, M., & Goldstein, O. (2014). ICT Integration in teaching and teacher training by faculty members in Israeli colleges of education, 2013. In M. Searson & M. Ochoa (Eds.), *Proceedings of Society for Information Technology & Teacher Education International Conference 2014* (pp. 2655–2660). Chesapeake, VA: Association for the Advancement of Computing in Education (AACE).

Shonfeld, M., Hoter, E., & Ganayem, A. (2013). Connecting cultures in conflict through ICT in Israel. In R. S. P. Austin & W. J. Hunter (Eds.), *Online learning and community cohesion: Linking schools* (pp. 42–58). New York, NY: Routledge Taylor & Francis Group.

Shonfeld, M., Resta, P., & Yaniv, H. (2011). Engagement and social presence in a virtual world (Second Life) learning environment. In M. Koehler & P. Mishra (Eds.), *Proceedings of Society for Information Technology & Teacher Education International Conference 2011* (pp. 740–745). Chesapeake, VA: Association for the Advancement of Computing in Education (AACE).

Slavin, R. E. (2010). Instruction based on cooperative learning. In R. Mayer (Ed.), *Handbook of research on learning and instruction* (pp. 344–360). London, UK: Taylor and Francis.

Spears, L. R. (2012). *Social presence, social interaction, collaborative learning, and satisfaction in online and face-to-face courses.* (Doctoral dissertation). University of Iowa. Retrieved from http://lib.dr.iastate.edu/cgi/viewcontent.cgi?article=3983&context=etd

Stahl, G. (2006). *Group cognition: Computer support for building collaborative knowledge.* Cambridge, MA: MIT Press.

Strauss, A., & Corbin, J. M., (Eds.) (1997). *Grounded theory in practice.* Thousand Oaks, CA: SAGE.

Tsuei, M. (2011). Development of a peer-assisted learning strategy in computer-supported collaborative learning environments for elementary school students. *British Journal of Educational Technology, 42*(2), 214–232.

Vygotsky, L. S. (1978). *Mind in society: The development of higher psychological processes.* Cambridge, MA: Harvard University Press.

Walther, J. B., & Bunz, U. (2005). The rules of virtual groups: Trust, liking, and performance in computer-mediated communication. *Journal of Communication, 55*(4), 828–846.

Walther, J. B., Hoter, E., Ganayem, A., & Shonfeld, M. (2015). Computer-mediated communication and the reduction of prejudice: A controlled longitudinal field experiment among Jews and Arabs in Israel. *Computers in Human Behavior, 52*, 550–558.

Warschauer, M., & Grimes, D. (2007). Audience, authorship, and artifact: The emergent semiotics of Web 2.0. *Annual Review of Applied Linguistics, 27*, 1–23.

Weinberger, Y. (2017). Empathy as a virtuous pedagogy. In N. Aloni & L. Weintrob (Eds.), *Beyond bystanders: Educational leadership for a humane culture in a globalizing reality* (pp. 191–204). Rotterdam: Sense Publishers.

Weinberger, Y. (2018). Strategies for effecting system-wide pedagogical change: Identifying and addressing the gap between organizational and pedagogical implementation. *Professional Development in Education, 44*(1), 47–61. doi:10.1080/19415257.2017.1345776.

Yogev, E., & Michaeli, N. (2009). Teachers as involved intellectuals in society and the community: A democratic civic education model. *International Journal of Learning, 16*(2), 129–142.

Zygouris-Coe, V. (2012). Collaborative learning in an online teacher education course: Lessons learned. *ICICTE 2012 Proceedings, 332–342.*

CHAPTER 12

CONNECTING UNIVERSITY STUDENTS FROM ISRAEL AND GERMANY

Claudia Finkbeiner, Miriam Muchow,
Einat Rozner, and Miri Shonfeld

This chapter describes a collaboration project between graduate students from Israel and Germany which used mobile devices such as laptops, tablets, and mobile phones to work together. The chapter reports on the advantages and challenges that evolved during the online collaboration and shares lessons learned. The online cooperation between the two university campuses in Tel Aviv and Kassel took place in two cycles in the winter terms of 2013/2014 and 2014/2015. Over each of the two study cycles, diverse student groups were formed on each occasion. Each group consisted of three students from the campus in Tel Aviv and three from Kassel. All students on the Tel Aviv campus were enrolled in a technology-in-education program. The majority of the students on the Kassel campus were enrolled in teacher-education programs, some in an English and American language and business program preparing them for the workplace. Specific online environments were created to allow the groups productive and creative work on the topic of distance learning. The highlight of the online cooperation was a video

Collaborative Online Learning in a Global World, pages 175–194.
Copyright © 2019 by Information Age Publishing
All rights of reproduction in any form reserved.

conference which was held at the end of the project. English was used as a *lingua franca* to allow group communication.

The collaboration brought together a diverse group of Jewish and Arab students from the Kibbutzim College in Tel Aviv, Israel, as well as a diverse group of students from the University of Kassel, Germany, to form an academic online community. The instructors intentionally decided to create a transnational, joint cyberspace community that represented heterogeneity within homogeneity. On the one hand, homogeneity resulted from all participants being university students either in education or business programs. On the other hand, heterogeneity was an underlying paradigm because a diverse group of students was included on both campuses. This was created by an agreed-upon common academic frame and goal before the work started.

As exemplified in the Learner-Moderator-Researcher Plus (LMR Plus) Model (Finkbeiner, 2001, 2004) all participants who were involved—students, tutors, and instructors—adopted interchangeable roles of learners, moderators, and researchers. The joint university class learned about the basic principles of distance learning in the plenary sessions and focused on different aspects of the topic within the group sessions, the results of which were presented to the whole class at the end in the video conference. These aspects included topics such as lifelong learning, global learning, intercultural learning, etc. The interaction was based on the TEC (Technology, Education, and Cultural diversity) model (Shonfeld, Hoter, & Ganayem, 2013), where collaboration and communication happened gradually, starting from textual communication, continuing with audio communication, and concluding with visual communication. The groups' products were based on their collaborative learning and included a module for teaching and learning regarding their subject.

This research analyzes the communication and the results of the tasks of two systematically selected groups of the second cycle. It focuses on the language used during the project. Furthermore, attention is paid to the professional versus personal level of communication. A particular focus is on the personal contact and the quality of group results (e.g., group wiki page). It is hypothesized that the quality and quantity of the group contact has an effect on the quality of the group work and group result.

THEORETICAL BACKGROUND

Learning in the 21st century is rapidly changing and has turned into a lifelong necessity (Finkbeiner, 2006). Two influences, technology and social media, have transformed personal as well as business communication (Finkbeiner & Knierim, 2008). The production of information in business, science, and the arts among others occurs in collaborative forums and has an influence on education. The distance between continents, people, and cultures seems to be "shortened," and numerous teams work together internationally (Shonfeld, 2017). Despite this, distance between cultures and groups can also be increased through the use of technological devices and social media (Finkbeiner & White, 2017) and as a result they separate people. Due to the nature of modern technology, online information processes are fast and often unpredictable. Collaboration is part of 21st-century skills and the basis for survival and development (Harasim, 2012). Therefore, it is important to supply learners with collaborative skills together with critical literacy skills (Finkbeiner, 2004; 2006). Students who have experienced collaborative learning themselves and have faced challenges will more carefully consider each single step in planning collaborative projects (Capdeferro & Romero, 2012).

Collaborative Learning

Johnson and Johnson (1987) define collaboration as work that is performed together by group members in order to achieve a common goal, where all the individuals in the group expect results that will be beneficial to every member of the group. Finkbeiner (2003) defines the term collaboration together with cooperation as complementary: "the two terms highlight[ed] two important ends of group dynamics: a) cooperation focuses on the 'opus,' the product, and b) collaboration focuses on the 'labor,' the process" (p. 15).

It is possible to apply the definition of collaboration to online environments, where the activities of sharing knowledge and collaborative construction of knowledge are enabled through the connections that the Internet provides (Dalsgaard, 2008; Finkbeiner & Knierim, 2008). More recently, collaborative learning has been integrated into higher education in the hope of improving pedagogic effectiveness (Wang, Dannenhoffer, Davidson, & Spector, 2005). However, even though the underlying policy in quite a few institutions is to encourage lecturers to develop expertise in teamwork through collaboration with their colleagues, they often are not given the appropriate tools and skills that would enable them to have the positive experiences of the process of working in a group (Murray & Lonne, 2006). Walther and Bunz (2005) claim that online students have to follow a set of rules in order to succeed at working in groups. The rules include the following: *Start immediately; Communicate frequently; Overtly acknowledge and feed back to one another's messages; Be clear about expectations and progress; Multitask organizing work and the generation of substantive content simultaneously; and Stick to deadlines.* Those rules were tested in intercultural groups and were found to be factors that increased the trust in the group (Shonfeld, Ganayem, Hoter, & Walther, 2015). The project described here relates to the literature claims and suggestions by enabling participants to develop expertise in an online learning environment specifically designed for this task.

The LMR Plus Model

The implementation of the joint online-learning class followed the LMR Plus approach (Finkbeiner, 2001, 2004). The LMR Plus model can be implemented in the university as well as the school or business level. In this project, it targeted prospective teachers who were studying English as a foreign or second language, technology in education, or English language and culture business M.A. programs.

The term LMR Plus can be explained as follows (Finkbeiner, 2001, 2004): L stands for learner, M stands for moderator (or teacher), R stands for researcher, and "Plus" refers to the use of a foreign language as a means for classroom communication. The LMR Plus Model draws on Vygotsky's theory of social interaction (1982) as well as on Cohen's Model of Complex Instruction (Cohen & Lotan, 1997). It adopts Vygotsky's underlying paradigm that higher-mental-order processes are socially or culturally mediated. This means that cooperation and collaboration are not only assets but non-questionable pre-conditions for effective, deep-level learning (Finkbeiner, 2006). Higher-order thinking as proposed by Vygotsky has also been integrated into Cohen's Model of Complex Instruction (Cohen & Lotan, 1997). Important factors are diversity and group work (see below), with a special focus on teaching strategies and skill building (Cohen, 1994).

In the LMR-Plus classroom (Finkbeiner, 2001, 2004), cooperation and collaboration take place between all participants in their roles as teachers, tutors, and learners, as well as all of them in their roles as researchers. Roles are considered to be constantly changing as well as interchangeable. As the LMR-Plus relies on different competencies in the different stages, the students must learn and acquire these competencies throughout the process. The LMR-Plus model supports the idea of lifelong learning. The change in the role allocation can be challenging in the beginning, but in the long run, it will lead to a beneficial learning environment for students as well as teachers. In the online learning environment described below, students are given learning opportunities for each role.

The TEC Model

The TEC Model (Shonfeld, Hoter, & Ganayem, 2013) is basically a model for trust building in online collaborative environments. Educators implement the model by forming small teams from diverse cultures, who progress from online communication (written, oral, video) to face-to-face interaction, in order to gradually build trust between participants (Hoter, Shonfeld, & Ganayem, 2009). The model works through online collaboration via joint assignments over an extended period of time. Team members get to know each other, develop mutual respect, eliminate stigmas, and reduce mutual prejudices. The TEC model was derived from the contact hypothesis (Allport, 1954; Pettigrew & Tropp, 2000), collaboration theories (Johnson & Johnson 1987; Slavin, 1990), and models of online collaborative learning (Austin, 2006; Salomon, 2011).

Similar to the LMR-Plus model and the TEC models, Cohen (1994) claimed that efficient group work requires small groups so every student has the possibility to participate on required tasks. More importantly, group work means that the students work mostly on their own without the immediate help of the teacher. However, the teachers are still important moderators and often may indirectly help by eliciting students' learning strategies to develop their autonomy in facilitating cognitive as well as meta-cognitive learning processes (Finkbeiner et al., 2012).

Students work autonomously on the tasks that are suggested by the teachers, negotiated and adapted by the class, and individually chosen by the groups. The groups are held accountable for the final products of their group work. The students are free to plan and choose a learning path which seems to be most suitable to achieve their final goal. Cohen suggests that students should take their own lead on solving a task without the constant supervision of the teacher. The learning process requires that the students work together; give each group member the chance to verbalize his or her opinions, criticism, and suggestions; and talk about important aspects of the collective task as well as individual tasks in order to put together the final product. Cohen recommends groups of four or five students to reduce the risk of individual students being left out, because the number of free riders has the potential to increase if the group number is too high. The best number has to be found out individually for each class.

Online and Distance Collaborative Learning

Distance learning is an educational means that becomes more and more popular as people wish to expand their knowledge and skills but, for example, a) might not want to or cannot leave their jobs, b) are tied to the home for personal reasons but still do not want to opt out with respect to education and training, or c) work or study at one location but would like to cooperate with participants elsewhere. Distance learning is becoming an integral part of school and university education across the world.

The project discussed here required distance learning as a necessity to enable cooperation between university students from Germany and Israel who would otherwise not have been able to meet. Face-to-face meetings were no option due to the long distance as well as curricular and funding constraints. Distance learning therefore allowed learning between participants who would not otherwise have had the chance to cooperate with each other.

According to Garrison and Cleveland-Innes (2005), important aspects of online learning are the physical presence at each end and the participation of the learners. However, ideal interaction in online learning does not simply include social interaction and good communication between the participants but also "various combinations of interaction among content, teachers, and students" (p. 134). As online learning is used as a means of education, Garrison and Cleveland-Innes state that the quality of the interaction has to be improved: "A community of inquiry is the integration of cognitive, social, and teaching presence" (p. 134). They combine high qualitative interaction with the standards of higher education. Obviously, the deep approach is desirable for higher education in general and in online learning.

The field of research on collaborative online communities is continually expanding in an attempt to understand the dynamic processes that occur in these learning environments (Brindley, Blaschke, & Walti, 2009; Watson, 2008). In addition, many researchers see the level of interaction between the participants in distance learning as a means of predicting the success of the experience of distance learning (Brindley et al., 2009) and suggest that the experiences of students who do not actively participate in the course are much more negative than students who succeed in creating interaction and collaboration (Nummenmaa & Nummenmaa, 2008; Wadmany, Rimor, & Rozner, 2011). It has to be noted that it is important to encourage student discussion and student-to-student interaction to achieve higher-order thinking in the group (Finkbeiner, 2004; Schrire, 2004; Vygotsky, 1982).

Description of the Project and Time Frame

The online collaborative-learning project was organized as a series of joint seminars for students at the Kibbutzim College, Israel, and at the University of Kassel, Germany. The classes were announced in both online university calendars with the title "Research in Distance Learning: Forming a Cyberspace Community between students in Tel Aviv and students in Kassel" (Figure 12.1). The classes were highly attractive: the demand was so high that more than double the number of participants who could finally be admitted to the courses registered. Therefore, a criteria-based selection of participants created a sample of n=60; 30 students were selected at each university for the joint classroom. Most were in teacher-education programs; a few were in business programs. All were advanced students. The classes were conducted as intensive, blended-learning classes, and they consisted of a preparatory face-to-face phase on each campus followed by an intense virtual transnational collaboration phase of eight weeks. The language of instruction during the online collaboration was English as *lingua franca*.

FIGURE 12.1.   Yin and Yang Welcome Flags

The first run served as a pilot. For the second run, a comparable sample of university students was drawn. In this chapter, the focus will be on the second run. Within the topic of distance learning, 10 sub-topics were suggested by the instructors to the students and discussed with them at the beginning in the face-to-face sessions before the virtual phase. The topics were mobile technology, lifelong learning, global learning, online collaborative learning, intercultural learning, history of media, digital equity, MOOCs, teachers' role in online learning, and evaluation in online collaborative learning. The 10 topics represented the work frame for 10 groups. As suggested by Cohen (1994), the instructors decided to give the students as much choice as possible and, therefore, did not assign students to each topic. Rather, the students chose and registered for a group topic they were interested in. Within a given time frame, all students had to self-enroll in one of the 10 groups. The principle was *first come, first served*. Each group consisted of six members: three from the campus in Germany and three from the campus in Israel.

ONLINE LEARNING ENVIRONMENT AND GROUP TASKS

All students were introduced to the specific issues connected to the Blackboard-Online Platforms at the beginning and—when necessary for task completion—new information was given in the follow-up sessions. There was tutorial help and tech support throughout the course.

As soon as their accounts were activated, the participants signed up for a topic/group by creating a blog entry with the name of their university in the title and four words to describe themselves in the body of the message. The project was tightly timed, and time management for each assignment was important (see Table 12.1: Online Collaboration–Joint Class Tel Aviv-Kassel, Winter 2014/2015). The seminar consisted of the following activities:

Four-Word Activity (Finkbeiner & Koplin, 2002): This is a group-forming and warm-up activity: getting to know each other in the group by writing four words about oneself. These words can be nouns, adjectives, or verbs. After all group members have individually entered their four words, the participants read the four words, find similarities and differences, ask each other questions, and discuss the entries.

Tech ABCs: This activity is an adaptation of the ABCs of Cultural Understanding and Communication (Finkbeiner & Lazar, 2015; Schmidt & Finkbeiner, 2006). Each group member creates an online page with text and pictures on his or her memories with respect to technology. The group members then ask each other questions on their tech memories. In the third step, the whole group meets and creates a Group Venn Diagram to find out about the similarities and differences in their memories.

Article Search on Group Topic: Each student has to search for an article on the group topic, post it into the group article forum, and write a short introduction about the article. After this process is completed, there are as many articles in each group forum posted as group participants. In this case, there were six articles per group.

Group Discussion of Article Content: The whole group discusses the articles that have been posted into their forum to find a structure and important content for their WIKI page.

WIKI Page Construction: The students create a WIKI page with online activities on their topic. Ten WIKI pages on the 10 topics were created in the study presented here.

WIKI Page Evaluation: Every participant evaluates two WIKI pages.

Preparation of Group Mini Presentation for Video Conference: The group members prepare the structure for their final mini-presentation for the video conference.

Video conference: Final, large, joint conference with group mini-presentations, discussion, and evaluation. Each group has five minutes to present their topic and reflect on the teamwork inside the group.

Feedback Week: In the week after the final video conference, the students write feedback about the course into the feedback section.

Parallel to the official class sessions, groups were expected to meet synchronously at least once a week as well as to contribute asynchronously at least twice per week on workdays.

TABLE 12.1. Online Collaboration Activities

Online Collaboration: Joint Class Tel Aviv-Kassel, winter 2014/2015				
Week	**Activity**	**Group/Individual**	**Product**	**Description of Activity**
Week 1	Getting to know each other	Individual and Group	Four words	The students post four words that describe themselves (Finkbeiner & Koplin, 2002) into their group blog and respond to their group members' entries.
Week 2	Getting to know each other Technology Memory	Individual and Group Individual	Four words: final comments Tech ABCs on Tech Memory	The students write an autobiography with regard to memories about technology (adapted after the ABCs: Schmidt & Finkbeiner, 2006; Finkbeiner & Lazar, 2015).
Week 3	Venn Diagram	Group	Venn Diagram	The students ask each other questions; they create a Venn Diagram filling in similarities and differences of their tech-memories (Edwards, 2004; Schmidt & Finkbeiner, 2006).
Week 4	Articles	Individual	Articles on group topic	Every student posts an article with regard to the group's topic into the forum and writes a short introduction about the article
Week 5	Articles	Individual, Group	Articles	The students discuss the articles that were posted into their forum to find a structure and content for their WIKI page.
Week 6	WIKI - Online Activity	Group	Online Activity	The students create an online activity on their WIKI page for the other participants of the course
Week 7	WIKI	Group	WIKI Page	The students elaborate on their WIKI pages
Week 8	Evaluate WIKIs Prepare and conduct video conference	Plenary, Individual Group	Evaluation Presentations for video conference	Every participant evaluates two WIKI pages The group members prepare and implement the structure for their presentation during the video conference

Instructor Collaboration: The instructors met weekly over a period of eight months. This included a time period of four months before the project in order to systematically plan the joint class, eight weeks during the project for constant feedback and adjustment, and eight weeks after the project for course evaluation and further planning. Each meeting was one-and-a-half hours long. Minutes were taken at each meeting. The content was, for example:

- Learning about each other's university and teacher-education programs
- Finding a valid core curriculum which applied to both campuses
- Defining the topics and sub-topics
- Writing the online university-calendar course announcement
- Time management, considering cultural differences (Shabbat, Sunday) with respect to, for example, religious holidays, time differences, etc.
- Learning about differences in cultural work script
- Defining group selection and group management
- Establishing the joint syllabus
- Constructing the pre- and post-questionnaire
- Preparing qualitative data collection
- Evaluation of the class, group collaboration, tasks, etc.

Google Docs was used for the common curriculum development. The instructors discussed all details of the content. They were involved in developing and testing all activities prior to class implementation; these tests were used as a priori analyses. Furthermore, a three-day-long, face-to-face meeting was organized between the first and second run in May 2014.

Significance of the Study

The cooperation between Germany and Israel was important. The political and diplomatic cooperation between both countries started 50 years earlier, after Adenauer and Ben Gurion had met in New York on neutral ground to discuss German support for Israel. Soon after the meeting, young-adult cooperation within the framework of "Aktion Sühnezeichen," a peace program founded in Germany in 1958, began. Since then, several diplomatic cooperation projects had been launched. Despite this, cooperation between university students from each country is still rare. It is important to mention that the university groups on both campuses were diverse, representing today's university student diversity, including Arab and Jewish students in Tel Aviv, and Turkish-German, American, Russian, and German students in Kassel. All participants shared book and media knowledge but no personal knowledge with their partners. One of the tutors on the Kassel campus had lived and worked in Israel for a year under the auspices of "Aktion Sühnezeichen." In this program, young people from Germany go to Israel for a year and work voluntarily with people in need. The tutor's information was used in all courses as it turned out to be highly valuable.

Research Questions

1. *What kind of language is used in the group communication?*

   To answer this research question, the entire online communication throughout the project of two selected focus groups was examined, including blog and forum entries as well as comments made during the task completion. Special attention was paid to turn taking, quantity and quality of the entries, depth of the communication, and personal (emotional) versus non-personal language use.

2. *Do the quantity and quality of the group communication have an effect on the outcome of the tasks and group results?*

   To answer this research question, process and product data had to be triangulated. Therefore, the quality and quantity of the group communication were related to the task outcome.

METHOD

Participants

The participants in the project were n = 60 advanced students from the two universities, 30 students from each, one located in Israel and the other in Germany. Most of the students were in teacher-education programs. All students from the Kassel campus were enrolled in English-as-a-foreign-language teacher-education or business programs. All students from the Kibbutzim College of Education campus were enrolled in a graduate program in technology in education. All students were able to use English as a *lingua franca* in academic discourse. All groups therefore had language and tech expertise. Of the 10 groups, two were systematically chosen for the research analysis (n=10 students). This was due to the limited resources in a non-funded and voluntary project.

Instruments and Procedure

First, the entire text corpus of all entries for all 10 groups was transferred from the platform into a codable work version for each blog and forum as well as for each task. The text corpus was examined with respect to conspicuous phenomena and categories that would emerge. It was striking that some groups seemed to have had an active communication across time, whereas others did not. Following the "extreme group" approach, two opposing groups (a successful group with good results and a non-successful group with poor results) with respect to group activity and group results were chosen for comparison. It was assumed that filtering out the most obvious differences could help explain probable reasons for the group results.

The following criteria were used to allow systematic selection of the two groups: quantity and quality of entries. The frequency of the blog and forum entries was considered significant for the communication between the group members. The number of entries in the blog and forum show how much the group members communicated with each other. Also, it is important to look at the time that passed between an entry and its direct answer by another group member. This is distinctive, as it shows how often the students logged into the Moodle course and therefore how committed they were to the group.

First, a quantitative approach was chosen via a count of the number of entries per time and date. This was complemented by a qualitative content analysis. Categories were formed both top down drawing on theories, such as the LMR-Plus model (Finkbeiner, 2001, 2004), the Group Work by Cohen (1994), the TEC Model (Shonfeld et al., 2013) as well as the Content Analysis by Krippendorff (1980). The focus of the analysis was on turn taking, personal vs. non-personal communication style, reference to what was said before, etc.

Findings on Research Question One: Language Used in the Two Focus Groups

Research Question One addresses the kind of language that is used in both focus groups throughout the project.

Turn Taking

The usage of turn taking is one criterion to answer Question One. Turn taking is a phenomenon which describes how communication is organized and when contributions alter between participants. A special focus here is on whether participants refer back to other group members' previous messages once turn taking has happened.

Group A used turn taking continuously. As a matter of fact, turn taking was used each time two group members engaged in a conversation. Most of the posts were followed by comments or questions of other group members, which were answered or commented on in return. Hence, all conversations show turn taking.

The turn taking in Group B, however, was not as successful. In fact, it rarely occurred. First, there were hardly any questions addressed to the other group members. Second, the few questions posed were not answered. Third, only a few rare posts resulted in a conversation. Most of the posts remained without comments, which excludes the possibility of turn taking.

Frequency of Posts and Reaction Time

Another aspect was the frequency of the posts. Post frequency can be taken as an implied measurement of active or passive participation of the group members. The group members of group A were frequently online and active. A closer look at the entries of Group A members reveals that within the group some members were more active than others. Nevertheless, there was a significant difference in reaction time between posts of even the slowest group member in Group A and the slowest one in Group B. In Group A, the longest reaction time of one member was four days; in Group B, it was 19 days!

The average reaction time of a group member in Group A did not exceed two days. For Group B, the reaction time was a lot longer. It was difficult to determine the exact length as there were only irregular comments in the blog over a given time period and entries were not regularly posted during the whole project.

Language Proficiency and Negotiation Of Meaning

The language-proficiency level varied in both groups A and B. In group A, one student apparently had severe language problems in contrast to her partner. However, the analysis shows that the student with the poorer language proficiency used adequate compensation methods to get her point across, for example, in the *Tech ABCs*. She actively used the tech media and uploaded pictures and quotes, for example. The verbal data analysis shows that despite the obvious differences in the level of language proficiency of the two partners in focus in Group A, they worked together frequently and on a high level. The strong language-proficiency student included and actively addressed the student with the poorer proficiency in her posts and, therefore, made her a fully recognized part of the cooperation without forcing her to actively expose a particular language struggle. There was no situation which was face-threatening; owing to the politeness in the group, the self-image of each participant was not challenged.

In Group B, this kind of cooperative attitude of reaching out to the other and adopting group responsibility was not observed. Generally speaking, the communication in Group B was a lot more difficult to assess. Avoidance strategies were used, which resulted in fewer written texts produced in comparison to the number produced in Group A.

Depth of Communication and Personal vs. Non-Personal Language Use

The final aspect of Research Question One was to explore the depth of the communication among the group members. One focus was the issue of a personal or non-personal, even superficial, communication level. With respect to the discourse among group members of Group A, it is safe to say that all of them communicated not only on a professional but also on a personal level. Only one student seemed a bit reluctant at the beginning.

The personal group and relationship building began right at the beginning with the first task, the "Four words about your own self activity" (Finkbeiner & Koplin, 2002). This activity led to many discussions and conversations about the four words the students had entered to describe themselves, and through this process, a lot of personal information was exchanged, triggered by the four words, as shown in Figure 12.2. Additionally, it became apparent in the discourse that the members of Group A had become eager to meet each other face-to-face as they tried to find time slots and dates to meet via Blackboard or Skype several times, even though they had already had a short face-to-face session.

FIGURE 12.2   First activity in the group's blog

Furthermore, the group members at the Tel Aviv campus were highly committed to creating a conflict-free environment. For example, the discourse analysis shows that they expressed worries but no reproach when their partners had not instantaneously reacted, getting back to them and asking if something was wrong. This kind of conversation can be considered an interpersonal meta-communication, which does not focus on content but on the interpersonal relationship. It seems to form a necessary pre-condition to enable content discussion later on, particularly when misunderstandings or conflicts occur. These misunderstandings can be caused by silence or slow response time.

There is evidence in the data that the discourse in Group A solely focused on the personal relationship between the group members when such a conflict occurred. In that case, work completion was not mentioned, and one can assume it was to avoid additional pressure. Also, the appreciation of the individual work of each group member was highly valued as there were several appreciative comments praising others individually. Moreover, the final posts and comments on the posts showed gratitude for the cooperation and the personal relationships of the group members, highlighted by statements such as "You are wonderful." One can conclude that the Group A members developed personal relationships from pretty early on, which became deeper during the course of the project.

In contrast to Group A, the depth of conversation in Group B remained rather superficial. The data show that conversations and discussions hardly evolved. Without discourse, it is not possible to build group and personal relationships in an online environment. The only conversations that developed in Group B occurred in the blog. However, there were no comments on posts in the forum; hence, no conversation ensued in the forum. Additionally, the conversation in the blog can barely be classified as conversation. Most of the entries were single comments or questions by different group members. Most of the time, the original writer of the post remained silent throughout the comments, and most questions were not answered or elaborated upon. Only one group member put effort into forming a conversation as she offered further information about herself without being asked for by her group members. However, her efforts did not lead to further depth in the group conversation. Hence, the members of Group B did not succeed in creating any personal relationships.

Findings on Research Question Two: Group Communication and Task Results

To answer Research Question Two, the quantity and quality of the group communication have to be related to the outcome of the tasks and group results. The goal was to find evidence of whether the group communication had an effect on the task execution.

As assessed during the analysis and reported in the results on Research Question One, the analysis of the verbal data of Group A showed that all its members practiced a successful and personal communication throughout the project. The task analysis shows that all tasks were completed successfully, from the introduction by the four words, to the tech memories (adapted from Schmidt & Finkbeiner, 2006), to the Venn diagram (Schmidt & Finkbeiner, 2006), to the choice and discussion of the chosen articles, and finally to the construction of the final wiki page.

However, there were some minor obstacles in the completion of some tasks. For example, one text on tech memory of one group member was a bit short due to her language problems, and the article the same member had posted had a questionable source. This individual weakness of this group member did not however

Group A
Global Learning

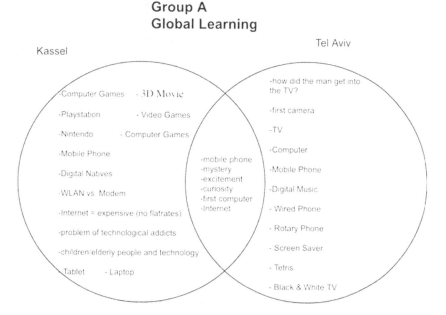

FIGURE 12.3.   Venn Diagram of Group A

disrupt the cohesion and success of Group A. All members of Group A completed all tasks as they used mutual support and discourse structures. The Venn diagram, as we can see in Figure 12.3, was nearly completed and only missed minor aspects of the Tech ABCS on tech memories.

The final wiki page was the most important product of the group collaboration. The wiki page of Group A was well-structured, neatly arranged, creative, and informative. It contained different media, such as texts, pictures, videos, and a quiz. The wiki was a result of the cooperation of the whole group, as can be seen by analyzing the discussions in the forum entries concerning the wiki construction. Every group member had a specific task to complete. The group members helped each other with problems or challenges. Hence, the wiki page turned out to be an overall success. This was also approved by the final student evaluation by all participants (n=60).

The group members of Group B did not fulfill all tasks. The first activity, "Four words about your own self," was misunderstood by two members. This was not clarified among the group members. Therefore, this activity did not really work as a springboard into a conversation about each other. Also, the *Tech ABCs* on tech memories were not successfully completed by two members, as only one short aspect was mentioned. The Venn diagram was incomplete. The articles of all group members but one were not adequate with respect to the task requirement. Additionally, one member did not post any article at all. The final group product, the wiki page, was not structured well, was inconsistent, and was not constructed by all group members but only by a few who obviously struggled. Despite these shortcomings, the online activity of Group B turned out to be surprisingly creative. Nevertheless, the wiki page of group B was insufficient.

Hence, with regard to the comparison of the two focus groups, who were comparable with respect to language and tech expertise, it becomes apparent that the group whose members communicated well and also did so on a personal level (Group A) had more success in completing the tasks than the group whose members barely communicated with each other (Group B).

DISCUSSION

The results and comparison of the two focus groups that were analyzed show that members of Group A not only communicated well and but also produced good group results. Their wiki page was highly convincing, while members of Group B struggled from the beginning. They had a hard time communicating with each other, and their group results, for example, the wiki page, left a lot of room for improvement.

Therefore, at first glance, one could conclude that there is a direct connection between the group communication and the final results. Well-functioning communication should be a predictor of a successful group result. However, this would be an over-simplification, and there are a few research limitations.

First, even though the results yield important and valuable hints with respect to a probable connection of quality and quantity of the group communication and quality of the group result, these research results cannot be generalized as only two groups out of 10 were analyzed.

Furthermore, we have not investigated the factors that could help in finding an explanation for group involvement and commitment versus group distance. One could assume that the members of Group B were not motivated to participate, perhaps as a result of external circumstances. This will have to be investigated further. In any case, a direct intervention should take place while the project is proceeding.

Despite the striking differences between Group A and Group B, both groups had members who participated more than others. One member of Group A was more reluctant to participate and less active than the others. However, as the majority of the group members conducted a well-functioning communication and engaged her personally, the results were successful. In this case, the less-involved member benefited from a highly supportive group.

The same applies to Group B but the other way around. One member was really active, posting more comments than all the others combined. However, the active group member's increased participation could not compensate for the others. Furthermore, the one active group member was not successful in improving the group's results. Nevertheless, it is apparent that there were members of both groups who significantly altered the overall pattern of participation.

One can conclude that when the majority of the group members exhibit strong communication skills, a less-active member can be integrated and will not disrupt the overall result. In cases where the majority of the group members exhibit weak or less-active communications skills, an individually active member alone will most likely not succeed in producing a good task outcome.

In the case of these two groups, communication played an important role in the outcome of the final product. Obviously, language awareness comes into play and needs to become an integral part next to technology and content matters (Finkbeiner & Svalberg, 2012).

Furthermore, the quality of communication inside a group definitely needs to be further investigated, and group cohesion strategies, such as turn taking and frequency as well as reference to what was said before, ought to be taught. In addition, it may also be necessary to check whether a positive attitude toward online learning is related to high level of participation (Wadmany, Rimor, & Rozner, 2011). Resta and Shonfeld (2014) point out that in order to succeed in collaborative learning, time should be provided for students to become familiar with the virtual environment before they engage in a time-constrained, collaborative-learning task. However, as the time of the reported study was limited, the cooperation between the group members had begun right from the start, which is why the students were asked to respond to all blog entries of their group and get to know each other during the first week. The students had a big workload and felt time pressure in their task completion. In future projects, more time ought to be allocated at the beginning of the project for group members to get to know each other to create group cohesion. If all participants have the feeling that it is worthwhile to engage in group conversation as others are interested in what one has to say, then the quality of the group communication will change over time, as will the quality of the completed task.

Walther and Bunz (2005) suggest encouraging online students to convert socioemotional and task-oriented messages into written, verbal form, and to accelerate the rate of message exchanges to compensate for the relatively slower speed of information exchange via online communication. The set of rules they suggest seems to be part of the behaviors that made Group A's results better than Group B's. Those rules were tested also in other groups and were found to increase the trust in the group (Shonfeld, Ganayem, Hoter, & Walther, 2015). It is important to teach the students and prepare them to work in groups (Finkbeiner, 2004; Shonfeld, 2017).

CONCLUSION

Several lessons were learned from the project. No matter whether the group cooperation was at its best or could be improved, all students stated in their final evaluations that they had really learned a lot about distance learning from their involvement in it. A lot of them could imagine implementing such an online environment in the future for their own students.

There were quite a few unexpected challenges, for example, how differently Shabbat and Sunday were considered as well as the role of family across the two diverse campuses. This had a strong impact on the group schedule.

The video conference was considered the absolute highlight, as students could present themselves as a group to the others and also explain their group results. This is why in the next project video conferences will be implemented at an earlier point in the project and will be held more often. Furthermore, more time will be allocated to direct, synchronous group cooperation.

The majority of the students stated in the final evaluation that they had participated in the class to learn about distance learning and that these expectations were absolutely fulfilled. Quite a few added that they had not expected to meet such wonderful people and even build friendships.

This is why we are already preparing for our third cycle, which will give us new insights. The one thing we learned throughout the project is that without strong commitment on each side, no matter whether we look at students, tutors, or instructors aligned with good IT support, such a project might not work. However, if commitment and support are given, the project will be a win-win, as it is not only about distance learning but also learning about other cultures and languages. With our project, we succeeded in mirroring the macro-cosmos of the world in the micro-cosmos of our classrooms.

REFERENCES

Allport, G. W. (1954). *The nature of prejudice*. Cambridge, MA: Addison-Wesley.

Brindley, J., Blaschke, L. M., & Walti, C. (2009). Creating effective collaborative learning groups in an online environment. *The International Review of Research in Open and Distributed Learning, 10*(3), 1–18.

Capdeferro, N., & Romero, M. (2012). Are online learners frustrated with collaborative learning experiences? *The International Review of Research in Open and Distributed Learning, 13*(2), 26–44.

Cohen, E. (1994). *Designing groupwork*. New York, NY: Teachers College Press.

Cohen, E., & Lotan, R. (Eds.). (1997). *Working for equity in heterogeneous classrooms: Sociological theory in action*. New York, NY: Teachers College Press.

Dalsgaard, C. (2008). Social networking sites: Transparency in online education. *Proceedings from European University Information Systems Organisation*. June 24–27, 2008. Downloaded from http://eunis.dk/papers/p41.pdf

Finkbeiner, C. (2001). One and all in CALL? Learner—Moderator—Researcher. *Computer Assisted Language Learning, 14*(3–4), 129–151.

Finkbeiner, C. (2003). Cooperative learning and teaching in Germany. *International Association for the Study of Cooperation in Education Newsletter, 22*(3), 14–16.

Finkbeiner, C. (2004). Cooperation and collaboration in a foreign language teacher training program: The LMR-Plus model. In E. Cohen, C. Brody, & M. Sapon-Shevin (Eds.),

Learning to teach with cooperative learning: Challenges in teacher education (pp. 111–127). Albany, NY: State University of New York Press.

Finkbeiner, C. (2006). EFL and ESL knowledgeable reading: A critical element for viable membership in global communities. *Babylonia, 3,* 45–50.

Finkbeiner, C., & Knierim, M. (2008). Developing L2 strategic competence online. In F. Zhang & B. Barber (Eds.), *Handbook of research on computer-enhanced language acquisition and learning* (pp. 377–402). Hershey, PA: IGI Global.

Finkbeiner, C., Knierim M., Smasal, M., & Ludwig, P. (2012). Self-regulated cooperative EFL reading tasks: Students' strategy use and teachers' support, *Language Awareness, 21*(1–2), 57–83.

Finkbeiner, C., & Koplin, C. (2002). A cooperative approach for facilitating intercultural education. *Reading Online, 6*(3). Retrieved from http://www.readingonline.org/

Finkbeiner, C., & Lazar, A. (Eds.) (2015). *Getting to know ourselves and others through the ABCs: A journey toward intercultural understanding.* Charlotte, NC: Information Age Publishing.

Finkbeiner, C., & Svalberg, A. (Eds.) (2012). Culture language literacy. Special issue. *Language Awareness, 21*(1–2).

Finkbeiner, C., & White, J. (2017). Language awareness and multilingualism: A historical overview. In J. Cenoz et al. (Eds.), *Language awareness and multilingualism; Encyclopedia of language and education* (pp. 2–15).

Garrison, D. R., & Cleveland-Innes, M. (2005). Facilitating cognitive presence in online learning: Interaction is not enough. *The American Journal of Distance Education, 19*(3), 133–148.

Harasim, L. (2012). *Learning theory and online technology: How new technologies are transforming learning opportunities.* New York, NY: Routledge Press.

Hoter, E., Shonfeld, M., & Ganayem, A. (2009). Information and communication technology (ICT) in the service of multiculturalism. *International Review of Research in Open and Distributed Learning, 10*(2).

Johnson, D.W., & Johnson, R.T. (1987). *Learning together and alone: Cooperative, competitive, and individualistic.* Englewood Cliffs, NJ: Prentice Hall.

Krippendorff, K. (1980). *Content analysis. An introduction to its methodology.* Beverly Hills, CA: Sage.

Murray, M., & Lonne, R. (2006). An innovative use of the web to build graduate skills. *Teaching in Higher Education, 11*(1), 63–77.

Nummenmaa, M., & Nummenmaa, L. (2008). University students' emotions, interest and activities in a web-based learning environment. *British Psychological Society, 78*(1), 163–178.

Pettigrew, T. F., & Tropp, L. R. (2000). Does intergroup contact reduce prejudice? Recent meta-analytic findings. In S. Oskamp (Ed.), *Reducing prejudice and discrimination: The Claremont Symposium on Applied Social Psychology* (pp. 93–114). Mahwah, NJ: Erlbaum.

Resta, R., & Shonfeld, M. (2016). Challenges and strategies in designing cross-national learning team projects in virtual worlds. In S. Gregory, M. J. W. Lee, B. Dalgarno, & B. Tynan (Eds.). Learning in virtual worlds: Research and applications (pp. 261–275). Canada: Athabasca University Press.

Schmidt, P. R., & Finkbeiner, C. (Eds.) (2006). *The ABC's of cultural understanding and communication: National and international adaptations.* Greenwich, CT: Information Age Publishing.

Shonfeld, M., Ganayem, A., Hoter, E., & Walter, J. B. (2015). Online teams, trust and prejudice. *Issues in Israeli Society, 19,* 40–47. [Hebrew]

Shonfeld, M., Hoter, E., & Ganayem, A. (2013). Connecting cultures in conflict through ICT in Israel. In R. S. P. Austin & W. J. Hunter (Eds.), *Linking schools: Online learning and community cohesion* (pp. 42–58). New York, NY: Routledge.

Schrire, S. (2004). Interaction and cognition in asynchronous computer conferencing. *Instructional Science, 32*(6), 475–502.

Slavin, R. E. (1990). *Cooperative learning: Theory, research and practice.* Englewood Cliffs, NJ: Prentice-Hall

Vygotsky, L. S. (1982). *Collected works* (Vol. 2). Moscow: Pedagocica.

Wadmany, R., Rimor, R., & Rozner, E. (2011). The relationship between attitude, thinking and activity of students in an e-learning course. *Research on Education and Media. 3*(1), 103–121.

Walther, J. B., & Bunz, U. (2005). The rules of virtual groups: Trust, liking, and performance in computer-mediated communication. *Journal of Communication, 55*(4), 828–846.

Wang, X., Dannenhoffer, J. F., Davidson, B. D., & Spector, J. M. (2005). Design issues in a cross-institutional collaboration on a distance education course. *Distance Education, 26*(3), *405–423.*

Watson, J. (2008). The inclusion of intentional ethos enablers in electronic distance learning opportunities of Christian institutions. *American Journal of Distance Education, 22*(4), 195–206.

CHAPTER 13

PROMOTING ONLINE COLLABORATION COMPETENCE AMONG PRE-SERVICE TEACHERS OF ENGLISH AS A FOREIGN LANGUAGE

Tina Waldman and Efrat Harel

Pre-service teachers of English as a foreign language (EFL) in a teacher-training college in central Israel and a university in Germany teamed up to create an online, inter-cultural, collaborative learning experience. The goals of the experience were three-fold: first, to give the student teachers an authentic opportunity to learn about and work with international peers and increase their understanding of teaching EFL in other countries; second, to provide an online collaboration experience demonstrating ways in which technology can be used in education to transcend classroom walls; and third, to enhance the pre-service teachers' self-efficacy to facilitate online projects in the future.

The collaboration involved an international Project Based Learning Task (PBLT) in which intensive communication occurred between the Israeli and German students over a period of five weeks. During this time, they compared

Collaborative Online Learning in a Global World, pages 195–210.
Copyright © 2019 by Information Age Publishing

and contrasted facets of their respective cultures and specific aspects of teaching, testing, and learning EFL in their education systems.

This chapter reports on research involving the Israeli students based in part on quantitative data collected in a survey distributed both pre- and post-collaboration as well as on qualitative data collected via personal interviews conducted with the students following the collaboration. The findings show that online collaboration experience integrated into teacher training contributes to teacher development.

LITERATURE REVIEW

The value of online collaborative learning (OCL) in higher education (HE) has been increasingly recognized. OCL has its roots in constructivist approaches to learning and online communication (Harasim, 2012). When instructors implement OCL, they support their students in working together and creating knowledge through synchronous and asynchronous online discussion. In OCL contexts in HE, students from different institutions, communities, and countries work online collaboratively in pairs or teams. The instructors, who act as facilitators, design student-centered tasks that involve a final product and assessment. Generally, the teams comprise members from each of the communities, allowing maximum opportunity for communication and exchange of knowledge between members of different cultures. The teams are engaged in tasks on specific topics or problems that are relevant to the communities. Consequently, the OCL process is learner centered, with an emphasis on building knowledge through communication. It provides a form of virtual mobility, allowing the students to develop intercultural communication skills and to learn about other cultures and contexts, hence fostering global competence.

Organizations such as the European Commission for Educational Reform recognize the potential of OCL in meeting challenges in HE in preparing students for the global workplace. European higher education also faces the major challenge and the ensuing opportunities of globalization and accelerated technological developments with new providers, new learners, and new types of learning. Student-centered learning and mobility will help students develop the competencies they need in a changing labor market and will empower them to become active and responsible citizens (The Bologna Process 2020, 2009).

Online Collaboration

Online collaborative learning engages classes of students in different countries in intercultural exchanges primarily for the purpose of development of language, intercultural competence, and online literacies (Belz, 2003; Helm & Guth, 2010). Klapper (2006) suggests that in the case of language learning and teaching, "perhaps the most exciting application of the web in language learning is its capacity for bringing together students and native speakers" (p. 191). While this is true, today, when the number of second-language speakers of some languages is greater than the number of native speakers, online collaborations in a *lingua franca* have also proven successful in terms of language development and intercultural understanding (O'Dowd & Waire, 2009; Oztok et al., 2013).

Online collaboration is closely linked to current principles of foreign-language teaching. It takes a communicative approach, emphasizes authenticity of tasks and materials, and promotes learner autonomy. In addition, it supports theories of how language and culture are bound together, thus fostering intercultural awareness (Ware, 2005) and expanding the repertoire of identities and communication strategies (Kern, Ware, & Warschauer, 2004).

Benefits of Online Collaboration

The benefits of online collaboration for gaining knowledge, for improving intercultural competence, and for language learning have been documented by a number of researchers. Resta and Laferriere (2007) identify three instructional motives for using technology to support collaborative learning with an emphasis on gaining knowledge. These benefits include practicing collaboration skills and knowledge creation to prepare students for the knowledge society, flexibility of time and space enhancing students' deep understanding, and student engagement and communication enhancing language production and literacy skills.

Other achievements gained in online collaboration were noted by Oztok et al. (2013) in their overview of research on asynchronous and synchronous methods of collaboration in HE. Within asynchronous collaboration contexts, such as when the students used digital tools like email or discussion forums, benefits were linked to time and flexibility. These factors enabled reflection and in-depth, thoughtful interaction and communication. In synchronous collaboration contexts, such as when the students used video conferencing or chat software, the benefits were found to create a sense of urgency in terms of the task or debate at hand. Synchronous collaboration was also shown to produce student engagement in learning and to foster social contact and activity between participants.

Benefits to intercultural competence among learners can either arise incidentally or may be one of the main goals of collaborative learning. Byram (1997) defines intercultural competence as being able to interact effectively using linguistic and non-linguistic resources with people from another country. This means, among other things, to be able to overcome stereotypes, to be empathic, to understand otherness, and also to some extent to avoid misunderstandings. Online, collaborative, task-based learning units often require the learners to analyze or compare cultural products and to identify different cultural perspectives while negotiating between themselves and their partners from the different culture, hence fostering understanding of cultural values and why people behave as they do.

The quality of the relationship between the team members in an online collaboration has been found to be a key feature of the learning process. Engagement between learners, promoted by social presence (Lawrence, 2013), refers to the students' ability to project their personal characteristics within the "community of inquiry" (Garrison, Anderson, & Archer, 2000) by expressing emotions, being open to communication, and using personal means to establish team cohesion. In a transnational wiki-writing project, researchers found that learner "identity investment" was a key factor in facilitating engagement in the learning environment and the intercultural and language-learning processes (Lawrence et al., 2009). Potts (2005) also reported that in a graduate online language-learning community, the participants' enhanced knowledge of each other encouraged a high degree of respect and interdependence. Furthermore, Waldman and Harel (2015) found that acceptance of members of the team, interpersonal relations, and commitment to task were influential motivational factors.

Online collaboration benefits language learning by enabling learners to practice language in authentic situations without taking them beyond the classroom walls. Online collaboration exchanges involve either the learners of a foreign language collaborating with native speakers of the target language or learners of a foreign language collaborating with other learners of the same language. The activity of online task collaboration has good potential for the negotiation of linguistic meaning. O'Dowd and Waire's (2009) meta-analysis of online collaboration tasks reveals that task type as well as technological tools can influence language outcomes. The researchers reviewed over 40 reports on online exchanges from peer-reviewed journals and organized the online tasks into three main categories: information exchange–as in personal introductions and sharing personal biographies; comparison and analysis–as in sharing information and establishing similarities and differences; and finally, collaboration involving not only information exchange and analysis but also the production of a joint product–for example, a report or a text translation.

In online tasks involving information exchange, the development of fluency in the target language was noted in the findings of Vinagre (2005) and Lee (2006). Tasks in which students engaged in comparison and analysis, especially those with a cultural focus, were found to promote learners' language skills in terms of "discourse, pragmatics and the connotations of words and phrases" (O'Dowd & Waire, 2009, p. 178). The most influential tasks in language use and development involved collaboration and product creation. Gains were found in improved metalinguistic awareness, linguistic accuracy, and fluency (Belz, 2007 ;Pellettieri, 2000).

There is a growing awareness among higher-education institutions (HEIs) that teachers must be globally competent and possess the digital skills to be able to integrate the characteristics and values of global competence into their teaching. "A globally competent teacher has knowledge of the world, critical global issues, their local impact, and the cultural backgrounds of learners; manifests intercultural sensitivity and acceptance of difference" (Soppelsa & Manise, 2015). Incorporating global competence skills into language teacher training is necessary so that graduating teachers can engage their pupils in constructive online language and intercultural learning. Newby et al. (2007) state in *The European Profile for Language Teacher Education*:

> ICTs (information and communication technology) play an increasingly central role in foreign language learning and require teachers to be familiar with information systems and computer-mediated communication. Collaborative learning environments as well as individual use of ICT information sources foster independent learning and, if appropriately employed, promote learner autonomy. (p. 44)

In the section of the European Profile document, which is used for self-assessment in language teacher training, a number of virtual-learning benchmarks relating to online collaboration are listed. For example, the user responds to statements such as:

- I can advise learners on how to find and evaluate appropriate ICT resources (web sites, search engines. computer programs, etc.).
- I can initiate and facilitate various learning environments (learning platforms, discussion forums, web pages, etc.).
- I can use various ICT resources (email, web sites, computer programs, etc.). (p. 49)

O'Dowd (2015) defines the skills necessary to organize, design, run, and assess online exchanges for the globally competent foreign-language teacher. These skills fall into three categories: emotional, pedagogical, and digital. In terms of emotional skills, the teacher must be able to work well with partner teachers and be responsive to the partner institutions' beliefs. Pedagogical skills include task design, defining task objectives, choosing culturally and linguistically appropriate topics, and creating assessment rubrics. Finally, the teacher should have a rich knowledge of digital tools and the ability to instruct their use, manage digital communication timeframes, and teach online etiquette and social presence.

Due to the complexity of the role of a globally competent foreign-language teacher, there is a need, as O'Dowd (2015) maintains, for trainees to gain the competencies of an online instructor through systematic learning in practice. In other words, trainees themselves should experience online exchanges from the perspective of participant. Learning from practice involves the trainees reflecting upon their own online experiences and sharing them and formulating notions of good practices.

Exposing student EFL teachers to the basic skills and technological tools in a single workshop on online collaboration is not likely to prepare them fully for the challenges involved. Therefore, in our research, we have engaged student EFL teachers studying at a teacher-training college in central Israel and a well-established university in Germany in an authentic, real-time online exchange over five weeks, hoping they will achieve fuller understanding of the competencies required to implement such collaborative learning in their future classrooms.

SETTING AND PARTICIPANTS

The study reported here was a joint project between the English-language education departments in both institutions. The lecturers, who teach various courses in applied linguistics to pre-service English teachers, met when the German professor visited the Israeli institution to initiate collaborative projects between the two schools. Following his visit, the lecturers created an online collaboration project to enable an intercultural exchange between students studying in both departments. The lecturers finalized details of the online collaboration through email correspondence and Skype video conferences.

The Israeli college, which is supervised by the Council for Higher Education, prepares educators and teachers for K–12 education settings. It serves a population of all sections of Israeli society, and its curriculum places emphasis on community involvement and social justice. In addition, the institution is interested in promoting the internationalization of teacher-education programs by creating agreements with colleges and universities all over the world. The English teaching department offers a four-year B.Ed. double major in English and education. The participants in the study were 33 student teachers of English in their third year of study. Their ages ranged from 25 to 40. Most spoke Hebrew as their mother tongue, but the group included three English native speakers and one Arabic native speaker.

The German university offers degree courses for initial teacher certification for primary and lower secondary school. The profile of the institution as a whole emphasizes European cultural studies, intercultural education, plurilingualism, and media education. The university works closely with partner universities in many other countries and has frequent exchanges for both students and lecturers. The 21 participants studying at the German university were in the second year of their studies. They were studying to be primary and lower secondary-school teachers of EFL and one more subject such as math, history, etc. The German participants were in their early 20s and native speakers of German.

IMPLEMENTATION OF THE INTERNATIONAL COLLABORATIVE PROJECT BASED LEARNING TASK (PBLT)

The implementation of the online collaboration followed a design developed by the Israeli researchers in an earlier project between Israeli and American students of education (Waldman & Harel, 2015). It included three stages: information exchange, comparison, and collaboration. Information exchange about personal details and aspects of home culture took place at the beginning of the process so that the students could get to know each other. Over the following weeks, student teams compared and critically analyzed the ways EFL is taught in Israel and Germany. Collaboration was implemented through the students' co-construction of electronic posters showcasing their findings. These posters were presented during a final synchronous videoconference.

The first synchronous videoconference was carried out simultaneously at each institution using Skype and a projector and screen, so that all the students could see and hear each other. After a brief introduction by the two lecturers, the participants began a lively exchange about why they chose to become teachers, different aspects of their student life, and the status of bilingualism and multiculturalism in their respective countries and educational systems.

Between the first and the second synchronous videoconferences, teams of students–three Israelis and two Germans–communicated using synchronous tools–Skype and WhatsApp (chat), and asynchronous tools–email, and Google Docs. The main goal of these interactions was to compare and contrast teaching English as a foreign language in the Israeli and the German public-education systems. The student teams decided among themselves which aspect of teaching EFL to focus on for their electronic poster presentation.

Following five weeks of teamwork, the second video conference took place at the institutions. The purpose of the videoconference was to create an authentic forum for the students to present their posters. Each presentation lasted for five minutes, and the student teachers from each country took turns talking about their findings. The posters and presentations were graded according to predetermined criteria.

The aim of this study was to provide experiential learning to foster participant reflection on online collaboration as a relevant tool for the EFL teacher. The primary question we sought to answer was whether integrating online collaboration into EFL teacher training enhances teacher development and a willingness to engage pupils in online language and intercultural learning.

Research Questions

1. Does online intercultural exchange increase a pre-service teachers' understanding of teaching EFL in a global context?
2. Can online collaboration contribute to understanding of online learning among student EFL teachers?
3. Does experiencing an online intercultural exchange enhance a pre-service teachers' self-efficacy to facilitate online projects in the future?

Data Collection

In order to answer the research questions, two sources of data were collected from the Israeli students. A quantitative survey was distributed before and after the online collaboration experience to document change in student attitudes and self-perceptions. We designed the survey based on a number of the descriptors provided in O'Dowd (2015). Qualitative data were collected from interviews conducted with all the students immediately following the collaboration experience.

The survey asked the students to assess the degree to which they agreed or disagreed with 18 statements. Six questions related to their understanding of teaching EFL in a global context; six asked them to reflect on learning through online collaboration among student teachers; and six asked them about their self-efficacy in facilitating online collaboration projects in their future classes.

Students responded using a five-point scale ranging from "Strongly Agree" to "Strongly Disagree" to the 18 statements. The statements asking about understanding of teaching EFL in a global context were:

> Culture plays a role in foreign language education; Learning about other students' cultural practices is important; Learning with overseas partners about L2 language teaching is meaningful; I am open to alternative pedagogical beliefs; I am open to alternative pedagogical aims; It is more beneficial for me to collaborate with a native speaker partner.

The statements asking about online learning among student teachers were:

> Telecollaboration plays an important role in language learning; It is important for me to feel social presence (the human touch) with partners in the telecollaboration; I am willing to deal with new messages as they emerge during the online exchange; It is valuable to try new online tasks proposed by partners; It is important to try new online tools proposed by partners; It is essential to have a degree of autonomy (from instructors) in the project.

The statements asking about self-efficacy using online collaboration in teaching were:

> I can organize an online exchange between my pupils and other pupils; I can design an online exchange project with a partner teacher in another culture; I can choose the appropriate online communication tool for a telecollaborative exchange; I can instruct my pupils on how to use online tools, e.g. chat for a telecollaborative exchange; I can design a relevant task in order to develop pupils' cultural and linguistic interaction; I can integrate appropriate assessment rubrics which reflect the activity I designed.

The personal interviews probed the students to report on their experience during the online collaboration project and to reflect on their learning and achievements at the conclusion of the project. Examples of questions are:

> Has your understanding of EFL in a global context improved due to the project? If so, how? Did it matter to you that you collaborated with people who speak English as L2/are not native speakers? How do you feel about digital communication as a way to share ideas, collaborate on creating a product? Could you see yourself initiating participation in similar projects when you are a practicing teacher?

Data Analysis

Quantitative analysis of the survey focused on the comparison between the means of each set of six ranked statements, which specifically targeted each research question, in the pre- and post-collaborative PBLT survey. We carried out group comparisons, first with the means of the six statements about teaching EFL globally, second with the means of the six statements about online learning, and third with the means of the six statements about self-efficacy in implementing an online collaboration project.

To examine the reliability of the survey, we conducted a reliability analysis for each of the three sets of statements. The Cronbach's alpha for the first set was 0.58, which was not high enough; hence, we removed one statement from the first set (about collaboration with a native/non-speaker partner). After doing so, the Cronbach's alpha for the first set was 0.7, which indicates a high level of internal consistency for our scale with this specific sample. The Cronbach's alpha for the second set was 0.74 and for the third set 0.86, indicating high levels of internal consistency.

Qualitative analysis was based on the students' reflections gathered via the interviews. The transcripts of the interviews were coded and categorized according to each research question.

FINDINGS

The findings from the quantitative analysis for each set of questions are presented below. The first set consists of five questions, and the other two sets consist of six questions each.

Table 13.1 shows the number of participating students (33), the mean, and standard deviation of pre- and post-collaboration survey scores for each set of statements. Although the mean scores for the post-survey were higher within the three sets of questions, one-way, repeated-measure analyses showed a main effect for time (pre- vs. post-survey) only within the third set of statements ($F(1,32)=24.23$, $p<0.001$)). These statements related to our third research question, asking about the students' self-efficacy to facilitate online projects independently. Indeed, the students reported higher self-efficacy in facilitating online collaboration projects in their future classes after participating in such a project themselves.

Qualitative Analysis of Interviews

We carried out the group interviews with the students at the end of the project, immediately after the second synchronous meeting, so the entire experience was

TABLE 13.1. Comparison of Student Response Means in the Pre- and Post-Survey

N = 33	Pre-survey		Post-Survey	
Set	Mean	SD	Mean	SD
1	4.3	0.43	4.4	0.5
2	3.84	0.52	4.0	0.4
3	3.8	0.59	4.29	0.54

still fresh in their minds. The qualitative analysis focused on evidence relating to the three research questions.

Our first research question asked whether the online intercultural exchange increased the pre-service teachers' understanding of teaching EFL in a global context: fostering intercultural understanding and communication skills. We found that the theme of global competence arose in various ways across the interview data. Some of the students showed overt awareness of cultural diversity. They had clearly reflected upon and interpreted the interaction with their German peers. Other participants referred to "feelings of surprise" and "different ways of doing things" but did not interpret these events in terms of intercultural learning.

One prominent issue that arose was the Israeli students' assumption that Internet communication culture is universal. The Israelis assumed that whatever online tool is used, communication should be immediate; they expected immediate answers whether they sent a message during the day or night or at the weekend. They were surprised to discover that the German Internet culture was different and that the German students did not always respond immediately to messages, nor did they communicate over the weekend. While some Israelis expressed frustration, they also revealed an awareness that perhaps they could be perceived as "pushy" by not giving up until they got a response. "Pushing them made them mad, because they do things quietly, in different pace, more relaxed" (Group 8). The Israeli students also sensed that their own pace of doing things was hurried in comparison to others and that different cultures keep pace to a different drummer. This knowledge was critical for them as future teachers when they would manage online collaboration projects in their own teaching careers.

The theme of global competence also arose in the interviews with the Israeli students in their comments on using English as the *lingua franca*. Their comments showed that, following the online collaboration experience, the students preferred interaction with L2 English-speaking peers to native speakers because they believed that it eased communication. They contended that they were less likely to be judged harshly for making language errors by an EFL speaker. In addition, when either they or their German partners had difficulty expressing an idea, they described undergoing a two-step process: first they empathized with each other; then they reflected together on language use and the effects of L1 influence. These conversations reveal meta-cognition about language learning and the shared predicaments of L2 language users across cultures.

Some researchers have expressed concerns that learner engagement in online collaboration is not authentic, and while safe, is also limiting (Hanna & de Nooy, 2009). But the students in our study saw online learner engagement in a positive light, as such interaction leads to reflection about language learning and use, and also to confidence building. Furthermore, in today's global society where English is the *lingua franca* for two thirds of Europeans and its use is rapidly spreading worldwide, it is more likely that communication with L2 speakers is going to occur in authentic situations such as business, travel, research, etc. than with L1 speakers.

The students' engagement with the PBLT also revealed learning over a broad range of subjects relating to teaching EFL globally. During the interviews, some of the students claimed that the PBLT opened their eyes to the fact that teaching EFL is different in other cultures. The teams' electronic poster projects included comparison of textbooks, comparison of teaching methods, approaches to bilingual and multilingual pupils, teacher autonomy, and assessment methods, among other topics. The students discovered that unlike in Israel, where there is a centralized curriculum for teaching EFL that includes a graduated system with theoretical foundations (various low- and high-order thinking skills that must be achieved by the end of high school), there is no centralized curriculum in Germany. Hence, unlike the Israeli English teacher who has to follow strict guidelines prescribed by the Ministry of Education, teachers in Germany follow the published teacher's guide which accompanies a textbook. Similarly, whereas in Israel, national assessment begins in the fifth grade, in Germany, it begins only in the 10th grade.

Comparisons of textbooks for the same grade level revealed that books in both countries are organized according to thematic units and the vocabulary presented is similar. For example, elementary-school books in both countries present high-frequency vocabulary and recycle topics like pets and animals. However, in Israel, the books place emphasis on reading and fill-in-gap (receptive skills) activities, whereas in Germany the books emphasize communicative speaking activities. In Germany, in general, there is greater emphasis on oral production, and teachers tend to use English only in the classroom, whereas in Israel, the teachers tend to switch back and forth between Hebrew and English, often providing Hebrew translation. The PBLT raised the Israeli students' awareness and appreciation of differences in teaching EFL globally. They concluded that "there is no one way of teaching a language" (Group 1).

Our second research question asked whether the online collaboration experience enhanced the students' understanding of online learning. In all, the students reported that this experience had provided them with practical insights into the complexities, challenges, and benefits of integrating technology into language learning. They focused in particular on the challenge of sustaining a social presence and reported that on the whole they enjoyed working with the German students because the Germans projected themselves as real people (i.e., with their full personalities and lives) through online communication. The Israeli students also felt that they projected themselves socially and emotionally, and some of them mentioned that they used emoticons in their communication to emphasize their feelings to the German students.

The student teams that worked exceptionally well together revealed that they were open to each other's proposals about ways of working. In terms of using online tools, they were ready to adapt their preferred ways of working in order to resolve difficulties arising from some of the German students not having the Microsoft software package by working with Google Docs and Google slides.

In addition, the students mentioned that they felt it was important to participate in both synchronous and asynchronous communication. On the one hand, synchronous communication such as Skype conferences were important because they highlighted the human element–the students were able to see each other, chat about subjects other than the project, and reveal their personalities to each other. On the other hand, they also noted that email communication was equally important because it gave them time to think about the information that the German students were sharing with them and gave them time to respond thoughtfully.

Our third research question investigated whether participating in the online collaboration developed student self-efficacy to facilitate online projects in the future. Both qualitative and quantitative data findings showed that all the students were positive about the experience and it had raised self-efficacy. They said they "loved" it and had the desire to apply it to their future teaching. However, some of the students also emphasized that through engaging in the experience, they had come to realize many of the difficulties that arise in terms of administrating and monitoring online collaborations, and, therefore, they were not sure whether they would attempt to set up an online collaboration as a beginner teacher. They perceived that the instructor, if working with school-age children, would have to take on a greater role than a facilitator, and they expressed concern about the work load. Specifically, they thought they must make themselves available around the clock for the duration of the project. Also, they were worried about a lack of digital support in the schools.

As a solution to some of these problems, a few of the students suggested setting up an online collaboration with another EFL class in Israel to practice their skills and gain confidence. Other students, however, felt the online collaboration experience had prepared them to implement online collaboration in their teaching immediately. "We are ready to carry it out now. We can use the model of our own project with our students" (Group 2). Some of these students were even looking for sites that offer online collaboration support and partner-finding solutions. One student claimed to have spoken to the English coordinator about setting up an online collaboration project in the coming school term. These enthusiastic students emphasized the need for online collaboration to provide not only language-learning opportunities for pupils but also opportunities to learn about other cultures and to be ambassadors for their own country.

CONCLUSION

This chapter reports research carried out on Israeli trainee EFL teachers participating in an international online collaboration. The findings are based on quantitative data collected in a survey distributed both pre- and post-collaboration as well as on qualitative data collected via personal interviews conducted with the students following the collaboration. The main findings revealed that experiential learning via online collaboration participation enhanced teacher development in two ways. First, it raised the student-teachers' self-efficacy in using online collaboration as a language-teaching tool. Second, it enhanced teacher development through providing an understanding of the connections between the theory and practice of intercultural online collaborative learning.

To start with our main finding, the students reported that the online collaboration experience provided them with a model they felt they could learn from and adapt to use with their future pupils. Moreover, the experiential learning caused the learners to reflect on their assumptions and expectations about online intercultural learning. Exposure and reflection led to a deeper understanding of online collaboration. With understanding comes empowerment and an increase in self-efficacy. Hence, our initial assumption that integrating online collaboration experience into teacher training is essential if we want teachers to use it in their own teaching practice was confirmed.

Although the survey questions about learning English globally did not yield a significant difference in the post-survey data, the interview data revealed that the students had reflected on developing intercultural skills and their importance for participating in a community of learners in a global society. Their comments revealed raised awareness of the value of the input of culturally and linguistically diverse peers (not only L1 speakers). They had greater understanding of cross-cultural interaction as shown through their desire to understand Internet-communication culture broadly. They realized the importance of establishing personal relations and the significance of empathy in creating healthy working relationships. Possibly, we did not see overall significant results in the post-survey because the statements we designed were limited to beliefs about the role of culture in learning. It is also possible that a five-week intervention may engage students in reflection of assumptions but not provide enough time for a full re-assessment of beliefs.

Similarly, the survey questions about online learning (our second research question) did not yield a significant difference in the post-survey data, while the interview data revealed raised awareness among the students of online collaboration as a model of teaching that integrates knowledge-sharing activities with the learner at the center. The students spoke about the impact that exchanging and comparing knowledge with the German students had on them in broadening their views of teaching EFL. They understood the value of a model of learning through discovery and thought that it would appeal to their future pupils, offering an alternative to traditional learning with textbooks and standardized tests. Furthermore, they liked the idea of integrating the Internet into EFL teaching and showed awareness of the advantages, fine-grain details, and pitfalls of using technology in the classroom. Online collaboration, they felt, provided meaningful uses of the internet beyond the recent trend of electronic textbooks and games like Kahoot. They had reflected on the details of an exchange to the extent of how to position a camera, whether to have the pupils teleconference in pairs or teams, and how to organize presentation of products at the end of the learning process. However, the deeper understanding also brought to the surface the student-teachers' fears and worries about classroom management and lack of technical support when implementing online collaboration. These fears have to be acknowledged, and effective solutions should be explored between teacher educators and student teachers.

Limitations and Challenges

This chapter provides only a partial view of our research, as only the Israeli-student perspective is reported. The next step is to compare it to the German-student perspective of the online collaboration experience. In addition, we are aware of the limitations in our research. The online collaboration lasted for only five weeks, which provided little time in terms of affecting student beliefs and intercultural understanding. We see an advantage in doubling the online collaboration to about 10 weeks, which would allow time for more developed relations to take place among participants and for more meaningful learning. Extending the collaboration could provide a better model of learning and allow the participants to gain skills in new technologies through teacher-initiated scaffolding. Students could learn and practice using digital tools that promote language learning like cartoon-creation tools and avatar software. This would broaden their repertoire of digital tools, which would aid them in designing their own classroom online collaboration projects.

Finally, our research investigated the students' mental shift in attitude and self-perception following experiential learning. We see value in investigating the process of learning through online collaboration, so we can understand more about the integration of content, materials, technology, and interaction in teaching EFL. More importantly, we see value in our student teachers exploring these processes while collaborating online with others, so they can employ this tool competently and critically.

REFERENCES

Belz, J. (2003). Linguistic perspectives on the development of intercultural competence in online collaboration. *Language Learning & Technology, 7*(2), 68–99. Retrieved from http://llt.msu.edu/vol7num2/belz/

Belz, J. (2007). The development of intercultural communicative competence in telecollaborative partnerships. In R. O'Dowd (Ed.), *Online intercultural exchange: An introduction for foreign language teachers. Languages for international communication and education 15* (pp. 127–166). Clevedon, UK: Multilingual Matters.

Byram, M. (1997). *Teaching and assessing intercultural competence*. Clevedon, UK: Multilingual Matters.

Garrison, D. R., Anderson, T., & Archer, W. (2000). Critical inquiry in a text-based environment: Computer conferencing in higher education. *The Internet and Higher Education, 2*(2–3), 87–105.

Hanna, B., & de Nooy, J. (2009). *Learning language and culture via public internet discussion forums.* New York, NY: Palgrave Macmillan.

Harasim, L. (2012). *Learning theory and online technology: How new technologies are transforming learning opportunities.* New York, NY: Routledge Press.

Helm, F., & Guth, S. (2010). The multifarious goals of telecollaboration 2.0: Theoretical and practical implications. In F. Helm, & S.Guth (Eds.), *Telecollaboration 2.0: Language literacies and intercultural learning in the 21st Century* (pp. 69–106). New York, NY: Peter Lang.

Kern, R., Ware, P., & Warschauer M. (2004). Crossing frontiers: New directions in online pedagogy and research. *Annual Review of Applied Linguistics, 24,* 243–260.

Klapper, J. (2006). *Understanding and developing good practice: Language teaching in higher education.* London, UK: CILT.

Lawrence, G. (2013). A working model for intercultural learning and engagement in collaborative online language learning environments. *Intercultural Education, 24*(4), 303–314. doi: 10.1080/14675986.2013.809247

Lawrence, G., Young, C., Owen, H., & Compton, T. (2009). Using wikis for collaborative writing and intercultural learning. In M. Dantas-Whitney & S. Rilling (Eds.), *Authenticity in the adult language classroom* (pp. 199–212). Alexandria, VA: TESOL.

Lee, L. (2006). A study of native and non-native speakers' feedback and responses in Spanish-American networked collaborative interaction. In J. Belz & S. Thorne (Eds.), *Internet-mediated intercultural foreign language education* (pp. 147–176). Boston: Heinle & Heinle.

Newby, D., Allan, R., Feener, A., Jones, B., Komorowska, H., & Soghikyan, K. (2007). *European portfolio for European teachers of languages.* Retrieved from http://archive.ecml.at/mtp2/Fte/pdf/C3_Epostl_E.pdf

O'Dowd, R. (2015). Supporting in-service language educators in learning to telecollaborate. *Language Learning & Technology, 19*(1), 63–82.

O'Dowd R., & Waire, P. (2009). Critical issues in online task design. *Computer Assisted Language Learning, 22*(2), 173–188.

Oztok, M., Zingaro, D., Brett, C., & Hewitt, J. (2013). Exploring asynchronous and synchronous tool use in online courses. *Computers and Education, 60,* 87–94.

Pellettieri, J. (2000). Negotiation in cyberspace: The role of chatting in the development of grammatical competence. In M. Warschauer & R. Kern (Eds.), *Network-based language teaching: Concepts and practice* (pp. 59–86). Cambridge, UK: Cambridge University Press.

Potts, D. (2005). Pedagogy, purpose, and the second language learner in on-line communities. *Canadian Modern Language Review, 62*(1), 137–160.

Resta, P., & Laferrière, T. (2007). Technology in support of collaborative learning. *Educational Psychology Review, 19,* 65–83.

Soppelsa, B., & Manise, J. (2015). *The top 10 characteristics of globally competent teachers* [Blog post]. Retrieved from http://blogs.edweek.org/edweek/global_learning/2015/08/the_top_10_characteristics_of_globally_competent_teachers.html

The Bologna Process 2020. (2009, April 28–29). *The European higher education area in the new decade Communiqué of the Conference of European Ministers Responsible for Higher Education, Leuven and Louvain-la-Neuve.* Retrieved from http://www.ehea.info/Uploads/Declarations/Leuven_Louvain-la-Neuve_Communiqu%C3%A9_April_2009.pdf

Vinagre, M. (2005). Fostering language learning via e-mail: An English-Spanish exchange. *Computer Assisted Language Learning, 18*(5), 369–388.

Waldman, T., & Harel, E. (2015). Participating in a technology-enhanced internationalization project to promote students' foreign language motivation. In D. Schwartzer & B. Bridglall (Eds.), *Promoting global competence and social justice in teacher education: Successes and challenges within local and international contexts* (pp. 149–172). Plymouth, UK: Lexington Books.

Ware, P. (2005). "Missed" communication in online communication: Tensions in a German-American online collaboration. *Language Learning & Technology, 9*(2) 64–89.

CHAPTER 14

THE FORUM OF EXCELLENT STUDENTS

A Model for Cooperative Learning in a Multicultural Environment

Liat Eyal, Rama Klavir, and Naomi Magid

Israel is a country characterized by cultural pluralism. It includes sub-groups that differ from one another on the basis of religion, nationality, and ethnicity. The country's social pluralism is reflected in the education system, including teacher-training colleges. Some colleges are designed for specific sectors of society (e.g. Arab or Jewish only), and at the same time there are colleges where students from different sectors learn together.

This chapter presents a study conducted in an inter-college forum, a joint framework for excellent students from all colleges in the country to learn together. The research examined the contribution of cooperative learning to the multicultural environment that served as a context for the student learning experience and also examined the contribution of cooperative learning to their educational perceptions. First, we discuss theoretically the terms "cooperative learning" and "cultural pluralism" in the Israeli context. We then review some challenges of teacher education in Israel's multicultural context. The study also

Collaborative Online Learning in a Global World, pages 211–229.
Copyright © 2019 by Information Age Publishing
211

examines the uniqueness of the Excellent Students program and the learning objectives of the inter-college forum. The chapter shares our research findings and conclusions, which are based on forum participants' responses to quantitative and qualitative questions.

Cooperative Learning in a Multicultural Environment

Cooperative learning and group learning have seen ups and downs in Israel in accordance with the country's development and the needs of the times. The policies of the Kibbutz Movement, a combination of socialist and humanist ideas, promulgated cooperative learning, which was subsequently shunted from center stage with the mass immigration in the first years of the nascent State of Israel and replaced by melting-pot policies and a centralized education system that extolled frontal teaching. However, the 1970s and '80s saw a significant wave of criticism leveled by researchers (Sharan & Sharan, 1976) against frontal teaching. Numerous books and studies were published about group learning, groups of experts were established, and the status of cooperative learning was strengthened concurrently with educational processes that were taking place all over the world (Hertz-Lazarowitz & Zelinker, 1999). Following the success of cooperative learning in the United States, it developed into a field of research that produced a variety of methods. Adoption of the cooperative-learning approach in Israel was attended by adjustments to suit Israeli culture. One such adjustment was emphasizing the aspect of cooperation over competition and on motivation that is not based on extrinsic incentives.

In recent years, group learning, and especially cooperative learning, has enjoyed a revival in Israel, especially in heterogeneous classrooms. This heterogeneity may be academic, ethnic, religious, sectorial, gendered, socioeconomic, and learning-style based. Israeli cooperative-learning methods were thereby oriented towards complex learning assignments that encouraged high-order thinking (Sharan & Hertz-Lazarowitz, 1980; Sharan & Sharan, 1976). In Israel, the metaphorical emphasis on cooperative learning is expressed as "a community of learners."

Nowadays, the conceptual framework of cooperative learning emphasizes knowledge-construction processes and a perception of learning that is driven by intrinsic rather than extrinsic factors (Hertz-Lazarowitz & Zelinker, 1999; Johnson & Johnson, 1975; Sharan & Sharan, 1976). Consequently, the more advanced cooperative-learning approaches propose that interrelationships structured on a behavioral basis of cooperative learning should be substituted for open or unstructured cooperation and collaboration. Learning in small groups encourages knowledge construction by means of processes of discourse, negotiation, and inquiry, which facilitate the application of equal rather than competitive cooperation (Damon & Phelps, 1989; Schaps, 1999). This cooperative-learning approach combines the ideas propounded by Vygotsky (1978) and Dewey (1929) and introduces aspects of active, progressive, and engaged learning.

In the learning environment developing today, cooperative-teaching methods also include a technological element. This creates new and interesting combinations that add to the accumulating experience in the field of cooperative learning. However, implementation of cooperative learning is still limited, especially in high schools and higher-education institutions, including teacher-training colleges. The reasons for this are complex and include attempts to meet education system requirements to achieve high scores in the matriculation examinations, which encourages high-school teachers to focus their efforts on teaching the specified content and covering the material by means of frontal teaching; teachers' in-principle objection to change; lack of support for teachers in change processes; and absence of an effective instructional system that brings about change in attitudes. In higher-education institutions, the reasons are lack of pedagogical training for lecturers, who continue to adhere to the traditional, familiar methods of teaching in academe, namely lectures (Koller, 2014); Israeli reality with its intercultural rifts and pitfalls; and technological developments and global reality that pose new educational and pedagogical challenges in terms of training teachers to educate for multiculturalism.

Cultural Pluralism in Israel

Israel is a multicultural country, comprising sub-groups that differ from one another in religion, nationality, and ethnicity. Israeli society acknowledges this cultural heterogeneity and respects the rights of individuals to express the unique values and norms of the group they belong to. According to Yogev (2001), this acknowledgement is manifested in two ways or reflects two different approaches: (1) The multicultural-pluralistic approach, which reflects the willingness of groups to include other groups in society and encourages the groups to learn about and develop empathy towards one another (similar to programs developed in the U.S., Canada, and Australia); and (2) the particularistic-pluralistic approach, which embarks from the thinking that on the one hand every group in society has the right to live in accordance with its preferences and enjoy equal rights and on the other from an understanding that the deep rifts between the sub-groups cannot be bridged and educational institutions should be allowed to operate separately for members of the different groups, which is the case in Israel.

Thus, for example, there are separate schools and academic institutions for the Arab and Jewish sectors in which the studies are conducted in the respective sector's language. There are differentiated schools for the various religious streams (i.e., state schools, state religious schools, and ultra-Orthodox schools), and the curricula are adapted to each sector's requirements.

Various researchers contend that in order to open up the ethnocentric seclusion of different groups and conduct an egalitarian, inclusive, and tolerant dialogue in which all the participants are of equal value, the different groups need to learn together (Tamir, 1998; Yonah, 1998). Various attempts have been made in Israel to implement the multicultural-pluralistic approach (e.g., mixed Jewish-Arab educational frameworks). Some of these attempts failed due to a pronounced preference for the culture of the majority Jewish group, which also constitutes the power group in society. There have been successes, such as bilingual schools, but they constitute "islands" and are not widespread.

According to Yogev (2001), to successfully implement the multicultural-pluralistic approach, Israel needs to adopt a policy that will be applied in a number of stages: (1) The Ministry of Education needs to define social pluralism as a value; (2) A systemic-structural change needs to be made that on the one hand provides educational autonomy for each sector and on the other mandates their cooperation concerning agreed values; (3) Unique curricula need to be developed whose principal aim is multicultural education that includes inculcation of knowledge on the subject, ideological discussions, and exposure to the different narratives; (4) A comprehensive change in the majority of curricula must be made so that the multicultural education constitutes a latitudinal objective; (5) Teacher-training programs need to be updated to accord a central place to education for social pluralism (Yogev, 2001).

Training Teachers for Cultural Pluralism

Despite the pressing need for cultural understanding, not only have the majority of teacher educators in the colleges of education not been trained to train teachers for multiculturalism (Merryfield, 2000) but also their attitudes towards multicultural education and what it should include are many and varied. Some challenge the policy and ignore the issue, while others incorporate discussions on subjects such as ethnicity, feminism, and racism. However, even these cases are mostly limited to courses that in any case engage in these unique subjects, when what is actually required is engagement with education for multiculturalism by addressing the values of social justice and equality (Ladson-Billings, 2000).

In their study, Ezer, Millet, and Patkin (2006) present the stories of teacher educators in a multicultural context in order to examine the connection between their life experiences and worldviews and educating teachers for multicultural-ism. They conducted content analysis of the narratives of three lecturers in teacher-training colleges representing native Israeli Jews, new Jewish immigrants, and native Israeli Arabs and found that they all acknowledge the importance of educating for multiculturalism, albeit from different points of departure. Each of them believed that they put their understanding of multiculturalism into practice in their teacher-training work, but in their own way. The "new immigrant" teacher naturally fostered equality and understanding of the other as a subliminal message through sensitivity towards the other, especially her minority group. The second teacher strived to express his Arab cultural uniqueness by working in a Hebrew-speaking institution, while the third teacher, a native Israeli, believed in fostering multiculturalism but found it difficult to do herself. According to the researchers, bringing the life stories of teacher educators to the surface and their reflective self-examination concerning their perception of multiculturalism is the first stage toward fostering awareness of educating for multiculturalism.

The personal-experience component is also of paramount importance in shaping an educational outlook towards multiculturalism. In her study, Merryfield (2000) examined the correlations between the actual experiences of teacher educators and development of their outlooks and practical work. She examined experiences that were described as retrospective reflections and concluded that the majority of the teachers' experiences consisted of encounters with others who differed from them in incidents of social, institutional, or personal discrimination. The experiences displayed contradictions between beliefs, expectations, and knowledge, which led to reflection and the ability to use these experiences to teach student teachers about the dynamics of power and culture and to develop a critical conscience. However, teachers who come from a uniform cultural perspective and who have not had experiences of otherness and culture are unable to assimilate these values in teacher training. Consequently, according to the researcher, consideration should be given to the recruitment of teacher educators based on their experiences and knowledge which are consistent with the objectives of the training program.

A study conducted by Diab, Bar Shalom, and Rousseau (2008) on an educational program entitled "Difference and Diversity in Israeli Society," with a study population consisting of 155 students from different population sectors, concluded that it is important for the workshop instructors to experience similar workshops themselves, since the component of the instructor's "self" greatly influences the program's operation. Additionally, the researchers recommended forming heterogeneous groups that cross study tracks and in which the group members are not necessarily previously acquainted, since such previous acquaintance preserves separation and impedes the creation of a synergic atmosphere among group members.

Laron and Lev-Ari (2006) reinforce this argument in a study conducted in Israel at a teacher-training college attended by students from a variety of population sectors. The college holds courses on cultural and national identity that set themselves the objective of conducting a dialogue and listening to the different voices of peers that reflect the multiculturalism in Israeli society as a tool for investigating and expanding personal identity. The researchers administered an attitude test to the students before and after the course. The findings of their study reinforce the argument that Israel's social and cultural structure, as well as the teacher-training system, encourage educating for particularistic-pluralism, and thus each sector knows its own culture but has very little exposure to the cultures of other sectors. However, the students' exposure to multiculturalism in courses indicates a trend of positive change in the students' social identity, and in this respect the college serves as a socialization agent. Consequently, the college environment and the courses provided play an important role in educating for multiculturalism.

THE REGEV PROGRAM FOR EXCELLENT STUDENT TRACHERS

The REGEV Program for Excellent Student Teachers in Israel's colleges of education has been operating for 18 years. The idea for establishing the program emerged from the desire to improve the quality of personnel turning to teaching in general and colleges of education in particular and to raise the prestige of the profession (Klavir, 2010). The REGEV Program aims to foster educational elite from personal, social, and academic perspectives. The general objective of the program is to recruit high-ability student teachers and train them in a specialized, quality program to become leading teachers, excellent educators, and educational leaders (Ministry of Education, 2015).

Since the aim of the program is to train these quality students to be excellent teachers, the program's leaders identified three unique components in prospective students that can constitute a basis for a specialized training program: (1) high cognitive and academic abilities that position them in the top 5% to 10% of student teachers in the country, (2) high motivation to engage in education and teaching, (3) high diversity. The first two are personal components and constitute conditions for acceptance into the program. The third characterizes the group as a whole and derives from the fact that the program operates in 21 colleges in Israel. The diversity is manifested in geography, population sector (Jews and Arabs, religious, ultra-Orthodox, and secular), gender, and college ethos. The combination of these components, which is unique to the REGEV Program, serves as one of the central resources for the program's leaders to develop personal and professional excellence in the course of the training.

To utilize this precious and unique resource, a number of frameworks have been developed in the program for encounters between students from the REGEV programs in all the colleges. These include, for example, student conferences and an intercollegiate student forum. In the present article, we shall focus on the Intercollegiate Student Forum.

THE INTERCOLLEGIATE STUDENT FORUM

The Intercollegiate Student Forum is a joint framework for excellent students representing all the academic colleges of education and is designed to develop a perception of leadership consistent with the program's objectives: fostering excellent educators and educational leaders. This framework focuses on engaged learning in a multicultural environment for REGEV program students.

The forum gives expression to the high abilities of its participants; their motivation; and their academic, cultural, and ideological diversity (Shayshon, & Popper-Giveon, 2016). The participants come from all the REGEV programs in the academic colleges of education: Jews and Arabs, religious and secular, and Israel's northern and southern regions. Every academic year, with the new cohort of students, the forum convenes anew, and its activities are held at the MOFET Institute, a research and development center for teacher training in Israel, which participates in leading the forum and gives academic accreditation to its participants. The forum's objectives as defined by its leaders:

- To develop a leading group from the students attending the REGEV program in all the academic colleges of education;
- To provide an unconventional learning encounter with a diverse peer group in order to enable the students to formulate a pedagogic-educational vision and outlook consistent with excellence in teaching and educating;
- To build a learning environment based on choice, joint exchange, high-order thinking, learning through different representations, and joint experience;
- To provide guidance, assistance, and monitoring for the forum participants in planning and leading educational processes in the classroom, the school, the community, and the education system;
- To contend with educational, ideological, and ethical dilemmas and develop varied and diverse methods to contend with them;
- To encourage teamwork in heterogeneous groups comprising students from different colleges and to develop a learning social network;
- To produce a concluding project in the classroom or educational framework by planning and building a discipline-based teaching unit which includes experience, reflection, and learning from successes and difficulties;
- To disseminate the products of the process, including the knowledge and its construction process, to the REGEV programs in particular and colleges of education in general.

The Forum's Activities

Several long study days offering two credits for 60 academic hours are held in the course of the academic year. The study days include lectures, tours, and activity workshops, and distance learning is maintained between meetings. Each study day either begins or ends with activity in the "parliament": time devoted to an actively guided discussion between all the students on a variety of shared educational issues, designed to foster critical and creative thinking and develop rhetorical ability. During the rest of the day, the students engage in a subject of their choice from four different channels in both content and character. In each channel, the choice is based on the connection between the channels and the program's objectives. The first channel, "Talking Education," involves discussions and debates on educational issues and the educator's role. The second, "Visual Journey," examines the connection between learning/teaching and the camera and visual communication. The third, "Creativity Changes Learning," focuses on developing the participants' creative thinking so that they in turn can develop creativity in their own students. The fourth channel, "Learning to Play," helps the future generation of teachers learn how to develop learning games using advanced digital tools.

Designing the forum's teaching and guidance method was based on the aspiration to build a framework of joyful, experiential, respectful, challenging, and empowering learning. Two instructors were chosen to work simultaneously in each channel, and all the forum's instructors maintain a relationship of cooperation, constant flow of ideas, and coordination from a shared desire for the endeavor to be different from any other learning framework in which they teach or in which the students study. The forum has a coordinator who unites the activities of all the channels into a single, unique body of work. The learning methods in the plenum and the forum's channels include lectures, workshops, and independent work as well as tours of educational frameworks and planning and implementing group projects.

The high demand from students in recent years to participate in the forum has led to a number of decisions: (1) To expand its spheres of activity, content, and work methods; (2) To ensure that multicultural groups are included in each channel so that the forum is typified by cultural, social, religious, and geographic diversity; (3) To utilize the multicultural diversity to develop advanced educational outlooks that acknowledge diversity as a value and use it to nurture human capital potential and achieve the program's objectives; (4) To deepen the processes of involving the students in learning in each channel and in the general "parliament."

Thus, in our view, the social wealth and diversity of the Intercollegiate Student Forum can serve as fertile soil for cooperative learning, for training quality teachers, and for expanding multiculturalism in education. Based on the program's unique context and on the professional literature, we formulated two research questions.

Research Questions

1. What is the contribution of cooperative learning in a multicultural environment, such as that which takes place in the forum, to the students' learning experience? (Experience as learners)
2. What is the contribution of participation in the forum to the students' educational outlooks concerning multiculturalism and cooperative learning as future teachers? (Adopting for teaching)

Methodology

Study Population

The study population included 110 students who participated in the Intercollegiate Student Forum during the 2014–2015 academic year. At the end of the academic year and conclusion of the forum's activities, an online questionnaire was administered to the students on Google Docs. One reminder was sent. Seventy-six percent of the students (N=69) responded to the questionnaire, 53% of them first-year, 38% second-year, and 9% third-year students. Twenty-two percent of the students were male and 78% female, which was consistent with the gender ratio in the forum. Forty-one percent were secular Jews, 39% religious Jews, and 20% were Arabs, which was consistent with the ratio in the forum. Of the respondents, 37% were graduates of the "Creativity Creates Learning" channel, 33% the "Visual Journey" channel, 18% the "Talking Education" channel, and 12% the "Learning to Play" channel.

The Questionnaire

The questionnaire was sent to the students as an online Google Form. It consisted of 16 closed questions and eight open ones. The questions included economic data, the influence of the forum's social and cultural diversity on the learning experience, the contribution of the atmosphere to the learning experience, the forum's contribution to training the students to become educators, exposure to cooperative learning strategies and their efficacy, and the likelihood of incorporation of cooperative learning in the student's future teaching.

There were two types of closed questions in the questionnaire: Yes/No questions and questions to which answers were arranged hierarchically on a five-point Likert scale, e.g., 5-to a great degree; 4-to a significant degree; 3-to an average degree; 2-to a low degree; 1-not at all. In the open questions, the respondents were asked to write the reasons for their choices of answers to the closed questions. The respondents were also asked questions in which they were required to address a specific issue in their own words (e.g.: "Here you can write freely about your thoughts, difficulties, tensions, problems, dilemmas, and anything else you feel is associated with the forum.") and a question in which each respondent was asked to choose a metaphor for the forum ("In my view the forum is like….").

Method of Analysis

The study employed both quantitative and qualitative methods. The quantitative part of the study was based on a statistical analysis of the answers to the closed questions, whereas the qualitative part included content analysis of the students' answers to the open questions in the questionnaire and the metaphors they chose to describe the Intercollegiate Student Forum.

Employing metaphors is based on the premise that they can serve as a means for researchers to discover the meanings, perceptions, feeling, beliefs, and experiences respondents enfold in them (Lakoff & Johnson, 1981). Indeed, many researchers employ metaphors provided by different respondents to reveal their perceptions, beliefs, and feelings towards a variety of complex subjects such as teaching, learning, and mentoring (e.g., Gasner, 1997; Goldstein, 2005; Kupferberg, 2008; Michael & Katerina, 2009; Saban, Kocbeker, & Saban, 2007; Schmitt, 2005). Analysis of the metaphors consisted of several layers: the first, finding the direction of the metaphor–negative or positive; the second, attributing the metaphor to the central research concepts–cooperative and multicultural learning–and examining the connection to them; and the third, classifying the metaphors into subgroups according to central themes, indicating the value of participation in the forum for the student (Schmitt, 2005).

FINDINGS

1. What is the contribution of cooperative learning in a multicultural environment, such as that which takes place in the forum, to the students' learning experience?

To answer this question, we first analyzed all the students' answers to the three relevant closed questions in the questionnaire. The distribution of the answers was as follows:

1. *To what degree did the forum's sociocultural diversity influence your learning experience?* About 75% (51 respondents out of 69) stated that the sociocultural diversity greatly influenced (to a great degree, to a significant degree) their learning experience. Only 3% (2 respondents) stated that the sociocultural diversity had very little or no influence on their learning experience.

2. *To what degree did the atmosphere in the forum influence your learning experience?* Eighty-four percent (58 respondents) stated that the atmosphere in the forum contributed to a great or significant degree to their learning experience. As with the previous question, the same two respondents (3%) stated that the atmosphere in the forum had little or no influence on their learning experience.

3. *To what degree were you exposed in the forum to cooperative learning strategies?* Seventy percent (49 respondents) stated that the forum exposed them to a great or significant degree to cooperative learning strategies. Six respondents (9%) stated that they were exposed to cooperative learning strategies to a low degree. None of the respondents stated that they had not been exposed to cooperative learning strategies at all.

Additionally, to examine the nature of the contribution of learning in the forum to the students as learners, we analyzed the metaphors. Analysis of the metaphors indicates a number of findings:

All the metaphors (58) indicate a positive experience at the forum and a positive influence on the participants. Example metaphors included "coming out into a new world," "window of opportunity," "sauce for spaghetti," "a drop falling in the ocean and creating ripples."

In most of the metaphors (83%), the respondents emphasized diversity and cooperative learning as central components in their positive experience at the forum (see Table 14.1).

The 48 metaphors that emphasized multiculturalism and cooperative learning can be divided into three groups: Group 1 includes the largest number of

TABLE 14.1.   Examples and Frequency of Metaphors from the Three Groups

Frequency		Examples
Group 1:		
"Cooperative learning in a multicultural environment"	38 (79%)	Fruit salad: Each student has his own flavor, characteristics, background, color, and so forth, and these characteristics were expressed in the forum, but each student did not remain on his own, just as each fruit in a fruit salad does not remain on its own; there is juice that connects them all and enables all the fruits to absorb flavor from other fruits, just as each student influenced others and was influenced by others.
		Summer camp: The Intercollegiate Student Forum is like a summer camp–I met new people from different places, sectors, and backgrounds, we carried out different activities together, and I brought myself.
		Vegetable garden: A wide range of vegetables can be grown in it, each vegetable has its own conditions and needs, but they all grow in the same soil. Thus, it was evident that everyone came from a different place, a different background, and had different needs, and at the same time, we were one group that learned and developed together.
Group 2:		
"Cooperative learning"	4 (8%)	A hot furnace in the artist's hand: Like a fountainhead in a craftsman's hand, or like a blacksmith or metal smith who put a basic raw material into a hot furnace (sand, metal) and transform it into a work of art, so is the forum, we came as raw material that can be worked, we learned a lot and were given directions and openness to ideas and works in the different subjects, in the context of education and life as well.
		A time generator: In an era in which everything is shorthand, visual, and rapid! You need a kind of spiral that will shorten processes, there are teachers who haven't got the strength or time to think of creative ideas, and now there's a team that's been set up and done all the work for them, all they have to do is choose an idea and apply it in the classroom.
		I don't have a metaphor: But it's an interesting encounter between future educators that to a certain extent shape the future of teaching in Israel.
Group 3:		
"Multiculturalism"	6 (13%)	An island of hues: An island because suddenly in the middle of the routine of life and studies you travel to Tel Aviv for a different kind of day, a routine breaker. And hues because of the human diversity there.
		Opening a door to a new world: In my view the forum is like a door that's always closed, then someone comes and suddenly opens it, the door out of the sector.
		An end-of-school candy: The forum is a release from the framework, and somewhat different learning. It's meeting students from all the sectors. At my college there's a relatively very homogeneous representation of society.
Total	48 (100%)	

metaphors (38; 79%) that do not draw a distinction between the two components, indicating that the students' experience at the forum was based on cooperative learning in a multicultural environment. Group 2 includes four metaphors (8%) that position cooperative learning at the center of the forum experience. Group 3 includes six metaphors (13%) that position multiculturalism at the center of their forum experience. See Table 14.1 for examples of metaphors from each of the three groups.

Finally, we examined how the students explained the contribution of their experience in cooperative learning in a multicultural environment in the framework of the forum; what in its blend led in their view to their feeling that it was a positive and meaningful experience for them. In an analysis of the Group 1 metaphors, in which this blend gains expression, three main groups of explanations emerge:

- Enjoyment due to the different experience, unlike anything they usually experience.

The students encountered people different from those they usually met for the purpose of learning together, subjects that were different to those they routinely studied, employing learning methods that were very different from those they generally experienced, in a different place, and at different times, creating the sense of an enjoyable, refreshing, new, unique experience that broke everyday routines. Cooperative learning with people they were not accustomed to meeting, and certainly studying, speaking, and thinking with, made participation in the forum a learning celebration: different, exciting, joyful, colorful. Examples of metaphors included "summer camp," "train station," "traveling the world."

- Enjoyment stemming from the discovery that cooperative learning first of all enables exposure to and creation of commonalities among very different learners.

The forum was a powerful experience of successfully focusing on or creating commonalities. The sense of success was actually reinforced, contrary to the prevailing expectation that diversity makes it difficult or impossible to create commonalities due to fundamental differences between people who are so different. If not for the forum, the students would not have had the opportunity to meet and certainly would not have talked to each other. They discovered that it is possible to work on joint assignments, think together, discuss, and discover numerous meeting points on education despite their differences. This discovery came as a surprise to the students, fascinated them, strengthened their sense of success, and aroused a desire in them to delve into and develop their commonalities. Examples of metaphors were "bubble" (only in a bubble is it possible for people separated by huge gaps [religion, culture, etc.] to sit in the same place without their differences preventing them from talking and thinking together), "family event" (meeting people who always seem new but you always find something in common), "vegetable garden," "rainbow."

- Discovery and insight that the participation of different people from different backgrounds brings a wealth of ideas, outlooks, beliefs, fields of interest, and knowledge to the learning process, which in turn leads to innovation, enrichment, and a heightened quality of learning and its products.

Combining the differences into cooperative learning groups brings diverse points of view and perspectives to the groups and enriches the learning process and its products on both the individual and group levels. Examples of metaphors were "a broad and colorful mosaic," "a jigsaw puzzle that together creates a picture," "pencil box," "a painting on a huge sheet of paper" (that includes all the colors in the world which together create perfect and visually pleasing harmony), "ras el hanout" (a spice mix influenced by the composition of spices included in it; consequently, it is a unique blend).

2.   What is the contribution of participating in the forum to the students' educational outlooks concerning multiculturalism and cooperative learning as future teachers?

Analysis of the findings concerning this question was carried out in two stages. In the first stage, the findings pertained to the question, What is the degree of contribution of participating in the forum to the students' educational outlooks and their training as teachers? (Question 1). In the second stage, we attempted to discover the degree to which cooperative learning in a multicultural environment is part of this contribution and what its contribution is (Question 2). The findings pertaining to Question 1 derive from a number of closed questions in the questionnaire and the quantitative analysis. The findings pertaining to Question 2 derive from a number of open questions in the questionnaire and the qualitative analysis.

2.1.   What is the degree of contribution of participating in the forum to the students' educational outlooks and their training as teachers?

Virtually all of the respondents (99%) stated that participating in the forum had added value to their college studies. With regard to their training as teachers, 76% stated that the forum exposed them to new teaching methods to a great or significant degree, 78% stated that in the forum they acquired new knowledge to a great or significant degree, and 63% (54 of 69 respondents) stated that participating in the forum influenced their educational outlooks to a great or significant degree.

Additionally, as stated at the beginning of this article, the objective of the forum is to develop a perception of leadership consistent with the objectives of the REGEV program: to foster excellent educators and educational leaders. Three closed questions referred to the degree to which the program's objectives were achieved through the forum in an attempt to examine how much the forum indeed contributed to achieving them:

1. Forum contribution to training students as educators: Seventy-one percent of the students stated that the forum contributed to a great or significant degree to their training as educators, 23% stated that it contributed to an average degree, and 6% stated that the forum had little or no influence.

2. Forum contribution to training students as educational leaders: Sixty-eight percent of the students stated that the forum contributed to a great or significant degree to their training as educational leaders, 22% stated that it contributed to an average degree, and 10% stated that the forum had little or no influence.

3. Forum contribution to training students as excellent teachers: Seventy-one percent of the students stated that the forum contributed to a great or significant degree to their training as excellent teachers, 17% stated that it contributed to an average degree, and 12% stated that the forum had little or no influence.

2.2. To what degree is cooperative learning in a multicultural environment part of this contribution, and what is its contribution?

1. The reasons provided by the students as to why in their view the forum influenced their educational outlooks to a great or significant degree were varied and were associated with the learned content: the new and diverse teaching practices they experienced; the creative, respectful, and tolerant approach of the instructors in the different channels; and the atmosphere of joy and adventure in the forum and its channels. All enabled them to reach the insight that good teaching can be both experiential and meaningful, with no contradiction between the two. Almost half of the respondents (47%) stated that participating in the forum influenced their educational outlooks and attributed the forum's influence on their educational outlooks to the cooperative and participative learning they experienced in its multicultural environment. At this juncture, it is important to note that of the students belonging to this group, only a few (four) emphasized just one of the components in the blend, as stated above in the findings presented concerning the first research question, which connects cooperative learning with the multicultural environment.

2. What reasons did the students in this group provide for how this blend influenced their outlooks? Some stated that the cooperative learning they experienced as students in the forum's multicultural environment helped them to become acquainted with different

opinions and outlooks, and according to them, this influenced their understanding that, as teachers, it was worth their while to view the differences between pupils as a valuable resource that the teacher should utilize for the purpose of enriching and deepening their learning:

Participating [in the forum] influenced my outlook and highlighted certain points. For example, in such a diverse encounter of people I learned that it's not beneficial to "avoid" the diversity, and sometimes it's even essential to bring the sensitive issues up for discussion, especially if you really want to have a cooperative group. Beyond that, it was nice to get to know students from different colleges, and it was especially nice to work on the project that really "required" it to give expression to what is being done and learned in the encounters. Apart from that, it was very interesting to see other people's projects and learn from them, it completely opened my mind to new directions.

Others stated that they understood that the other needs to be respected and listened to in order to eliminate prejudices and misconceptions: "I was exposed to different cultures, sectors and people I hadn't known before. By getting to know them, the stigmas and prejudices were erased."

Others stated that they understood that cooperative learning with others is reinforcing since it helps to discover (to their surprise at times) that, despite the vast differences between group members, they have a great deal in common. The students who expressed this explained that for them this discovery strengthened the feeling that they were not alone; that others in the forum shared a similar sense of vocation as teachers in general and excellent teachers in particular; and that, when discussing common educational issues, diversity contributes to the shared issues on the one hand and to the formulation of their personal outlooks on the other:

The forum provided me with an opportunity to connect with a diverse variety of people from different sectors and ethnicities who all share an objective–to improve the future education of the next generation. The shared vision infected me too, and I found myself daring to dream and imagine a better future.

3. Most of the respondents (87%) stated that they had acquired new colleagues at the forum, and 63% thought that they would continue to maintain personal or professional contact with them in the future. All of the students stated that cooperative learning would be part of their teaching routine in the future, with 80% stating that they would do so to a great or significant degree.

4. Strategies and tools for cooperative learning and adoption for teaching: To deepen the understanding of the students' ability to adopt the cooperative-learning approach in their future teaching, they were asked which strategies and tools they were exposed to in the course of learning in the forum and which of them they would adopt in the future. In their answers, the respondents noted the cooperative learning strategies to which they were exposed, among them working in teams, studying together, Jigsaw, division of functions, online cooperative-learning environments, exhibition, time and space for free, and evolving discussion. They also explicitly stated that they would adopt the tools and ideas they had experienced, such as co-teaching, creating heterogeneous groups during activities with different methods (e.g., random distribution of stickers), group evaluation and feedback processes, learning-promoting group discourse and listening ability, containment, granting team responsibility for learning, and peer teaching.

CONCLUSIONS

In the learning setting of the REGEV program's Intercollegiate Student Forum, an attempt is being made to adopt the pluralistic-multicultural approach as presented by Yogev (2001) and thus meet the educational and pedagogical challenge for teacher training. To educate for multiculturalism, it is not enough to seat learners of different cultures in a shared setting; it is necessary to create opportunities for an active, egalitarian dialogue and enable participants to experience cooperative learning themselves.

Cooperative learning in a multicultural environment had a considerable influence on the students' learning experience. The forum's atmosphere that encourages an egalitarian dialogue, as proposed by innovative cooperative-learning models (Damon & Phelps, 1989; Schaps, 1999), contributed considerably to a positive learning experience, and the vast majority of the participants described it by means of metaphors emphasizing both multiculturalism and cooperative learning as central, inseparably intertwined components in this experience. The learning experience was accompanied by enjoyment resulting from its novelty, a sense of success in solving joint assignments, and value that learning of this kind added to the products. The learning was combined with tours, experiential-respite activities, discourse-inviting recesses, and a concluding encounter devoted to displaying the products of the activities in the different channels: workshops on educational dilemmas, photography workshops, experiencing games developed by the students, and a poster conference on creative teaching products. Participating in the forum greatly influenced the students' self-perceptions as leaders, excellent educators, and teachers who view diversity as a value and resource for good learning.

The students experienced a range of cooperative learning strategies. Experience is crucially important for changing outlooks, influencing attitudes, and adopting tools (Bar Shalom, Diab, & Rousseau, 2008; Laron & Lev-Ari, 2006; Merryfield, 2000), since the subject of cooperative learning in a multicultural environment was not specifically studied in and of itself but merely constituted part of the shared experience. The learners were exposed to diverse cooperative-learning strategies that now constitute part of their educational toolbox as future educators. As a student representing a minority population said,

> In my view the forum is a path of love and respect for one another, and gives hope for uniting students from the different populations in Israel. It brings together all the students from different sectors in the country and gives them the love and help to advance and succeed together.

REFERENCES

Bar Shalom, Y., Diab, K., & Rousseau, A. (2008) Sowing the seeds of change: Educating for diversity in the context of teacher training at an academic college of education in Jerusalem intercultural education. *Intercultural Education 19*(1), 1–14.

Damon, W., & Phelps, E. (1989). Strategic uses of peer learning in children's education. In T. J. Berndt & G. W. Ladd (Eds.), *Wiley series on personality processes. Peer relationships in child development* (pp. 135–157). Oxford, UK: John Wiley & Sons.

Dewey, J. (1929). *Experience and nature.* New York, NY: W. W. Norton & Co. Retrieved from: http://dx.doi.org/10.1037/13377-009

Diab, K., Bar Shalom, Y., & Rousseau, A. (2008). Expanding the encounter and mutual learning between students from different cultures in Israel: Case study in a teacher training framework at an academic college of education. *Bamichlala [At the college], 21*, 211–251.

Ezer, H., Millet, S., & Patkin, D. (2006). Multicultural perspectives in the curricula of two colleges of education in Israel: The curriculum is a cruel mirror of our society. *Teachers and Teaching: Theory and Practice, 12*(4), 391–406.

Gasner, T. (1997). Metaphors for mentoring: An exploratory study. *Mentor (1)*. Retrieved from http://www.mentors.net/journal/j1_ganser_metaph.php

Goldstein, L. S. (2005). Becoming a teacher as a hero's journey: Using metaphor in preservice teacher education. *Teacher Education Quarterly, 32*(1), 7–24.

Hertz-Lazarowitz R., & Zelniker, T. (1999). Alternative methods in teaching: Cooperative learning in Israel. In E. Peled (Ed.), Fifty years of Israeli education (vol. 2, pp. 349–367). Israel: Jerusalem Ministry of Education, Culture and Sport.

Israeli Ministry of Education. (2015). *Teaching personnel, training and professional development administration.* Director's circular on the Program for Excellent Students for 2015. Retrieved from http://cms.education.gov.il/EducationCMS/Units/Metzuyanut/HoraotNehalim/Hizer+2016.htm [Hebrew].

Johnson, D. W., & Johnson, R. T. (1975). *Learning together and alone: Cooperation, competition and individualization*. Englewood Cliffs, NJ: Prentice Hall.

Klavir, R. (2010). Excellent students–specialized training–excellent teachers. *Maof uma'ase (Vision and Practice), 13*, 166–194. [Hebrew].

Koller, D. (2014). Coursera: What we're learning from online education. *Hora'a BeAcademia (Academic Teaching), 4*, 4–8. Jerusalem, Israel: Israel Academy of Sciences and Humanities.

Kupferberg, I. (2008). Metaphorical expressions of thought in discourse: Implications for teacher training. *Shvilei Mehkar (Research Pathways), 15*, 108–113. MOFET Institute. [Hebrew].

Ladson-Billings, G. (2000). *Multicultural education in the 21st century: Multiple perspectives on its past, present, and future*. A symposium presented at the AERA Conference. New Orleans, LA.

Lakoff, G., & Johnson, M. (1981) *Metaphors we live by*. Chicago: University of Chicago Press.

Laron, D., & Lev-Ari, L. (2006). *Limudey tarbut vezehut Beoranim-Hashpa'atam al amadot mitkashrim lehora'a beheksher shel chinuch lerav-tarbutiut [Culture and identity studies in Oranim: Their influence on the attitudes of prospective teachers regarding multiculturalism]*. 8th Scientific Conference, Oranim College of Education. [Hebrew].

Merryfield, M. M. (2000). Why aren't teachers being prepared to teach for diversity, equity, and global interconnectedness? A study of lived experiences in the making of multicultural and global educators. *Teaching and Teacher Education, 16*, 429–443.

Michael, K., & Katerina, M. (2009). Exploring Greek teachers' beliefs using metaphor. *Australian Journal of Teacher Education, 34*(2), 64–83. Retrieved from http://ro.ecu.edu.au/ajte/vol34/iss2/6

Saban, A., Kocbeker, B. N., & Saban, A. (2007). Prospective teachers' conceptions of teaching and learning revealed through metaphor analysis. *Learning and Instruction, 17*(2), 123–139.

Schaps, E., & Lewis, C. (1999). Perils on an essential journey: Building school community. *Kappan, 81*, 215–218.

Schmitt, R. (2005). Systematic metaphor analysis as a method of qualitative research. *The Qualitative Report, 10*(2), 358–394. Retrieved from http://www.nova.edu/ssss/QR/QR10-2/schmitt.pdf

Sharan, S., & Hertz-Lazarowitz, R. (1980). A group investigation method of cooperative learning in the classroom. In S. Sharan, P. Hare, C. Webb, & R. Hertz-Lazarowitz (Eds.), *Cooperation in education* (pp. 14–46). Provo, UT: Brigham Young University Press.

Sharan, S., & Sharan, Y. (1976). *Small group teaching*. Englewood Cliffs, NJ: Educational Technology Publications.

Shayshon, B., & Popper-Giveon, A. (2016). "Leave out ideologies, just let us return home safely": Reflections of motivations and expectations in the professional development of students and graduates of the Program for Excellent Students at the David Yellin Academic College of Education in Jerusalem. *Dapim*, 98–126. [Hebrew].

Tamir, Y. (1998). Two concepts of multiculturalism. In M. Mautner, A. Sagi, & R. Shamir (Eds.), *Multiculturalism in a democratic Jewish state* (pp. 79–92). Tel Aviv: Ramot. [Hebrew].

Vygotsky, L.S. (1978). *Mind in society: The development of higher psychological processes*. Cambridge, MA: Harvard University Press.

Yogev, A. (2001). Approaches in value education in a pluralistic society. In Y. Iram, S. Scolnicov, J. Cohen, & E. Schachter (Eds.), *Arachim vehinuch bahevra Haisraelit [Crossroads: Values and education in Israeli society]* (pp. 355–379). Jerusalem: Israel Ministry of Education. [Hebrew].

Yonah, Y. (1998). Fifty years later: The scope and limits of liberal democracy in Israel. *Constellations, 6*(3), 411–428.

CHAPTER 15

ASSESSING PERSONAL LEARNING IN ONLINE, COLLABORATIVE PROBLEM SOLVING

David Gibson, Leah Irving, and Tami Seifert

Collaboration is understood as a continuous group activity addressing a mutually constructed problem or challenge (Roschelle & Teasley, 1995). If the problem or challenge does not hold the mutual interests of the parties, collaboration is impossible. In addition, during collaboration, an individual group member's contributions and influences on others comprise important aspects of the group experience, because without individuals there is neither group nor collaboration. At the same time, a group's ability to collaboratively solve a problem is more than the sum of individuals' contributions because unique synergies and added values emerge during the group's social-learning processes (Slavin, 2010). Therefore, assessing personal learning is bound up with assessing the group's collaborative problem-solving processes. This chapter focuses on assessing personal learning through challenges that contain open-ended, unresolved problems, which in turn bring forth higher-order thinking processes, communications, critical thinking, and creativity.

Collaborative Online Learning in a Global World, pages 231–248.

231

The chapter will define and discuss key terms–personal learning, collaboration, problem solving–and will outline a design framework for creating open-ended challenges and group problem-solving activities for online task spaces or scenarios that elicit measurable individual and group performances linked to an assessment argument for personal learning. Assessment entails an opportunity to perform a current or previously acquired competency, a domain model of what that performance looks like when a target concept is evidenced, and a chain of reasoning from evidence to an inference about what the learner knows and can do (Mislevy, Steinberg, & Almond, 1999; Pellegrino, Chudowsky, & Glaser, 2001). The narrative will first describe the domain model and assessment targets, then propose and discuss a design framework and process, and finally illustrate the theory with a case example.

DOMAIN MODEL AND ASSESSMENT TARGETS

The domain model of an assessment is a conceptual representation of the key performance indicators that experts "might see people say, do, or make as evidence, and situations and activities that evoke it–in short, the elements of assessment arguments" (Mislevy, 2011, p. 13). For the assessment discussed here, the dimensions of the domain model are personal learning, collaboration, and problem solving, which are defined as:

- *Personal learning*: acquisition of knowledge (e.g. new insights, capacities for thinking, acting, and employing skills) that is evidenced for outside observers as well as an individual's own reflection and metacognition.
- *Collaboration*: coordinated group activity resulting from continuous attempts to construct and maintain a shared conception of a problem (Roschelle & Teasley, 1995)
- *Problem solving*: cognitive processing directed at achieving a goal when no solution method is obvious (Mayer & Wittrock, 1996).

Assessment targets of this domain model are the specific objectives set for the process of gathering and evaluating performance-based evidence. The qualifier *performance-based* draws attention to the fact that, in order to have externally observable and measurable evidence of learning, someone must act upon or within the real world, which leaves traces or artifacts of that performance. Learning that leaves no trace in the real world cannot be measured by an observer, including the self as observer. Metacognition, for example, requires one to recognize and reflect on how one learns by becoming aware of sensations and patterns of thinking (Hartman, 2001; Weinert & Kluwe, 1987).

Assessment targets also draw attention to the alignment of the assessment's purpose with the learning and the expressive or performative affordances given to the learner in order for the assessment to provide fair and adequate evidence of the knowledge, skill, or capability being measured. In this case, the challenge or problem must be comprised of opportunities to perform actions that would leave evidence of personal learning (PL), collaboration (C), and problem solving (PS), which will be referred to as the PL-C-PS model. For example, if the assessment is targeting the skill of solving an open-ended problem, then the learning opportunities as well as the assessment prompts given to the learner need to speak to, exhibit, and elicit openness. Otherwise, the assessment can't measure the targeted concept for the lack of an opportunity to perform. The concept of openness that is emphasized here in relation to problem solving entails agency, decision-making, and a lack of a previously known right answer, which adds to the design criteria outlined below for the PL-C-PS assessment-targets' structure.

The dimension of personal learning (PL) competencies enables assessment of individual achievement in a real group setting and is thus important in real-world online collaborative problem solving. The aim of the PL-C-PS model is to frame how an individual's pathway as a group member changes over time, interacts with the elements of the group's collaboration and problem solving, and contributes to the participant's learning experience as well as the group's journey in collaborative problem solving. The personal-learning competencies (PL) outlined below are supported by a theory of dialog based in research that indicates a critical role for a cycle of individual inquiry and expression in a group context (Friedrichs, 2000; Friedrichs & Gibson, 2003). The theory is consistent with research findings concerned with authenticity, use of technology to create problem-centered learning teams, representation of complex dynamics in educational settings, and online learning. (Carroll, 2000; Gibson & Clarke, 2000; Newmann & Wehlage, 1995; NSDC-NICI, 2001; Wiggins, 1989). Friedrichs (2000) discusses four distinct dialogue stages that manifest themselves in a personalized learning process; her framework maps onto an action research cycle of planning and thinking, doing, analyzing, and taking action but focuses these activities on the personal level of meaning-making by an individual.

Personal Learning

1. Sharing experience. Listening to own and others' inner speech and natural attitude about a skill or concept;
2. Expressing and examining diverse concepts. Recognizing conflicts; analyzing old and new concepts, models and beliefs; working in one's zone of proximal development;
3. Articulating, applying and building understanding. Practicing new skills; combining old and new concepts; using others' ideas; using scaffolds to renegotiate understandings;
4. Communicating new powers and creations. Celebrating effects of critical analysis.

The Organization for Economic and Community Development (OECD) developed an assessment domain model for collaborative problem solving with targets situated at the intersection of two sets of the competencies drawn upon here (PISA, 2013):

Collaboration

1. Establishing and maintaining shared understanding
2. Taking appropriate action to solve the problem
3. Establishing and maintaining team organization

Problem solving

1. Exploring and understanding
2. Representing and formulating
3. Planning and executing
4. Monitoring and reflecting

Examples of assessment targets for collaboration (C) and problem solving (PS) include the intersection of C1 and PS1–"Discovering perspectives and abilities of team members"—and the intersection of C2 and PS2—"Identifying and describing tasks to be completed" (PISA, 2013). Webb and Gibson (2015) analyze the OECD PISA model in greater detail. The assessment at the 12 intersections of C and PS is delivered online to an individual who interacts with a software agent mimicking a collaborative-learning partner. So, the focus is on individual competency in a virtualized, collaborative, problem-solving simulator. The C-PS model is here extended to include features needed for personal learning (PL) in a real-world, team-based, learning context. Assessment purposes of the new PL-C-PS model include an instructor who wants to assess the degree of successful teamwork, the degree of success of the team in creating a collaborative solution, and the degree of individual learning attained by each team member.

The collaborative group's *social learning capacity* is defined by the balance of relationships of each member's PL configuration over time (Figure 15.1). This claim is supported and analyzed by noting that if the group as a whole does not have the capacity to share experience (PL1) or the ability to recognize and resolve conflicts (PL2), then the members will not listen to each other or be sensitive to one another's perspectives, and this will prevent the group from achieving a shared understanding (C1) and may find it difficult to explore the problem (PS1) and maintain the group's organization (C3). If the group cannot articulate current understandings and negotiate new ones (PL3), then formulating a mutually agreeable solution (PS2) will be impossible. Other similar supportive arguments can be made that involve all the constructs of the framework with and among each other.

It seems reasonable to infer that if any individual member of the group lacks the requisite construct capacities, the group's overall collaborative capacity will be diminished, especially if we insist that collaborative activity engages and im-

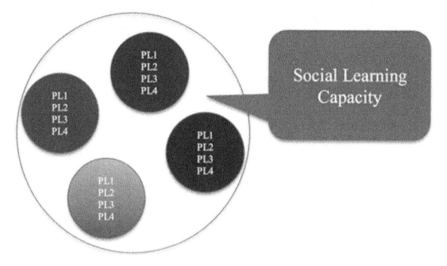

FIGURE 15.1. Social learning capacity is the combined personal learning capacities and experiences of its members.

pacts all participants. Note that this stance promotes equity of learning opportunity by having all members of the team make progress; the model would not count a solution reached by only part of the team as collaborative. This analysis suggests that for best group functioning, each individual needs to have opportunities for experiencing the PL stages with appropriate dialogic support (e.g. inclusion, belonging) and feedback (e.g. sensitive critical friendship, guidance) from the group. For example, early in the group's formative period, each member could be prompted to tell the others about his or her strengths, interests, and aspirations (PL1) and how these unique characteristics can contribute to the group's success (PL2). The PL stages can be seen as a process that scaffolds both collaboration and problem solving, for example, by helping establish a rich, diverse view for improved understanding (C1) and helping explore how the group might think about and approach the problem (PS2).

A group's *cohesion* around a challenge or problem is envisioned as the interplay of individual influences and trajectories as the group traverses the problem-solving and collaboration workspace (Figure 15.2). Cohesion is the degree of overlap in the model's measures of each individual that become evident when measuring each member's status in PL, C, and PS. Lack of overlap might be thought of as a degree of separation among the members of the group. The more the group stays together or *coheres* through the process of collaboration and problem solving, it is hypothesized that the group will experience concentrated and similar levels of individual success, which may be most appropriate for a group experiencing its first collaborative challenge. A complementary hypothesis is that

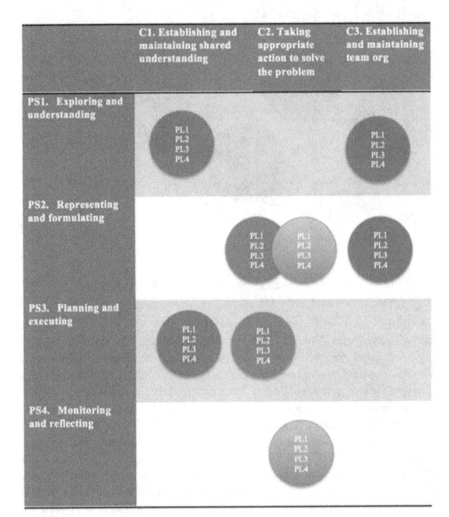

FIGURE 15.2. Snapshot of evidence from a collaborative problem-solving team

by simultaneously exploring all the space of collaboration and problem solving, a less-cohesive group may be able to negotiate with more diversity of ideas and individual growth and reach a different level of success through diversity. Empirical studies are needed and might point to immature groups needing more-cohesive approaches while mature groups can operate with less-cohesive processes.

In any case, all members in a group have to experience the personal learning (PL) opportunities as they individually experience the intersection of the collaboration (C) and problem-solving (PS) opportunities. A performance landscape comprised of C crossed with PS thus forms a *CPS theater* or backdrop (Figure

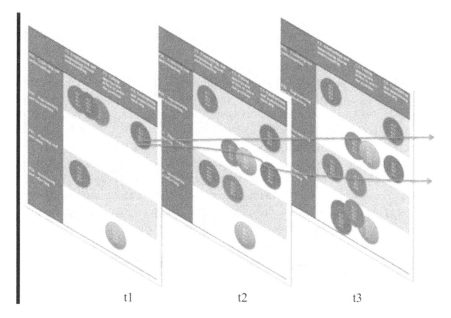

FIGURE 15.3. Trajectories of individual performance over times t1, t2, t3

15.2) for each individual's group-based experiences in PL while participating collaboratively to address a challenge or solve a problem. A snapshot of the group at a moment in time might place members at various locations in the CPS theater. In the documented observation in Figure 15.2, the red student is playing a lead role in keeping the group organized, while others are engaged in other group tasks.

If this account seems reasonable, then the assessment of the group's current and evolving interactions during collaborative problem solving can be thought of as a network of relationships evolving during the group's history with the current problem (Figure 15.3). At the first observation at time t1 in Figure 15.3, the red student is acting to keep the group organized and is participating in establishing a shared understanding of the problem. At the second observation at time t2, the red student has added the organizational role as the group moves into representing and formulating a proposed solution but has stopped participating openly in building the shared understanding. At the third observation at time t3, the red student has rejoined the shared vision and action during reflection while maintaining a role as group organizer.

DESIGN FRAMEWORK

The challenge for e-learning designers who intend to promote personalized learning through collaborative problem solving is to scaffold the three sets of concepts just outlined (personal learning, collaboration, and problem solving) in a domain-free way that allows the group and its members to be self-determining. The design needs to be domain-free in order to re-use the model for many different kinds of problems and to underscore that processes such as personal learning, collaboration, and problem solving have a core a set of measurable, observable competencies-in-action, which can be taught, supported, and improved over time in a variety of contexts. This does not ignore the vital role of subject knowledge for problem solving in a particular domain such as music, science, medicine, or mining. Subject-specific practices and approaches to knowledge can be added to and integrated into the framework, for example, in setting up a scenario for performance such as using advanced technologies to solve problems in cell biology. Using the PL-C-PS model with different discipline-enriched scenarios over time emphasizes the foundational and repeatable role of the processes, knowledge, and skills that help promote equitable individual participation, successful group functioning, and addressing complex, open-ended problems in teams.

The assessment targets of personal learning, collaboration, and problem solving are relatively independent of one another. For example, the group might be able to establish a shared understanding of their problem as the group is forming and exploring their strengths as well as their ideas concerning the problem but then fail to maintain that understanding during the planning and execution stage of problem solving. Or a group may take appropriate action that looks different at each of the four stages of problem solving. The group might be able to explore, formulate an action, and execute it but then be unprepared or unable to evaluate and reflect on what was learned and how the group functioned. Ideally, a well-designed, online learning experience will help the group as well as each individual in the group to thoughtfully work through each stage, while giving each individual the chance to experience the full set of personalized learning opportunities.

Designing for Personal Learning in Online, Collaborative Problem Solving

As noted in Webb and Gibson (2015), although collaborative learning is known to have a positive impact on students' learning (Johnson, Johnson, & Stanne, 2000; Lee, Linn, Varma, & Liu, 2010), productive interactions between students are not easily achieved (Barron, 2003; Chan, 2012), and appropriate learning situations are challenging to implement (Bell, Urhahne, Schanze, & Ploetzner, 2009). The design structure needs to promote the personal learning cycle in order to gain the most from each individual's potential contribution to the whole. The design has to help ensure that all group members have an equal chance in each of the intersections of collaboration and problem solving to share what they know and are learning, add their ideas to the mix, actively build and play with the ideas and solution concepts, and celebrate "ah-ha" moments and new insights with others. The three stages of collaboration (shared understanding, appropriate action, team organization) are critical to the core definition of coordinated, synchronous group activity that continuously creates and maintains a shared conception of a problem.

So, the design for collaboration, at a minimum, has to promote productive team-member interactions that build a shared understanding, create action plans, and keep the group together. In a similar vein, the four stages of problem solving (understanding the problem, representing and formulating the problem, planning and executing solution ideas, monitoring and reflecting on those solutions) are critical to the core definition of achieving a goal when no solution method is obvious. Thus, the design for problem solving has to support the team in working within and then transitioning into each of the problem-solving stages.

This produces a three-part design that can shape the learning experience for any part of the collaborative process in which the group chooses to work. Suppose the group would like to work today on defining the problem. The online design structure could prompt the group to note the group's status on collaboration and problem solving, while giving each member a chance to experience part or all of the personal learning cycle. There is no one "most correct" way to traverse the framework. Although there are a few pathways that generally lead to next best moves for the group (e.g. it is generally better if the group has a clear representation of the problem before it designs actions), it does not hurt the group process to return to an earlier intersection for a second or third chance to see what might develop. For example, if the group jumps to solution ideas before exploring the problem, then there is a chance that it will discover later that other explorers have already found that line of thought unproductive. This ah-ha moment in the group's reflection might amount to a feeling of "time wasted," but on the other hand, the group might invent a completely new way of thinking about the problem, which breaks through a former "finding" of earlier researchers. Since the goal is to maximize agency, decision-making, and the learning journey that ensues, the three-part design model is not focused on the reproduction of knowledge but instead is most concerned about new knowledge production by the group. If a "best solution" is already known, then the challenge or problem itself is not appropriate because open-endedness has been violated and the context has not been properly set for collaborative problem solving.

Designing for Online Assessment

Principled assessment design is required in order for an online learning experience to provide trustworthy evidence of learning, and the design must incorporate and take account of the engagement of the audiences for the assessment as well as vary with the purposes and contexts of the assessment (Webb & Gibson, 2015). Technology-enhanced assessment enables in-depth unobtrusive documentation or "quiet assessment" of the many layers and dynamics of authentic performance and allows greater flexibility and dynamic interactions in and among the design features. The design process for assessment uses "evidence-centered design" (Mislevy et al., 1999), with attention to three perspectives on assessment that include assessment FOR learning, assessment OF learning, and assessment AS learning.

The stages of the evidence-centered design process include:

- Domain analysis and modeling to define the assessment problem space and shape its affordances;
- Use of the conceptual assessment framework to define the assessment task, performance model, and evidentiary rules that map from student performance to the domain model;
- Development of the delivery and sampling plan to define the media, range of problem space for tasks, and presentation issues.

Most important for assessment FOR learning are interactive features that allow the learner to turn up or down the intensity, amount, and sharpness of the information needed for self-absorption and adoption of the feedback. Most important in assessment OF learning are features that compare the learner with external standards of performance. Most important in "assessment AS learning" are features that allow multiple performances and a wide array of affordances for authentic action, communication, and the production of artifacts.

Design Process

The design process for creating the requisite digital-media learning space for personal learning in online, collaborative problem solving (PL-C-PS) is iterative and nonlinear and can start anywhere in the framework, unlike traditional instructional design processes that are often linear and top-down in orientation. The only top-down aspect of the PL-C-PS model is the choice of challenge or problem domain with open-ended questions and no pre-ordained or limited solution sets that are already known to be "correct" or "best." In the case study presented below, the Curtin University authoring team chose one of the *United Nations Sustainable Development Goals* (Table 15.1) as the team's problem domain. The example case of *Balance of the Planet* described below uses water resources as the problem domain, with the key question, "How can everyone on earth be granted access to adequate clean water?"

Once the problem domain is selected and is deemed suitable according to the criteria of open-endedness and evoking many possible solutions, then the PL-C-PS framework can be tapped to consider seven *construct-space perspectives* in any order, utilizing the 11 sub-constructs of the framework to generate ideas, explore overlapping integration points, and create and shape the learner experience (Figure 15.4). The seven perspectives are PL, C, PS; the three intersections of each pair (e.g. PL-C, PL-PS, and C-PS); and the integration of all three (PL-C-PS). The OECD PISA assessment focuses on individual capability in the C-PS construct space; the PL-C-PS framework allows other focusing points in any of the single constructs or their intersections.

For example, the design team can use a set of 11 key questions (Table 15.2) about the sub-constructs of the framework as experienced by the learner at a cur-

TABLE 15.1.   UN Sustainable Development Goals

GOAL 1	End poverty in all its forms everywhere
GOAL 2	End hunger, achieve food security and improved nutrition, and promote sustainable agriculture
GOAL 3	Ensure healthy lives and promote well-being for all at all ages
GOAL 4	Ensure inclusive and equitable quality education and promote lifelong learning opportunities for all
GOAL 5	Achieve gender equality and empower all women and girls
GOAL 6	Ensure availability and sustainable management of water and sanitation for all
GOAL 7	Ensure access to affordable, reliable, sustainable, and modern energy for all
GOAL 8	Promote sustained, inclusive, and sustainable economic growth; full and productive employment; and decent work for all
GOAL 9	Build resilient infrastructure, promote inclusive and sustainable industrialization, and foster innovation
GOAL 10	Reduce inequality within and among countries
GOAL 11	Make cities and human settlements inclusive, safe, resilient, and sustainable
GOAL 12	Ensure sustainable consumption and production patterns
GOAL 13	Take urgent action to combat climate change and its impacts*
GOAL 14	Conserve and sustainably use the oceans, seas, and marine resources for sustainable development
GOAL 15	Protect, restore, and promote sustainable use of terrestrial ecosystems; sustainably manage forests; combat desertification; halt and reverse land degradation; and halt biodiversity loss
GOAL 16	Promote peaceful and inclusive societies for sustainable development; provide access to justice for all; and build effective, accountable, and inclusive institutions at all levels
GOAL 17	Strengthen the means of implementation and revitalize the global partnership for sustainable development

rently considered stage or any future stage of the experience and, with that perspective, organize the design team's thinking into metaphoric *experience pages* with hyperlinks coming into and out of each page (or a graph-theory-based network structure with nodes and edges), forming an interconnected *branching storyline* (Aldrich, 2005) of the possible experience pathways. The network for a particular storyline does not have to be complete because the learner will have more than one scenario with performance opportunities to cover the network and provide multiple measures on each sub-construct.

As the design team considers where the learner has immediately come from (e.g. which page of the branching storyline, at what point in the process) and where he or she might go afterwards, the key questions help generate *activity ideas* for each page of the experience, where each activity to the extent possible

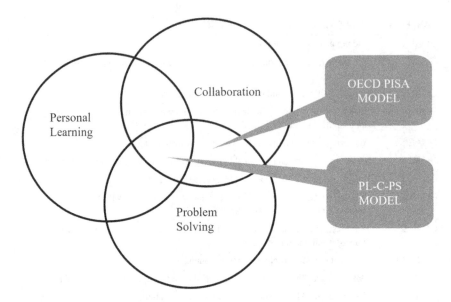

FIGURE 15.4.   Design framework for personal learning via collaborative problem solving.

TABLE 15.2.   Key Sub-Construct Questions

Personal Learning
How can the learner share his or her background, experience, and initial thoughts?
How can the learner be exposed to and reconcile differing ideas and viewpoints?
How can the learner create a critically reflective response-artifact that articulates a new understanding at this point in time?
How can the learner communicate and celebrate the results thus far?

Collaboration
How can the learner establish and maintain the group's shared understanding of the problem?
How can the learner take appropriate action to solve the problem?
How can the learner help establish and maintain the team organization?

Problem Solving
How can the learner explore and understand the problem?
How can the learner represent and formulate solution options?
How can the learner plan and execute appropriate actions?
How can the learner monitor and reflect on progress?

and feasible requires of the learner a thoughtful personal action (PL), an interaction with others in the group (C), and a mini-reflection on the group's progress on the solution (PS).

CASE STUDY: CURTIN UNIVERSITY'S BALANCE OF THE PLANET

In Curtin University's *Balance of the Planet*, the domain model, assessment, and design framework features outlined above are addressed by a set of connected and networked activities that help team members explore their own and others' strengths, interests, and aspirations in a collaborative context of a team that is solving a big challenge. The challenge undertaken by any team is its choice of one of the UN Sustainable Development Goals (Table 15.1), which have been validated and supported by an open process involving people across the world. *Challenge-based learning* is supported at Curtin University by a new, pedagogically driven, digital-learning platform called *Curtin Challenge,* which enables self-guided individual or group learning in game-inspired contexts. This case study section will briefly describe the ideas behind challenge-based learning, the platform, and the design of *Balance of the Planet* as a case example illustrating the theory and principles outlined above.

Challenge-Based Learning

Challenge-based learning builds on the practice of problem-based learning but with an exclusive focus on real-world problems being creatively addressed by diverse collaborative teams. In addition, several key distinctions add relevancy and urgency for students, especially when combined with game-inspired methods such as badges, levels, points, transparent goals, and clear progress-related feedback in self-paced learning. As noted by the New Media Consortium (Johnson, Smith, Smythe, & Varon, 2009):

> At the center of challenge-based learning is a call to action that inherently requires students to make something happen: they are compelled to research their topic, brainstorm strategies and solutions that are both credible and realistic in light of time and resources, and then develop and execute one of those solutions that addresses the challenge in ways both they themselves and others can see and measure. (p. 4)

Curtin University's approach adds game-based elements (Gibson, Aldrich, & Prensky, 2007; Gibson & Jakl, 2015), which creates increased self-empowerment for individuals in teams by making the learning process and higher-order goals explicit (not the solutions), providing assessable progress indicators of group-process evolution and product quality based on the PL-C-PS framework (rather than focusing on product delivery timelines and expert-only-scored quality feedback as in traditional assignments), and utilizing exogenous rewards, awards, and recognition that go beyond the current context. For example, a team selected as one of the best in the world this year for a solution in water quality might receive award certificates and recommendation letters that enhance the members' resumes, increase their opportunities for advanced study, and give them bragging rights for their successful collaborative efforts. It also doesn't hurt to have engaging, fun, light-heartedness, and wit embedded into self-guided learning experiences (Klopfer, Osterweil, & Salen, 2009; Malone & Lepper, 1987; Prensky, 2001), so we do not shy away from these aspects of game-based learning even though the purposes of the engagement are serious for both the participants and the real-world recipients of the team-based solutions and efforts.

Curtin Challenge

Curtin Challenge is a mobile-ready, interactive, learning-delivery platform that illustrates several features of game-inspired, challenge-based learning while adding a layer of big-data collection to enable research into teaching and learning. A learner interacts with Curtin Challenge content by pointing, clicking, sliding items, vocalizing, taking pictures, and drawing as well as watching, listening, reading, and writing as in traditional e-learning. The more highly engaging interactions occur more often (every few seconds) than in passive traditional e-learning. Key to engagement is having a compelling storyline, situating the learner as a prime actor in the story, and creating urgency of action through curiosity, humor, relevance, and individual or collaborative team pressures to produce and succeed.

The platform is being developed to support both individual and team-based learning in primarily open-ended, ill-structured problem-solving and project-based learning contexts. The platform can also support self-guided learning, automated feedback, branching story lines, self-organizing teams, and distributed processes of mentoring, learning support, and assessment.

The data traces captured by the platform are highly detailed, with many events per learning activity, which brings the potential for measuring indicators of physical, emotional, and cognitive states of the learner. The data innovation of the platform is the ability to capture event-based records of the higher-frequency and higher-dimensional aspects of learning engagement, which is in turn useful for analysis of the teaching effectiveness and impact on the physical, emotional, and cognitive layers of learning caused or influenced by the engagements. This forms a high-resolution analytics base on which people can conduct research into teaching and learning and into how to achieve better outcomes in scalable, digital-learning experiences (Gibson & Jakl, 2013, 2015).

Authoring content for the platform is a challenge for collaborating teams of discipline experts, digital instructional designers, and technologists. The team needs skills in systems thinking, mental models, game-based learning, and digital-delivery technologies in addition to the pedagogical and content knowledge of instruction in a field of knowledge. Curtin University meets this challenge by forming flexible teams of people from teaching and learning as well as the faculties and larger community to undertake authoring and implementing digital learning on Curtin Challenge.

Design of Balance of the Planet

Balance of the Planet is designed on the principles of challenge-based learning and is implemented on the Curtin Challenge platform, which adds new dimensions of self-organizing teams, self-determination of the challenge or problem domain, and a socially competitive environment for winning top awards and rewards from an external panel of judges. The learning-experience design utilizes the PL-C-PS framework to organize the activities and assessment and structure in three key phases.

Phase 1 (PL and C)

On registering for *Balance of the Planet*, participants provide basic profile information that is fleshed out through a number of individual activities aimed at sharing their background, interests, skills, aspirations, and the UN sustainability goal (see Table 15.1) they are most interested in. Participants can create a team and invite others with shared sustainability goal interests to join. Alternatively, they can browse or search for existing teams and ask to join one that has a vacancy. Developing skills for working in a distributed online team to make it a cohesive unit is an important learning outcome for *Balance of the Planet*. Once a team is formed, members work together through activities designed to guide and develop good teamwork practices including getting to know each other, understanding group processes, establishing ground rules for communication, reaching a consensus, responsibilities, project management, and strategies for working effectively together. The team identity is developed; team name and icon and later the mission statement will be included when they have worked on identifying the problem they will solve.

Phase 2 (C)

Open-ended exploration of authentic problem-solving can generate considerable cognitive load if not supported by guided instruction, according to Kirschner, Sweller, and Clark (2006); however, several features are built into the learning design of the challenge to support learners without relying on instruction. Guidance is through scaffolded activities, team mentors, expert mentors, and social networks (PL). The process of teamwork is captured through activities, assessment, and peer feedback, which also includes responding to feedback from team members, other teams, mentors, social networks, and experts. As the team works through activities, the problem is defined, the opportunities it may offer are identified, and the resources it requires are explored through research and posing questions (C). Rubric-driven assessment of individual and team learning and capability is embedded throughout the learning experience, and progress through activities is shown on the team page. Team progress in the overall challenge is published to a leaderboard that is visible to all other teams.

Phase 3 (C and PS)

Now that the problem has been identified and is deemed solvable, the team members work on developing a solution and expand their network to include experts and special-interest groups associated with their problem. The team uses an artifact that captures individual contributions to develop a Technical Innovation Plan (TIP), which is the first assessable artifact of the *Balance of the Planet* challenge. Teams can choose to exit at this point with a TIP badge. Teams wishing to complete the entire challenge can create prototypes of their solution or build a comprehensive business plan for the solution. Continuous feedback and advice on their solution is gained throughout the processes and assists in refining the plan or prototype (C-PS). Team members are asked to reflect on team function at each phase. The plan/prototype is voted on through social networks as a final stage prior to submission to an expert panel for judgment to earn their full *Balance of the Planet* badge and be eligible to win the challenge competition.

CONCLUSION

Designing learning experiences for personal learning, collaboration, and problem solving requires the development of a learning environment that provides opportunities for teams and individuals to engage in meaningful, measurable collaborative processes as well as via the production of artifacts. The environments form the backdrop for situations that evoke knowledge-in-use, and, as noted by Mislevy (2011), provide opportunities to capture data about what people say, do, or make as evidence for an assessment argument. Assessment of the personal learning of each team member, captured without disturbing the natural functioning of a group during collaborative problem solving, is now more technically feasible due to the availability of digital learning environments. Emerging technology platforms such as the Curtin Challenge provide data collection of the actions, communications, and products created by group members in a designed task space for self-directed individual and group learning. Evidence of learning from the analysis of these digital records can be used to infer how people engage in coordinated activity to construct and maintain a shared conception of how to tackle an open-ended, challenging problem.

REFERENCES

Aldrich, C. (2005). *Learning by doing: The essential guide to simulations, computer games, and pedagogy in e-learning and other educational experiences.* San Francisco, CA: Jossey-Bass.

Barron, B. (2003). When smart groups fail. *Journal of the Learning Sciences, 12*(3), 307–359.

Bell, T., Urhahne, D., Schanze, S., & Ploetzner, R. (2009). Collaborative inquiry learning: models, tools, and challenges. *International Journal of Science Education, 32*(3), 349–377.

Carroll, T. (2000). If we didn't have the schools we have today, would we create the schools we have today? *AACE/SITE conference*. San Diego, CA.

Chan, C. K. (2012). Co-regulation of learning in computer-supported collaborative learning environments: A discussion. *Metacognition and Learning, 7*(1), 63–73.

Friedrichs, A. (2000). *Continuous learning dialogues: An ethnography of personal learning plans' impact on four River High School learners*. (Doctoral dissertation). Burlington, VT: University of Vermont.

Friedrichs, A., & Gibson, D. (2003). Personalization and secondary school renewal. In J. DiMartino, J. Clarke, & D. Wolf (Eds.), *Personalized learning: Preparing high school students to create their futures*. (pp. 4–68.). Lanham, MD: Scarecrow Education.

Gibson, D., Aldrich, C., & Prensky, M. (Eds.). (2007). *Games and simulations in online learning: Research and development frameworks*. Hershey, PA: Information Science Publishing.

Gibson, D., & Clarke, J. (2000). Reflections on visual representation. In J. Clarke, J. Bossange, C. Erb, D. Gibson, & B. Nelligan (Eds.), *Dynamics of change in high school teaching: A study of innovation in five Vermont professional development schools*. (pp. 173–189). Providence, RI: Brown University.

Gibson, D., & Jakl, P. (2013). *Data challenges of leveraging a simulation to assess learning*. West Lake Village, CA. Retrieved from http://www.curveshift.com/images/Gibson_Jakl_data_challenges.pdf

Gibson, D., & Jakl, P. (2015). Theoretical considerations for game-based e-learning analytics. In T. Reiners & L. Wood (Eds.), *Gamification in education and business* (pp. 403–416). Springer. Retrieved from http://link.springer.com/chapter/10.1007/978-3-319-10208-5_20

Hartman, H. J. (2001). Metacognition in learning and instruction: Theory, research, and practice. *Neuropsychology and cognition* (Vol. 19)*. Dordrecht, Netherlands; Boston, MA: Kluwer Academic Publishers.

Johnson, D. W., Johnson, R. T., & Stanne, M. B. (2000). *Co-operative learning methods: A meta-analysis*. Minneapolis, MN: University of Minnesota.

Johnson, L., Smith, R., Smythe, J., & Varon, R. (2009). *Challenge-based learning: An approach for our time*. Austin, TX: The New Media Consortium. Retrieved from http://search.ebscohost.com/login.aspx?direct=true&db=eric&AN=ED505102&site=ehost-live

Kirschner, P., Sweller, J., & Clark, R. (2006). Why minimal guidance during instruction does not work: An analysis of the failure of constructivist, discovery, problem-based, experiential, and inquiry-based teaching. *Educational Psychologist, 41*(2), 75–86. Retrieved from https://doi.org/10.1207/s15326985ep4102_1

Klopfer, E., Osterweil, S., & Salen, K. (2009). *Moving learning games forward: Obstacles, opportunities, and openness. Flora*. Boston, MA: Massachusetts Institute of Technology. Retrieved from http://education.mit.edu/papers/MovingLearningGamesForward_EdArcade.pdf

Lee, H.-S., Linn, M. C., Varma, K., & Liu, O. L. (2010). How do technology-enhanced inquiry science units impact classroom learning? *Journal of Research in Science Teaching, 47*(1), 71–90.

Malone, T., & Lepper, M. (1987). Making learning fun: A taxonomy of intrinsic motivations for learning. In R. Snow & M. Farr (Eds.), *Aptitude, learning and instruction (Vol. 3): Cognitive and affective process analysis*. Englewood Cliffs, NJ: Erlbaum.

Mayer, R., & Wittrock, M. (1996). Problem-solving transfer. In D. Berliner & R. Calfee (Eds.), *Handbook of educational psychology* (pp. 47–62). New York, NY: Simon & Schuster Macmillan.

Mislevy, R. (2011). *Evidence-centered design for simulation-based assessment*. Los Angeles, CA: The National Center for Research on Evaluation, Standards, and Student Testing.

Mislevy, R., Steinberg, L., & Almond, R. (1999). *Evidence-centered assessment design*. Princeton, NJ: Educational Testing Service. Retrieved from http://www.education.umd.edu/EDMS/mislevy/papers/ECD_overview.html

Newmann, F. M., & Wehlage, G. G. (1995). *Successful school restructuring: A report to the public and educators*. Madison, WI: University of Wisconsin Center on Organization and Restructuring.

NSDC-NICI. (2001). *E-learning for educators: Implementing the standards for staff development*. National Staff Development Council & National Institutes for Community Innovations. Oxford, OH: National Staff Development Council.

Pellegrino, J., Chudowsky, N., & Glaser, R. (2001). Knowing what students know: The science and design of educational assessment. *Committee on the Foundations of Assessment, Board on Testing and Assessment, Center for Education, National Research Council*. Washington, DC: National Academy Press.

PISA. (2013). *Draft collaborative problem solving framework*. Paris: Organization for Economic and Community Development.

Prensky, M. (2001). *Digital game-based learning*. New York, NY: McGraw-Hill.

Roschelle, J., & Teasley, S. (1995). The construction of shared knowledge in collaborative problem-solving. In C. O'Malley (Ed.), *Computer-supported collaborative learning* (pp. 69–97). Berlin: Springer-Verlag.

Slavin, R. E. (2010). Cooperative learning. In *International Encyclopedia of Education* (pp. 177–183). doi:10.1016/B978-0-08-044894-7.00494-2

Webb, M., & Gibson, D. (2015, *June*). Technology enhanced assessment in complex collaborative settings. *Education and Information Technologies, 4*, 675–695. doi:10.1007/s10639-015-9413-5

Weinert, F. E., & Kluwe, R. (1987). *Metacognition, motivation, and understanding. The psychology of education and instruction*. Hillsdale, NJ: L. Erlbaum Associates.

Wiggins, G. (1989). Teaching to the (authentic) test. *Educational Leadership, 46*, 41–46.

CHAPTER 16

THE IMPACT OF AN ONLINE COLLABORATIVE LEARNING PROGRAM ON ATTITUDES TOWARD TECHNOLOGY IN TWO EDUCATION COLLEGES

Noga Magen-Nagar

The accelerated development of innovative technologies has created a new culture of digital communication and sharing that shape the individual, society, and education (Horizon Report, 2014). In universities and colleges, the requirement that technology be used in learning is increasing (Lambert et al., 2014). Higher-education institutions aim to adopt these technologies, but the implementation involves extensive organizational and pedagogical change in teaching courses and academic learning (Amirault, 2012). Interactive online learning can lead to collaborative learning, which is vital in the 21st century (Melamed et al., 2011; Resta & Carrol, 2010). Therefore, it is highly important that students experience online collaborative teaching and learning in teacher-training colleges. The experience described in this chapter is accompanied by research that may provide significant

Collaborative Online Learning in a Global World, pages 249–265.
Copyright © 2019 by Information Age Publishing
All rights of reproduction in any form reserved.

information leading toward understanding the processes and causes involved in the success of collaborative models in higher education.

ONLINE COLLABORATIVE LEARNING

Online Collaborative Learning (OCL) is one of the accepted teaching methods in distance learning. OCL is based on traditional collaborative learning, which includes five interwoven components: (1) positive mutual dependency; (2) personal accountability; (3) promoting interaction; (4) social skills; and (5) group process (Johnson & Johnson, 1999). When these components are included in the course of effective teaching, the academic achievements, involvement, responsibility, and intrinsic motivation of learners improve (Hanze & Berger, 2007). Online collaborative learning is similar to face-to-face collaborative learning, except that group members' meetings take place through the Internet in a synchronous or asynchronous way. Online collaborative-learning theory developed with the expansion of online learning in education systems (Harasim, 2012). Collaborative learning in online courses can play a very valuable role because it alleviates the student's loneliness in online courses in which communication takes place through written texts, pictures, and videos but without an interpersonal touch.

Collaborative learning in online courses creates interaction between the learners and a sense of social presence (Resta & Shonfeld, 2013). This contributes to improving learning, increasing the ability to adjust to different teaching methods, and enhancing the motivation and satisfaction of students (Abedin, 2012; Harasim, 2012; Palloff & Pratt, 2005). Salmon (2004) has developed a model for e-moderators that demarcates the progression of tasks that the online teacher moves through in the process of effectively moderating an online course. The stages include (1) individual access and motivation to use computer-mediated communication; (2) online socialization and formulation of online identities; (3) relevant information exchange among learners; (4) knowledge construction through collaborative discussion and interaction; and (5) development of meta-thinking and application of knowledge and online skills to learners' goals and purposes that are often exam-related. In each stage of the model, interaction and the learning level among the learners increase incrementally as they move to a higher stage (Salmon, Nie, & Edirisingha, 2010). Research shows that students who learn in online courses report high intrinsic motivation, which is expressed by enjoyment and interest, high self-efficacy, a sense of autonomy, and relaxed learning, which contribute to their success in the course (Callaghan, Graff, & Davies, 2013; Katz & Yablon, 2009). However, some students display technophobia, characterized by an unwillingness to use technology, having negative attitudes towards it, a lack of technological self-confidence, and fear of using technological devices (Sivakumaran & Lux, 2011).

The term "attitudes towards technology" refers to an individual's attitudes in three aspects: behavioral, including technological tendencies and the inclination to work with technology; cognitive, including technological self-confidence and the ability to perform digital tasks; and emotional, including technological anxiety, worry, or fear while using technology and anxiety about acquiring digital skills (Loyd & Gressard, 1984). This research project examined the contribution of collaboration, satisfaction, and intrinsic motivation to increasing positive attitudes towards the use of technology among students. The research is based on the assumption that teachers' attitudes, perceptions, and beliefs about technology affect the teaching in an ICT (Information Communication Technology) environment, and, moreover, they are the most significant factors in implementing change (Cunningham, 2009; De Freitas & Oliver, 2005; Halverson & Smith, 2010; Selwyn, 2010).

According to the Theory of Planned Behavior (Ajzen, 1991), attitude affects behavior through the process of planned decision making. The decision to behave in a certain way is rational and not spontaneous and is a result of the intention to perform the behavior and the amount of effort that the person is willing to put in. An intention to behave in a certain way may predict future behavior. Three factors affect intentions to behave in a certain way: 1. attitudes towards the behavior–how much the person values the behavior, positively or negatively; 2. subjective norms–the perception of what those who are important to the person might say about her or his behaving or not behaving in a certain way; 3. perceived behavioral control–how easy or difficult the person perceives the behavior to be. Researchers claim that the more positive the attitudes towards the behavior and the subjective norms, and the higher the perceived behavioral control, the stronger the behavioral intentions will be (Doll & Ajzen, 1992); and the higher the intentions, the greater the likelihood of performing the behavior (Schifter & Ajzen, 1985). The theory assumes that behavior is an indirect product of information or relevant beliefs towards the behavior, so that each of the intention factors is derived from relevant beliefs. This theoretical model may provide an approach to developing interventions aimed at changing human behavior (Ajzen, 2002). In this research, experience in online collaborative learning will serve as a model for collaborative learning in the classroom.

THE MEDTEC INTERVENTION PROGRAM

Pedagogical Perspective

An innovative syllabus based on online collaboration among students from different academic institutions was developed as part of advanced studies (i.e. the intervention in this study) in two education colleges in Israel. The syllabus drew on innovative pedagogical principles, including (1) informed use of digital teaching-learning processes in classes integrating technology, (2) teaching-learning processes based on personal and collaborative knowledge, (3) research-based self-learning including innovative technological tools, (4) newly created and accessible digital learning materials, (5) management of teaching-learning processes with online organizational tools, (6) expansion of class boundaries and effective learning times, and (7) provision for diversity and diverse learning styles. The chosen learning model was Technology, Education, and Cultural Diversity (TEC) (Shonfeld, Hoter, & Ganayem, 2013). This model is based on the conditions of contact theory (Allport, 1954): equality between participants, collaboration not competition, institutional support, and a long period of discussion and partnership within groups and not between individuals. In addition, the model suggests a gradual development in communication and strengthening trust within the groups during the group work through the Internet, in which it is possible to hold discussions without seeing or hearing one another. According to the TEC model, online collaborative learning begins with textual communication, after which comes verbal communication, then the online visual aspect, and finally a face-to-face meeting. Collaboration in learning develops gradually through joint performance of tasks, and it passes from the dialog stage to the synergetic collaboration stage as well as from using simple tools to complex network tools.

The study's intervention program included two main goals: first, comprehensive meaningful learning about distance-learning issues; second, experiencing distant learning while developing research skills, collaboration, and analytical thinking in an ICT environment. Each group in the intervention class explored a subject according to the research stages and scientific approach. The research processes were based on readings, discussions, interviews, and collaborative writing while using collaborative-technological tools that are a part of the TEC social network, such as the group blog, group discussions, group pages, and synchronous meetings (Shonfeld, Hoter, & Ganayem, 2013).

Implementing the Program

The program included three stages: Preparation, Introduction, and Research Process.

Stage A: Preparation

During the term break, the lecturers built the program and listed a variety of research subjects in the field of distance learning that are relevant to the education world, such as self-regulation in an ICT environment, digital gap and equality in education, the teachers' and students' roles in the digital era, and mobile learning. During the development of the program, gradual assimilation was emphasized. The program was built according to the number of sessions and the distribution of sessions among face-to-face, synchronous, and asynchronous meetings. In the first two sessions of the course, the lecturer at each college introduced the program to her students. Additionally, the lecturer introduced the social network and how to operate within it. Following that, each student chose a topic according to his or her own interest areas. Eight research groups were formed, with four to six students in each.

Stage B: Introduction–Who Are We?

For the group members to get to know each other, each wrote four words that were related to her or his personality and educational activity. After writing the four words, each student sent clarification questions to the group peers and answered questions. The communication took place in the group forum.

Stage C: Group Research Process

a. Brainstorming–each member of the group raised ideas and concepts related to the research subject.

b. Information searching–each member of the group searched for two information sources about the subject and wrote a summary in the forum.

c. Asking questions–the group members read the materials written by their colleagues, discussing issues and forming a fertile research question.

d. Information gathering–all members of the group posted a position interview guide on the group's wiki. They performed the interviews in a Blackboard environment. Each student interviewed a group member, recorded the interview, and wrote a summary of it.

e. Preparing a learning activity–the group wrote a general summary built from the research question, the insights that came from the interviews, and the research conclusions. After that, they planned a learning activity based on findings and conclusions from the research on the subject and distributed it to colleagues in the other groups.

f. Performing and evaluating an activity–each student performed a learning activity and evaluated it.

Figure 16.1 reflects the study process conducted in the six stages defined in time units, with some stages involving teamwork and some independent learning. The distance-learning topics studied varied and included innovative learning environments, mobile learning, project-based learning, social networks in education, and challenges of collaborative learning.

In contrast to the intervention program described above, a control group experienced a traditional online course, where contents were presented on a course website and divided into "lessons" in which the students were required to learn independently. The communication with students took place through a forum and the lecturer's email. Occasionally, the students were permitted to hand in assignments as a group. Usually the tasks were separated and required comprehension and analysis. The assessment of students was left to the lecturer and ranged from conventional to alternative methods (Cheng, Jordan, & Schallert, 2013).

Research Goal

The goal of the research was to examine the contribution of collaboration to predicting attitudes about advanced technology among students in the control compared to the intervention courses. The research question was "To what extent

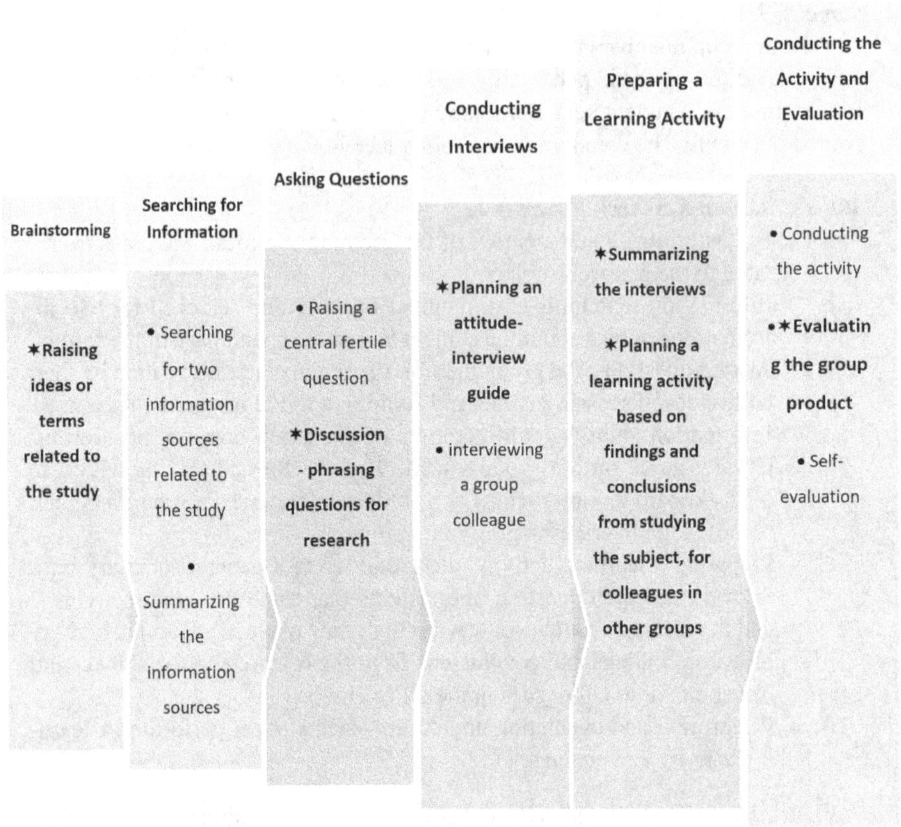

Conducting the
Activity and
Evaluation

Preparing a
Learning Activity

Conducting
Interviews

Asking Questions

Searching for
Information

Brainstorming

• Conducting
the activity

✳Summarizing
the interviews

✳Planning an
attitude-
interview
guide

• Raising a
central fertile
question

• Searching
for two
information
sources
related to
the study

✳Raising
ideas or
terms
related to
the study

•✳Evaluatin
g the group
product

✳Planning a
learning activity
based on
findings and
conclusions
from studying
the subject, for
colleagues in
other groups

• interviewing
a group
colleague

✳Discussion
- phrasing
questions for
research

• Self-
evaluation

•

Summarizing
the
information
sources

FIGURE 16.1. The study process in online collaborative groups

does collaboration between students in these two conditions affect satisfaction, intrinsic motivation, and positions towards advanced technology?"

Research Hypotheses

1. Collaboration contributes to explaining the variance in satisfaction with the course curriculum; thus, a stronger effect will be found in the intervention group than in the control group.

2. Collaboration contributes to explaining the variance of intrinsic motivation to perform the course's assignments; thus, a stronger effect will be found in the intervention group than in the control group.

3. Collaboration in the intervention group more than in the control group has an indirect effect on predicting satisfaction with and intrinsic motivation about advanced technology.

METHOD

This exploratory study was performed in two teacher-training colleges in Israel. Both colleges integrated the novel, collaborative, intervention program in online courses. The research design is a quantitative controlled experiment. One-time measurement was performed following an intervention in the study group and in the control group. This is a design used for preliminary testing of a phenomenon.

Participants

Ninety-two graduate M.Ed. students from two colleges of education participated. The intervention group had 47 students studying in an online course, of whom 32 (68.1%) were students at one college of education and 15 (31.9%) were students at the other. The control group included 45 students studying in a regular online course.

The average number of years that students in the intervention group had taught was 13.7 (SD=8.23) and in the control group, 15.16 (SD=7.14). Both groups consisted of a female majority (91.5% and 95.6%, respectively).

Research Tools

Four questionnaires were used during the study:

1. *Collaboration Questionnaire*: This questionnaire was taken from a subset of the collaborative learning, social presence, and satisfaction questionnaire developed by So & Brush (2008). The questionnaire's reliability was α=.92.
2. *Satisfaction Questionnaire*: This questionnaire was based on the Dayan and Magen-Nagar questionnaire (2013) and was adapted for this study. The questionnaire's reliability was α=.92.
3. *Intrinsic Motivation Questionnaire*: This questionnaire was based on the shortened intrinsic motivation questionnaire by Ryan, Koestner, and Deci (1991). The questionnaire's reliability was α=.91.
4. *Attitudes towards Advanced Technologies Questionnaire*: This questionnaire was based on the questionnaire by Francisa, Katz, and Jones (2000) developed from the questionnaire by Loyd and Gressard (1984). The questionnaire's reliability was α=.95. The questionnaire's indicators are technological anxiety, technological self-confidence, and technological inclination.

All the questionnaires used a Likert scale ranging from 1 ("strongly disagree") to 5 ("strongly agree").

Research Procedure

After having finished the online courses, the students were asked to complete self-report questionnaires online using a Google Forms application to evaluate integrating online courses in academic learning.

FINDINGS

In order to test the research hypotheses, Pearson correlations were conducted between the research variables (Table 16.1).

Table 16.1 shows that medium to strong, significant, positive relationships were found between all of the research variables except technological anxiety. This means that the more the students collaborated, reported satisfaction with the course curriculum, and had intrinsic motivation to perform the course's tasks, the more positive their attitudes towards technology were.

To test the contribution of collaboration, satisfaction, and intrinsic motivation of students to the prediction of attitudes towards technology, a path analysis model with structural equation modeling (SEM) was proposed, using the Analysis of Moment Structures (AMOS) 22.0 statistical software (Arbuckle, 2013; Blunch, 2008). This software allows examination of variables and their relationships simultaneously and improves the examination's reliability through reference to the measurement model and the structural model; thus, the analysis may reinforce or disprove the foundation of the theory upon which the research is based.

The first stage in structural equation analysis is assessment of the measurement model, which is done by testing the measures that indicate its fit to the model. The

TABLE 16.1. Pearson Correlation Matrix Between the Research Variables (N=92)

	Collaboration	Satisfaction from the Course Curriculum	Intrinsic Motivation for Course's Task Performance	M	SD
Collaboration				3.86	.83
Satisfaction from the Course Curriculum	.63**			3.77	.82
Intrinsic Motivation for Course's Task Performance	.62**	.72**		3.66	.59
Attitudes towards Technology	.26*	.43**	.44**	3.99	.68
Technological Anxiety	−.17	−.30**	−.29**	2.59	.43
Technological Self-Confidence	.25**	.39**	.40**	4.03	.74
Technological Inclination	.33**	.48**	.47**	3.86	.68

**P<.01; *P<.05

TABLE 16.2. Fit Measures of the Model for Predicting Attitudes Towards Technology

Fit Measures	Recommended Levels of Fit	Value of the Measure
χ^2	n.s. at p < .05	n.s.19.535
χ^2 / df	< 5	1.628
CFI	>.90	97.
NFI	>.90	93.
RMSEA	<.08	08.

four measures χ^2, RMSEA, NFI, and CFI are used to test the model best fit for reality (Bentler & Bonett, 1980; Kline, 2010). Table 16.2 shows the fit measures of the model for predicting attitudes towards technology.

The results of the measurement model's fit presented in Table 16.1 show that all terms were measured in a valid way; thus, they strengthen the theoretical basis that guided the choice of the different indicators for the two groups. Additionally, the findings of the measurement model indicate a good fit of the model to the research data.

Testing the Structural Model and Reinforcement of the Research Hypotheses

The second stage is the assessment of the structural model which estimates the causal relationships between variables of two kinds: exogenous variables, which are the independent variables and are not affected by other variables in the model, and endogenous variables, which are affected by variables in the model.

The exogenous variable was collaboration, and the endogenous variables were satisfaction, intrinsic motivation, and the three types of attitudes towards technology. The satisfaction variable is a mediating variable observed between collaboration and intrinsic motivation. The intrinsic motivation variable is a mediating variable observed between satisfaction and the three types of attitudes towards technology: technological anxiety, technological self-confidence, and technological inclination. Also, it is a mediating variable between collaboration and the three types of attitudes towards technology. Figure 16.2 presents the path analysis of the intervention group, students who were studying in an innovative online course, and Figure 16.3, the control group analysis of students who were studying in a regular online course. Figures 2 and 3 show the standardized effect coefficient (β) and the percentage of variance explained (R^2).

Figures 16.2 and 16.3 indicate that a similar picture of the intervention group and the control group was received at a high level of the percentage of variance explained of the students' satisfaction, explained by the level of collaboration (33% and 44% respectively). Also, a high level was received in the percentage

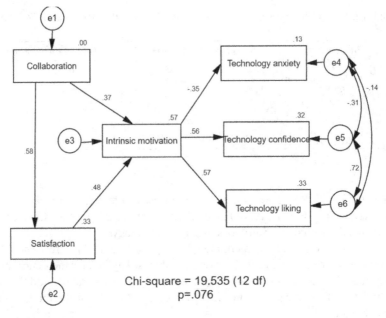

FIGURE 16.2.   Path Analysis for the Intervention Group

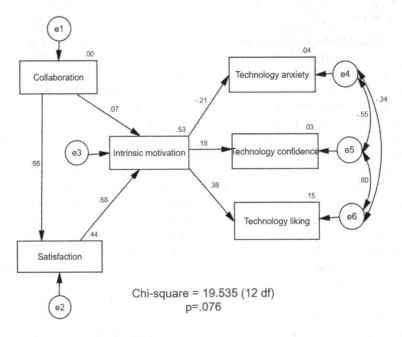

FIGURE 16.3.   Path Analysis for the Control GroupGroup

of variance explained of intrinsic motivation among students in the intervention group and the control group, which is explained by the level of collaboration and satisfaction (57% and 53% respectively). However, the types of attitudes towards technology (i.e. technological anxiety, technological self-confidence, and technological inclination among students in the intervention group) are explained by intrinsic motivation (between 13% and 33% of the explained variance), whereas among students in the control group, intrinsic motivation is explained somewhat by technological inclination (15%) and not by technological anxiety and technological self-confidence (4% and 3% respectively).

Testing the first hypothesis shows that among students in both the intervention group and the control group, collaboration had a strong, significant, positive effect on the level of satisfaction ($p<.001$; $\beta=.66$, $\beta=.58$, accordingly). This means that the higher the level of collaboration shown by the student, the higher the satisfaction from the course's curriculum. The hypothesis was not reinforced.

Testing the second hypothesis shows that among students of the intervention group, collaboration has a medium, significant, positive effect on the level of intrinsic motivation to complete the course's tasks ($p<.001$; $\beta=.37$). This means that the higher the level of collaboration shown by the student in the intervention group, the higher the intrinsic motivation to complete the course's tasks. However, among students in the control group, no effect of collaboration on the level of intrinsic motivation was found. The hypothesis was reinforced.

In examining the third research assumption, two sets of path analysis were taken. On one path, it is apparent that satisfaction has a strong, significant, positive effect on the level of intrinsic motivation among students in both the intervention group and the control group ($p<.001$; $\beta=.68$, $\beta=.48$, accordingly). That is, the higher the satisfaction of a student with the course program, the higher the intrinsic motivation to complete the course tasks. The assumption was not reinforced. Also, it was found that in the control group, collaboration had a meaningful indirect effect on predicting intrinsic motivation, more than in the intervention group. This means that in the control group the satisfaction variable was a meaningful mediator between collaboration and intrinsic motivation, more than in the intervention group.

The second path shows that among students in the intervention group, intrinsic motivation had a strong significant positive effect on technological self-confidence and technological inclination ($p<.001$; $\beta=.57$, $\beta=.56$, accordingly), and a medium significant positive effect on technological anxiety ($p<.01$; $\beta=-.35$). This means that the higher the level of intrinsic motivation shown by the student in the intervention group, the higher the technological self-confidence and technological inclination and the lower the technological anxiety. However, among students in the control group, intrinsic motivation had a medium, significant, positive effect on technological inclination ($p<.01$; $\beta=.38$), and there was no effect on technological self-confidence and technological anxiety. This means that the higher the

TABLE 16.3. Intrinsic Motivation Mediation Findings

| | MEDTEC Collaboration in the Intervention group | | Traditional Collaboration in the Control group | |
	With mediation of intrinsic motivation	Without mediation of intrinsic motivation	With mediation of intrinsic motivation	Without mediation of intrinsic motivation
Technological anxiety	n.s.	$p < .01$	n.s.	n.s.
Technological self-confidence	$p < .05$	$p < .001$	n.s.	n.s.
Technological inclination	$p < .001$	$p < .001$	n.s.	$p < .01$

level of intrinsic motivation shown by the student in the control group, the higher the technological inclination. The hypothesis was partially reinforced.

In order to examine the indirect effect compared to the direct effect between collaboration, motivation, and attitudes towards advanced technology, mediation tests were taken. Table 16.3 shows the results.

Table 16.3 shows that there were significant differences between the intervention group and the control group. Analysis of the indirect effect of collaboration on predicting attitudes towards advanced technologies showed that in the intervention group collaboration had a meaningful indirect effect on predicting measurements of positions about advanced technologies (technological anxiety, technological self-confidence, and technological tendency), more than in the control group. This means that in the intervention group, more than in the control group, the intrinsic motivation variable was a meaningful mediator between collaboration and attitudes towards advanced technologies. Therefore, the research assumption was reinforced.

DISCUSSION AND CONCLUSIONS

Educational reformers recommend integrating collaborative technologies as part of learning 21st-century skills (Harasim, 2012; OECD, 2013; Resta & Carol, 2010). Teacher-training colleges implement ICT and collaborative learning as part of Israel's Ministry of Education policy and have shown progress in the use of ICT with teachers and students. However, collaborative environments and collaborative teaching and learning methods have yet to be implemented as required (Magen-Nagar & Shamir-Inbal, 2014). The demand for the implementation of the TEC model is expanding in teacher training and in schools, but difficulties still arise in integrating online collaborative learning (Shonfeld, Hoter, & Ganayem, 2013). The findings described in this study may contribute to a better understanding of the implementation of collaborative learning both in higher education and in schools.

The path analysis shows that in the intervention group the student's level of collaboration in the group impacts intrinsic motivation and affects his or her attitudes towards technology. The most significant contribution is an inclination toward adopting advanced technology, then to self-confidence in using it, and finally to decreasing anxiety about it. Perhaps the uniqueness of the intervention program was the teaching method based on online collaborative learning that integrated group research learning. The interaction between the learners and a sense of social presence contributed to intrinsic motivation (Resta & Shonfeld, 2013; Zimmerman, 2012). Collaboration among these students was relevant and essential to learning, and so it increased or enhanced intrinsic motivation. It is possible that the pedagogy was innovative for the students and that is why they experienced excitement, curiosity, and enjoyment in learning. However, in the control group, the level of their collaboration in the group did not affect the students' intrinsic motivation. The regular online courses had forums and tasks that could be completed as a group. Usually, the collaboration required effort and time, and so it became a burden in an online course, even if students chose to perform tasks as a group.

The research findings show that in the control group, the higher the level of collaboration, the higher the satisfaction, and the latter affected intrinsic motivation. It is possible that the students in the control group saw the collaboration as an important value of innovative learning, and that is the reason why intrinsic motivation increased, regardless of the satisfaction derived from the course. The findings show that satisfaction is a significant mediator for a strong, positive relationship between collaboration and motivation. It is possible that the collaborative learning in the online course created satisfaction, which resulted in students' intrinsic desire to invest. However, in the intervention group, collaborative learning at a distance produced coordination and balance among the different students. It appears that the students were involved and understood the importance of collaborative learning in the course as well as for personal development; therefore, the intrinsic motivation increased.

It is possible that the satisfaction with the online innovative program was higher because it was more interesting to the students and contributed to their self-efficacy and sense of autonomy more than in a traditional course. Therefore, an online collaborative program that is meaningful for the student may promote positive attitudes towards technology. This claim requires further research. The research findings indicate a strong effect of intrinsic motivation on attitudes towards technology when the learning occurs in an ICT environment based on collaboration. Students' intrinsic motivation may promote positive attitudes towards technology when technology is considered an essential and effective tool for promoting their personal and professional needs. Indeed, Katz and Yablon (2009) found that students who study in a distance-learning environment report high intrinsic motivation. It can be assumed that after their experience in this innovative program, the students were ready to implement an online, collaborative-learning model in their work at school while focusing on teaching goals and not technology learning per se.

The collaboration effect in the intervention group was stronger than in the control group both for intrinsic motivation and satisfaction. Therefore, the intervention program influenced the professional development of the study's teacher participants (students). The students wrote: "To be a part of a process of distance learning–is true collaborative learning."; "The learning was enriching, interesting and an experience."; "I acquired knowledge in the field of technology and collaborative learning."; "I met a new, fascinating world." Quality collaboration in the group, social interactions, active participation, and involvement led to students' satisfaction (Abedin, 2012; Palloff & Pratt, 2005) with the course.

In the intervention group, the students' intrinsic motivation had a stronger significance influence on the relationship between collaboration and technological anxiety. In the control group, the motivation was not a mediator. Anxiety is a feeling of danger and deep stress, which is sometimes caused by rapid technological change. Collaboration does not affect anxiety unless the intrinsic motivation increases, meaning that collaboration that increases intrinsic motivation contributes to a decrease in technological anxiety. Therefore, it is important to raise students' awareness of the fact that even if they are unfamiliar with the advanced technologies and are weary of the complexity, but are willing to learn collaboratively, they will succeed in reducing their technological anxiety and will use advanced technology efficiently for their needs.

In the intervention group, the students' intrinsic motivation had a stronger significance in the relationship between collaboration and technological self-confidence and technological inclination. In true collaboration, everyone feels a part of the resulting product, the intrinsic motivation increases, and so does technological self-confidence and inclination.

The current research, due to its pioneering nature, is narrow. Therefore, more comprehensive research including many varied courses offered by colleges of education taking part in online collaborative programs is recommended. Additionally, the length of the intervention was relatively short, which made it difficult to examine the changes that the students experienced. Therefore, it is recommended that the intervention program be expanded and operated for the majority of the course, with the study examining attitudes towards technology and motivation to adopt it both before and after the intervention. Finally, to expand the research, interviews with students should be added and the content of the interim and final products of the study assignments be analyzed. These steps might offer a broader picture of the learning in the program and contribute to explaining the findings.

REFERENCES

Allport, G.W. (1954). *The nature of prejudice*. Reading, MA: AddisonWesley.

Abedin, B. (2012). Sense of community and learning outcomes in computer supported collaborative learning environments. *Proceeding of International Conference on Business and Information, Academy of Taiwan Information Systems Research* (pp. 964–969). Saporo, Japan.

Amirault, R. J. (2012). Distance learning in the 21st century university. *The Quarterly Review of Distance Education, 13*(4), 253–265.

Arbuckle, J. L. (2013). *AMOS 22.0 user's guide*. Chicago: SPSS Inc.

Ajzen, I. (1991). The theory of planned behavior. *Organizational Behavior and Human Decision Processes, 50*, 179–211.

Ajzen, I. (2002). Perceived behavioral control, self-efficacy, locus of control, and the theory of planned behavior. *Journal of Applied Social Psychology, 32*, 665–683.

Bentler, P. M., & Bonett, D. G. (1980). Significance tests and goodness of fit in the analysis of covariance structures. *Psychological Bulletin, 88*, 588–606.

Blunch, N. J. (2008). *Introduction to structural equation modelling using SPSS and AMOS*. London: SAGE Publications.

Callaghan, D.E., Graff, M., G. & Davies, J. (2013). Revealing all: Misleading self-disclosure rates in laboratory based on-line research. *Cyberpsychology, Behavior, and Social Networking, 16*(9), 690–694.

Cheng, A. C., Jordan, M. E., & Schallert, D. L. (2013). Reconsidering assessment in online/hybrid courses: Knowing versus learning. *Computers and Education, 68*, 51–59.

Cunningham, C. A. (2009). Transforming schooling through technology: Twenty-first century approaches to participatory learning. *Education and Culture, 25*(2), 46–61.

Dayan, R., & Magen-Nagar, N. (2013). Teachers' satisfaction following online courses in the ICT field. In Y. Yair & A. Shmueli (Eds.), *MEITAL's 11th National Convention Book: The world of open information–New technologies and the ways to evaluate them in online teaching and learning* (pp. 136–140). Jerusalem: The Hebrew University.

De Freitas, S., & Oliver, M. (2005). Does e-learning policy drive change in higher education? A case study relating models of organizational change to e-leaning implementation. *Journal of Higher Education Policy and Management, 27*(1), 81–95.

Doll, J., & Ajzen, I. (1992). Accessibility and stability of predictors in the theory of planned behavior. *Journal of Personality and Social Psychology, 63*, 754–765.

Francisa, L., Katzb, Y., & Jones, H. (2000). The reliability and validity of the Hebrew version of the Computer Attitude Scale. *Computers & Education, 35*, 149–159.

Halverson, R., & Smith, A. (2010). How new technologies have (and have not) changed teaching and learning in school. *Journal of Computing in Teacher Education, 26*(2), 16–49.

Harasim, L. (2012). *Learning theory and online technology: How new technologies are transforming learning opportunities*. New York, NY: Routledge Press.

Hanze, M., & Berger, R. (2007). Cooperative learning, motivational effects, and student characteristics: An experimental study comparing cooperative learning and direct instruction in 12th grade physics classes. *Learning & Instruction, 17*, 29–41.

Horizon Report. (2014). *Higher education edition. NMC*. Retrieved from http://www.nmc.org/publications/2014-horizon-report-higher-ed

Johnson, D. W., & Johnson, R. T. (1999). Making cooperative learning work. *Theory Into Practice, 38*(2), 67–73.

Katz, Y. J., & Yablon, Y. B. (2009). Mobile learning: A major e-learning platform. In A. Szucs, (Ed.), *New technology platforms for learning revisited* (pp. 121–126). LOGOS Conference proceedings. Budapest: European Distance and E-learning Network.

Kline, R. B. (2010). *Principles and practice of structural equation modeling* (3rd ed.). New York, NY: Guilford Press.

Lambert, C., Erickson, L., Alhramelah, A., Rhoton, D., Lindbeck, R., & Sammons, D. (2014). Technology and adult students in higher education: A review of the literature. *Issues and Trends in Educational Technology, 2*(1), 1–19. University of Arizona Libraries.

Loyd, B. H., & Gressard, C. P. (1984). Reliability and factorial validity of computer attitude scales. *Educational and Psychological Measurement, 44*, 501–505.

Melamed, U., Peled, R., Mor, N., Shonfeld, M., Harel, S., & Ben Shimon, I. (2011). *Tohnit lehasharat hamihlalot lmea ha21.* [*A program for adjusting teacher education colleges to the 21st century*]. Israel: Ministry of Education.

Magen-Nagar, N., & Shamir-Inbal, T. (2014). National ICT program—A Lever to Change Teachers' Work. *American Journal of Educational Research, 2*(9), 727–734.

OECD (2013). *Draft collaborative problem solving framework.* Retrieved from http://www.oecd.org/pisa/pisaproducts/Draft%20PISA%202015%20Collaborative%20Problem%20Solving%20Framework%20.pdf

Palloff, R. M., & Pratt, K. (2005). Online learning communities revisited. *21st Annual Conference on Distance Teaching and Learning.* Retrieved from http://www.uwex.edu/disted/conference/Resource_library/proceedings/05_1801.pdf

Ryan, R. M., Koestner, R., & Deci, E. L. (1991). Ego-involved persistence: When free-choice behavior is not intrinsically motivated. *Motivation and Emotion, 15*, 185–205.

Resta, P., & Carroll, T. (2010). *Redefining teacher education for digital age learners. Summit Report.* Austin, TX: University of Texas Press.

Resta, P., & Shonfeld, M. (2013). A study of trans-national learning teams in a virtual world. In R. McBride & M. Searson (Eds.), *Proceedings of Society for Information Technology & Teacher Education International Conference 2013* (pp. 2932–2940). Chesapeake, VA: AACE.

Salmon, G. (2004). *E-moderating: The key to teaching and learning online* (2nd ed.). New York, NY: Routledge Falmer.

Salmon, G., Nie, M., & Edirisingha, P. (2010). Developing a five-stage model of learning in Second Life. *Educational Research, 52*, 169–182.

Schifter, D. E., & Ajzen, I. (1985). Intentions, perceived control, and weight loss: An application of the theory of planned behavior. *Journal of Personality and Social Psychology, 49*, 843–851.

Selwyn, N. (2010). Looking beyond learning: Notes towards the critical study of educational technology. *Journal of Computer Assisted Learning, 26*(1), 65–73.

Sivakumaran, T., & Lux, A. (2011). Overcoming computer anxiety: A three-step process for adult learners. *US-China Education Review, 8*(5), 155–161.

Shonfeld, M., Hoter, E., & Ganayem, A. (2013). Israel: Connecting cultures in conflict. In R. Austin & B. Hunter (Eds.), *Online learning and community cohesion: Linking schools* (pp. 41–58). New York, NY and London: Routledge.

So, H. J., & Brush, T. A. (2008). Student perceptions of collaborative learning, social presence and satisfaction in a blended learning environment: Relationships and critical factors. *Computers & Education, 51*, 318–336.

Zimmerman, T. D. (2012). Exploring learner to content interaction as a success factor in online courses. *International Review of Research in Open and Distance Learning, 13*(4), 152–165.

POSTSCRIPT

David Gibson and Miri Shonfeld

Online collaborative learning involves interaction between learners through both social and professional communications, enabled by the accessibility and affordances offered by global networks. The practice fosters multicultural and international understanding via online collaborative processes that create, process, and produce knowledge. Online collaborative learning is increasingly positioned to become a dominant and pervasive online teaching method known by almost every digitally literate educator throughout the world. The practice will continue to progress because the underlying construct of social interdependence which it promotes leads to higher productivity, positive relationships, and psychological health while learning.

Presented here are a number of studies, examples, and reflections on the current and future use of online collaborative learning in response to global interdependence, the diversity and pluralism of students, and cultures reflected in schools, the need for 21st-century skills, and the expansion of democracies. This book itself was produced by the collaborative work of the editors and the writers and would have been impossible without global networks.

There are several take-away lessons from these authors concerning student learning, teaching, and assessing conceptual change. Online collaborative learning provides significant opportunities to:

Collaborative Online Learning in a Global World, pages 267–268.

- Accentuate the central role of writing and reflection in learning.
- Set up interactive roles that expand the number and quality of relationships in learning, including friendly group competition while learning.
- Build upon the design principles of challenge-based learning in a global context resulting from an extension of problem-based, project-based, and contextual teaching and learning.
- Create a new space for shared citizenship via blended contact that promotes community cohesion.
- Provide students with empowering and enjoyable dialogical learning experiences, which increases their appreciation of multiculturalism as a valuable resource for learning.
- Increase the exposure and number of approaches to technology-enhanced communication among participants, which promotes positive attitudes towards using technologies in learning.
- Develop critical reflection on local existing practices.
- Engender mutual respect through an increased awareness of the special needs of others such as pupils with disabilities.
- Challenge all students to present themselves in a new light and in new roles as people with equal rights.
- Assess personal learning in online collaborative problem solving by observing the actions, communications, and products created by group members in a designed task space as they engage in coordinated activity to construct and maintain a shared conception of an open-ended problem and achieve some goal in relation to the problem.
- Know how to design virtual spaces for performance assessment that support freedom, choice and openness in emergent collaborative learning, which is critical for progress in technology-enabled assessment.

Teachers' willingness to incorporate online collaborative learning in their classes is based on their knowledge, competency and readiness. At the same time, providing online collaboration learning experiences integrated into teacher training contributes to teacher development and increases the likelihood that they will utilize the superior methods for appropriate purposes.

We trust that you have found inspiring ideas here that motivate you to learn more, adapt new ideas in your context, and find colleagues here who share your energy and enthusiasm for online collaborative learning in a global world.

BIOGRAPHIES

EDITORS

David Gibson is Curtin University's Director Learning Futures, Education Theme Leader for the Curtin Institute of Computation and UNESCO Chair of Data Science in Higher Education Learning and Teaching. His research has extended from learning analytics, complex systems analysis and modeling of education to application of complexity via games and simulations in teacher education, web applications, and the future of learning. Dr. Gibson has also advanced the use of technology to personalize education via cognitive modeling, design, and implementation. His articles and books on games and simulations in learning led to applying game-based learning principles to the design and implementation of *The Global Challenge Award,* a cyber-infrastructure-supported, global problem-solving contest for students from 100 countries while he was a Research Professor of Computer Science at the University of Vermont, College of Engineering and Mathematical Sciences. That program led to creating the Curtin Challenge platform.

Miri Shonfeld has played an influential and instrumental role in many changes in teacher education in Israel. She was the head of ICT at Kibbutzim College of

Collaborative Online Learning in a Global World, pages 269–274.

Education, and as the head of the forum for ICT coordinators in teacher education, she worked to integrate technology in education. She was involved in writing the national program for the 21st century, as well as numerous position papers. She has been invited by universities all over the world to present her philosophy and pedagogy on using ICT in education. Her research deals with online learning environments, collaborative work, and intercultural links. She is the head of the Technology, Education, and Cultural Diversity (TEC) Center at Mofet Institute and a faculty member in the Education department at Kibbutzim College of Education in Tel-Aviv.

CONTRIBUTORS

Roger Austin is Emeritus Professor of Education at Ulster University in Northern Ireland. He has published research on the role of ICT in intercultural education in over 60 articles since 1988 and is the co-author of *E-schooling; Global Messages from a Small Island* (2008) and *Online Learning and Community Cohesion: Linking Schools* (2013).

Rivi Carmel has been a lecturer and pedagogical advisor in the English department at KCE for the last 17 years. She teaches literacy, didactics, and methodology in English as a second/foreign language. Her main areas of research are beginning teachers, induction into teaching, and intercultural and intergroup contact.

Liat Eyal is researcher and a faculty member at Levinsky College of Education, Tel-Aviv, Israel. Dr. Eyal is also an academic consulter for innovative schools at the "Experiment and Projects" Division at the Ministry of Education in Israel. Areas of her research interests include innovative pedagogy, learning technologies, educational leadership and action research.

Claudia Finkbeiner is a professor of Applied Linguistics, Foreign Language Research & Intercultural Communication at the University of Kassel, Germany. She specializes in the field of L2 and multilingual literacy development with a special focus on reading and writing strategies, language awareness and cultural awareness, interest, bilingual and multilingual factors as well as distance learning. She has been the chair of the Association for Language Awareness since 2006.

Efrat Harel, a lecturer in the EAP department in Kibbutzim College, is a researcher in the domain of language acquisition among bilingual children compared to monolingual peers. Her Ph.D. dissertation focused on the linguistic profile of typically developing bilingual children in preschool years. In addition, Efrat is part of an international project whose aim is to create a diagnostic tool designed for the bilingual population. Efrat trains student teachers in Kibbutzim College to deal with issues of multilingualism and multiculturalism at preschools and schools in Israel. Together with Dr. Waldman, Efrat has been participating in telecollaboration projects with New Jersey, USA, and recently in Germany.

Elaine Hoter is a senior faculty member and head of the M.Ed. program in English as an International language at Talpiot College of Education and earned her Ph.D. from the Hebrew University. She is an early pioneer in online learning, having taught the first collaborative online course in 1995 connecting student teachers and school children and developing the first online conference for teacher educators in 2001. In addition, Hoter has created award-winning courses connecting a variety of diverse populations through the Internet, including deaf and hearing, the diaspora and Israel, and in the last decade Arabs and Jews. A Fulbright alumna, she is one of the three founders of the Technology, Education, and Cultural diversity Center. Today, she is head of pedagogy for the TEC4SCHOOLS project, developing new technologies and programs *TEC Center*, including social networks, MOOCS, and virtual worlds. She has presented at numerous conferences and has been invited to lecture on every continent.

Leah Irving has many years of experience in designing, developing, and implementing technology-enhanced learning experiences including virtual worlds, simulations, and location-based augmented reality across education sectors. Her recent research examines the role of virtual worlds as pedagogical places, examining experiences of academic identity through the lenses of place, pedagogy, and embodiment. Leah is currently Deputy Director of Learning Design at Charles Sturt University in New South Wales.

Rama Klavir is assistant professor at Kaye Academic College of Education in Be'er-Sheva. Her research interests include thinking and learning, giftedness, creativity and excellence in schools and within the framework of teacher training. She was one of the founders of the program for training excellent students for education and is in charge of the program on behalf of the department of training education staff in the Israel Ministry of Education. The program has been running for 20 years in 23 Israeli colleges of education. She has published three books and many studies on these topics.

Miki Kritz is senior lecturer at Kibbutzim College and an academic-technological advisor in the field of ICT in teacher education. A coordinator of the Online Environment Team at Mofet Institute and the manager of the Amirim TEC program at the TEC Center, where students from different cultures collaborate via the Internet. Dr. Kritz has published three books about the Internet and many articles about progressive education and online teaching environments.

Dalit Levy is currently heading a unique B.A. program in Community Information Systems at Zefat Academic College. She has more than 20 years of international experience in research and development in the intersection of computer science education and educational technology. She earned her Ph.D. from the Technion–Israel Institute of Technology–and participated as a post-doctoral fellow in the TELS–Technology-Enhanced Learning in Science project–led by UC Berkeley and the Concord Consortium.

Noga Magen-Nagar is a senior lecturer at the Gordon Academic College of Education, and the head of the M.Ed. program of Teaching and Learning: Educators' Mentorship Training. She is an academic consultant in the national ICT program, in the Department of Science and Technology, Ministry of Education. Her areas of expertise and research focus on integrating ICT in education, quality of teaching, innovative learning environments, and evaluation in education.

Naomi Magid, Ph.D. in Biochemistry from Bar-Ilan University in Ramat Gan, Israel. Lecturer in Life Sciences and in charge of the program for Training Excellent Students for Education in Talpiyot Academic College for Education, Holon and the head of the Intercollegiate Students Forum of the program for Training Excellent Students for Education.

Miriam Muchow graduated with a teaching degree from the University of Kassel in 2016. She currently works as a teacher and on a Masters degree for German as a Second and Foreign Language. She did internships in Thailand and Alaska.

Rachel Peled is a lecturer at the School of Education, Levinsky College, Tel-Aviv. Educational Counselor at "Onn" school, Special education School-for pupils with cerebral palsy (CP), Tel-Aviv. She has expertise in the fields of: Participation and self-advocacy of adults with special needs in work, society and leisure and Collaboration of parents—teachers and students with special needs.

Paul Resta holds the Ruth Knight Millikan Chair in Learning Technology at The University of Texas at Austin. He is the founding president of the International Society for Technology in Education and served as President of the International Council for Computers in Education. He currently is President of the National Collaborative for Digital Equity in the United States.

Einat Rozner teaches at the Kibbutzim College of Education as a teacher educator, teaching computer science and computing technologies in education as well as working with faculty, teaching them how to teach online. She has been involved in The Center for Technology, Diversity, and Cultural Education (TEC) in planning and teaching courses for 10 years. Einat's research focuses on learning and instruction with computer-based online environment. Her publications include a co-authored book on computer science subjects published by the Centre for Educational Technology (CET). She received her Ph.D. from Ben-Gurion University.

Her doctoral thesis was on educational Innovation arising from practitioner entrepreneurship.

Katy Scott is a content creator, game producer and front end web developer with a background in journalism and marketing. She has worked on various online games, digital platforms, websites and marketing campaigns for Curtin University, and has a keen interest in creatively using the online space for student acquisition, engagement and retention. She has degrees in film and journalism.

Tami Seifert is currently a senior lecturer at Kibbutzim College of Education, Tel-Aviv. She served as head of the Department of Educational Computing, the head of Academic ICT and vice-director of the Teacher Training for Graduates Program at Kibbutzim College of Education (2007–2014). Courses Tami has taught in the past five years include: Innovative Technologies in Education, The Design of Online Instruction, Social Networking in Educational Contexts, Application of Video in Teaching.

Yael Sharan has over thirty years of international experience developing, training, and writing about cooperative learning in general and about Group Investigation in particular. Her book Expanding Cooperative Learning through Group Investigation (1992), published by Teachers College Press, was translated into Italian and Japanese. Yael is a board member of the International Association for the Study of Cooperation in Education. Her Google site is

Efrat Shoshani–Bachar is lecturer at the school of education, Ono Academic College and teaches "Technology in education" courses. Her M.Ed. in Technology in education from Kibbutzim Collage of education, Technology and Arts. She is a coordinator of the Municipalities program at the TEC (Technology, Education and Cultural Diversity) Center and an instructor and a program developer in TEC on-line collaborative learning programs. She teaches also in courses for medical staff about technological innovation in learning.

Betty Shrieber is a researcher and lecturer at the School of Education, Kibbutzim College, Tel-Aviv. She has expertise in the fields of Learning Disorder and ADHD, Assistive technology, Planning functions for adults with learning disabilities and ADHD and Executive Functions.

Tsafi Timor is the Head of a post-graduate program (M. Teach) and a senior lecturer in the Faculty of Education, in the Kibbutzim College of Education. Dr. Timor lectures on teachers' professional development, classroom management, educational leadership, pedagogy, special needs and learning disabilities, and inclusion. These are also her research interests. Tsafi has earned her M.Sc. degree in Applied Psychology from Leicester University, UK, and her Ph.D. from the center of Leadership & Management, School of Education, Leicester University, UK. She is a psycho-educational diagnostician and the author of the book "The Art of Diagnostic Teaching."

Tina Waldman is the head of the English for Academic Purposes Unit at Kibbutzim College of Education, Technology and the Arts in Tel Aviv, Israel, where she also lectures to trainee English teachers in applied linguistics. She received her Ph.D. from the University of Haifa, Israel where she compiled the Israeli Corpus of Learner English. Her research interests and publications include online intercultural collaboration, applied corpus linguistics and the acquisition of vocabulary in an additional language.

Yehudith Weinberger, B.Sc. (Biology), M.A. (Science Education), Ph.D. (Education), is the Rector of Kibbutzim College of Education, Technology and the Arts, the greatest teacher education college in Israel. She serves as a referent of the Ministry of Education for new academic programs that are submitted by Education Colleges to the Council for Higher Education in Israel. Her major areas of expertise are: development of higher order thinking, empathy in education, and teacher education.

CPSIA information can be obtained
at www.ICGtesting.com
Printed in the USA
LVHW081940280619
622714LV00003B/26/P